Developments in
Rational-Emotive Therapy

Developments in Rational-Emotive Therapy

Edited by

Windy Dryden and Peter Trower

Open University Press
Milton Keynes · Philadelphia

Open University Press
Open University Educational Enterprises Limited
12 Cofferidge Close
Stony Stratford
Milton Keynes MK11 1BY

and

242 Cherry Street
Philadelphia, PA 19106, USA

First Published 1988

British Library Cataloguing in Publication Data

Rational-emotive therapy : recent developments
in theory and practice.—2nd ed.
1. Medicine. Rational emotive therapy
I. Dryden, Windy II. Trower, Peter, *1938–*
616.89′14

ISBN 0–335–09534–8

Library of Congress Cataloging-in-Publication Data

Developments in rational-emotive therapy / edited by Windy
  Dryden and Peter Trower.
    p.   cm.
  Includes index.
  1. Rational-emotive psychotherapy.   I. Dryden, Windy.
II. Trower, Peter
RC489.R3D49   1988
616.89′14—dc 19   88–19641 CIP

ISBN 0-335-09534-8

Typeset by Inforum Ltd., Portsmouth
Printed in Great Britain by
St Edmundsbury Press, Bury St Edmunds

To Albert Ellis and the memory of Howard S. Young

Contents

Contents

Introduction

This book considers developments in the theory and practice of Rational-Emotive Therapy (RET) 33 years after Albert Ellis first gave his initial presentation on what was then called 'Rational Therapy'.

Theory

There have been several different recent attempts to expand the ABCs of RET. As Al Raitt notes in Chapter 13, some theorists prefer to group all cognitive activity under 'B', while others have chosen to stress that 'A' has cognitive components. An example of the latter approach is provided by Robert Moore in Chapter 1. Here Moore distinguishes between the objective and subjective aspects of 'A' and outlines several practical ways of assessing clients' inference chains.

In 1980, Ruth and Richard Wessler's book *The principles and practice of rational-emotive therapy* was published. In that text the Wesslers outlined an 8-step model of an emotional episode which again stressed that 'A' has different cognitive components, and in which 'B' was reserved for evaluative thinking. In Chapter 2, Ruth Wessler notes a difficulty inherent in this 1980 model, in that distinctions between evaluations of 'it' and evaluations of 'I' are not immediately apparent. She puts forward a solution to this problem by introducing the idea of evaluative rules.

In Chapter 3, Ray DiGiuseppe shows that clients often have thoughts about their affective reactions which may aid or hinder change. For example, clients may be reluctant to work on overcoming feelings of guilt if they believe they are supposed to feel guilty or if they evaluate guilt as an admirable emotion. RET therapists would be wise to undertake a thorough cognitive analysis of clients' affective states if they are to understand fully the ambivalent attitudes that clients sometimes have about changing disturbed emotions.

In Chapter 4, Windy Dryden encourages therapists to distinguish between words and their meaning in RET terminology. A number of key words have a specific meaning within the RET system. These words may be assigned a different meaning by clients who cannot be expected to understand spontaneously RET terminology. Dryden advises RET therapists to work towards developing a shared meaning framework with their clients, a process which often involves teaching clients the specific meaning of RET terms.

In Chapter 5, Naomi McCormick and Theresa Jordan review recent literature on the role played by irrational beliefs about relationships and sexuality in dysfunctional intimate relationships. An interesting feature of their review concerns certain gender differences in irrational beliefs about relationships.

In Chapter 6, Duncan Cramer and Albert Ellis debate two rival versions of the RET theory of inappropriateness of feelings. In the original version, inappropriateness of feelings was deemed by Ellis to be characterized by feeling strength, while in the latter version, Ellis considers that such inappropriateness is characterized by the nature of the feeling's underlying belief structure. The debate was prompted by Cramer's data which seemed to support the original version.

In Chapter 7, Richard Wessler notes several problems that characterize the design and conduct of RET outcome studies. He shows that what often passes for RET in such studies may not, in fact, be representative of good RET and advocates that future researchers study procedures rather than approaches.

Practice

In this section of the book, we have deliberately included chapters that address the practice of RET with difficult clinical populations and problems. In Chapters 8–10 the innovative work of Howard Young is presented. Howard, now deceased, practised in Huntington, West Virginia and developed some creative strategies and techniques while conducting therapy with lower-class clients, bible-belt Christians and other 'tough customers'. This work is featured in his three chapters. In Chapter 11, Naomi McCormick builds upon Howard Young's work and presents her work with clients from non-metropolitan communities which she aptly calls 'Rural RET'. A feature of her chapter is that her work is firmly based on a review of sociological and psychological research carried out with such populations.

In Chapter 12, Michael Bernard adapts his recent work in using RET with school-age children and includes some important suggestions concerning the practice of RET parent counselling and education.

Finally, in Chapters 13 and 14, difficult problems of self-discipline are addressed. In Chapter 13, Al Raitt presents his own experiences in applying RET to clients with weight control problems. He distinguishes between dieting problems based on a philosophy of Low Frustration Tolerance (LFT) and those related to ego anxiety. He counsels caution when dealing with clients' anxiety problems in this context. The danger here is that therapists may offer a service that clients have not sought. In Chapter 14, Emmett Velten deals with important theoretical and practical issues in helping clients to withdraw from heroin – an issue that has largely been neglected in the RET literature. Velten covers both methadone maintenance and abstinence maintenance in his wide-ranging chapter.

We would like to acknowledge the following for giving us their permission to publish the work presented in this book: all contributors, Michele Young (Chapters 8, 9 and 10) and the *Journal of Rational-Emotive Therapy* and Human Sciences Press (Chapter 4). All chapters (apart from Chapter 4) were initially published in the *British Journal of Cognitive Psychotherapy*.

London and Birmingham

Windy Dryden
Peter Trower

Part 1

Theory

Chapter 1

Inference as 'A' in rational-emotive therapy

Robert H. Moore

Routinely observable in clients' conceptualizations of the origins of their emotional disturbances is the tendency to attribute causality to events: past, present and future – 'Sue embarrassed me', 'Flying makes me nervous', 'Funerals depress me', etc. The linguistic structure is standard. The implication is clear and acceptable to the popular imagination: one's emotional upset is the result of external circumstances.

It is mainly in their contact with rational–emotive, or other cognitively-oriented therapists, that clients learn to challenge this errant causal attribution and to take personal responsibility for their own emotional/behavioural repertoire. A man, for example, comes to understand, in this connection, that it is not the *fact* that his wife made some stupid remarks at the annual dinner that embarrassed him, but some thoughts he had *about* the fact. He learns, accordingly, that neither aeroplanes, nor flying, is responsible for his nervousness, but that certain of his learned attitudes about them precipitate the reaction.

It is not uncommon, however, for clients to understand correctly that their thoughts, rather than events, cause their emotions, yet continue to misidentify event-level phenomena as primarily responsible for their disturbance. This is frequently seen where clients' descriptions of stimulus events are more the product of a cognitive, than a perceptual process. A client may grasp well that it was not the sceptical audience before her that caused her anxiety attack at the podium, but some thoughts she entertained at the time that triggered her reaction. And she is quite correct, in that regard. She is incorrect, however, when she identifies her thought that she 'could be passed over for promotion', if she is not sufficiently persuasive as a speaker, as the cognition responsible for her anxiety.

In this particularly common error in the application of rational-emotive therapy (RET), clients mistake a component of the inference structure, with which they project a future consequence of present action, for the disturbance-causing thought process. In doing so, they bypass (or seriously risk bypassing) those specific *evaluative* thoughts that actually produce their dissonant reactions.

This is not to say that the client is not correct in thinking that she could be passed over for promotion, if she is not sufficiently persuasive as a speaker. She *may* be quite correct in predicting this particular future *event*. Her anxiety, however, does not derive even from her *correct* prediction of failed promotion, but from her learned evaluation of such an eventuality, namely: 'How awful! I should never be able to look myself in the eye again! I must either win the promotion, or know that I am an utter slob with a slim chance of ever again succeeding at anything!' Evaluative thoughts of this quality have long been known to trigger anxiety reactions. Still, the newly initiated client and cognitive therapist routinely err in holding predicted events responsible for emotional reactions, on the grounds that they exist only as 'thoughts', in the client's cognitive repertoire.

Contributing significantly to the frequency with which clients make this particular error, in the author's view, is incomplete training in their use of Ellis' (1962) ABC model. With A defined only as an *external* reality, or stimulus, and B defined merely as *thought*, clients are invited to regard a considerable assortment of cognitive processes as culpable in the generation of their emotional responses (C). In point of fact, many clients' 'thoughts' (appraisals, attitudes, ideas, beliefs, postulates, predictions, interpretations and expectations) are not the disturbance-causing cognitions, or irrational ideations designated B in RET. Clients who regard them as such, therefore, risk falling into the unproductive habit of challenging innocent cognitions as though they were disturbance-causing.

Consider, for instance, the client who responded to (A) *addressing a group*, with (C) *anxiety*. Asked for her (B) 'thoughts', she will often respond to the effect:

Client: I thought everybody would notice that my knees were knocking. I was afraid I might throw up. I was sure I was going to stutter and stammer through the whole speech, and they'd all think I was completely incompetent.

Which, if any, of this common 'thought' activity qualifies as a disturbance-causing cognition (B), within the rational-emotive framework? None of it.

The first two items contain somatic manifestations of the client's emotional reaction:

1. I thought everybody would notice that *my knees were knocking*.
2. I was afraid I might *throw up*. (nausea)

These are appropriately listed at (C).

Note also, however, that each statement contains material appropriate for inclusion under A. Item 1 describes an event A which the client believed took place after the occurrence of the original anxiety response: '. . . *everybody would notice*'. And the somatic reactions of both items 1 and 2, the knocking knees and nausea, themselves, are appropriate for inclusion under A, given that the client identified these reactions (C) as additional events (A) worthy of her concern.

Items 3 and 4, contained in the client's last sentence, are similar to 1 and 2, in that they contain mainly references to a predicted anxiety reaction which, like those above, also can be considered a part of the event scenario (A):

3. I was sure I was going to *stutter and stammer* . . .

and to an event the client supposed took place in the minds of her audience:

4. . . . and *they'd think I was completely incompetent*.

In order to make RET work, of course, clients must be trained to identify their disturbance-causing, evaluative cognitions (B), apart from the various components of the stimulus event (A), and the various components of their emotional reaction (C). The irrational ideation, or evaluative cognitions (B) associated with anxiety are standard, allowing for a given client's particular turn of phrase:

It would be awful if (A) took place! I couldn't stand it if (A) took place! (A) must not take place! My self-esteem and/or emotional well-being depend on (A) not taking place! If (A) takes place it proves I'm a worthless person–complete failure/etc.

Whether the stimulus event (A) in question is failing to give a persuasive speech, being passed over for promotion, being caught with knocking knees, throwing up, being rejected in a love relationship, or dying, the thought process that triggers anxiety over it resembles that set out above. It is primarily such thoughts, therefore, that merit challenge. And it is primarily in successfully challenging such thoughts that clients relieve themselves of anxiety. They will not do themselves much good by challenging the 'thought' that they could get passed over for promotion, or the 'thought' that they could die in a 'plane crash, on the basis of its low probability. Low probability or high, these 'thoughts' represent events and, as such, belong in the A category, where they can only be challenged on the grounds of 'probability of occurrence'.

If clients were to challenge, or otherwise dispute or dispose of an event (inference, prediction, assumption, etc.), they would be talking themselves out of dealing with some aspect of their irrational thinking. Put another way: a client can't very well correct his/her faulty thinking (i.e. 'It would prove I'm worthless') *about* an event, if s/he has already discarded the event itself as a low-probability prediction. That would be a very poor and inefficacious application of RET. Alas, it all too frequently passes.

Just as important as getting clients to distinguish their inferences and predictions from evaluative cognitions – and more important than where they list them in their written, rational self-analyses – is the matter of getting clients to reveal, in the first place, the cognitive material with which they fully describe the event, or events (A) to which they react. More frequently overlooked than B, which is virtually axiomatic, given C, the emotional consequence, are those forecasts, predictions, assumptions, expectations and interpretations, without which we have only a fragment of the stimulus event (A). It is important, therefore, to solicit a client's inference structures in clinical inquiry, until one is satisfied that the full picture has been obtained. A relatively simple procedure, such an inquiry consists mainly of the two parts – 'then what?' and 'why?' As an example:

> **Therapist:** So, you might actually stutter and stammer, you say. *Then what?*
> **Client:** Well, they'd clearly see what a nervous wreck I was.
> **Therapist:** Yes, and *then . . . what?*
> **Client:** They'd think me quite incompetent.

At this point, the client's public speaking anxiety has evolved into a reaction to being thought incompetent. To accept this as the last word in definition of the stimulus event, however, would be to discontinue the pursuit of the client's inference chain prematurely. The proper inquiry continues:

> **Therapist:** Yes, I suppose they might think you incompetent. *And then?*
> **Client:** I might get passed over for promotion.

Indeed, the string of consequences is not complete and the stimulus event not fully defined, until the client has exhausted her supply of responses to the 'then what?' question. Before that point is reached, however, most clients will respond with at least a few evaluations (B) and reactions (C). In such a case, the clinical inquiry might look more like this:

Therapist: So, you might stutter and stammer, you say. *Then what?*
Client: I'd probably throw up.

Given a C response and wanting the client to continue her elaboration of A, the therapist ordinarily would continue the inquiry with the 'Why?' question, as follows:

Therapist: Throw up, eh. *Why's that?*
Client: Thinking they'd spotted (A) my nervousness. It would make me even more nervous.

In this instance, given that the C response (prediction of throwing up) also represents a component of the stimulus event (A) (a reaction to which the client is reacting), it is equally appropriate for the therapist to continue the inquiry in pursuit of A with the 'what?' question, in this fashion:

Therapist: Throw up, eh. And *then what?*
Client: They'd know for sure I was out of control. (A)
Therapist: And if they did notice . . . *then what?*
Client: I mustn't let that happen! (B)
Therapist: *Why not?*
Client: Because *(consequence) – (consequence) – (consequence)* . . . they'd probably fire me . . . I wouldn't be able to find another job . . . the bank would foreclose on my mortgage . . . etc.

The point to remember is none of these real or imaginary consequences is the cause of the client's anxiety. Each is simply a component of the circumstances (A) to which the client responds with anxiety. It is her learned, irrational thinking (B), her awfulizing, needing, self-downing and philosophy of low frustration tolerance, *with respect to the situation described in A*, that cause her anxiety. And she likely will continue to have anxiety, in the given circumstance, until she learns, as she would in RET, that the event(s) in A are *not* awful, that she does not *need* them not to occur, that she *can* bear them, and that they *do not* prove her worthless.

In the case of an anger reaction, we have a man whose rage (C) is directed at his wife. The stimulus event is, having sworn to have the house cleaned up and dinner on the table for his visiting boss, the woman stretched out for an afternoon nap and never awoke until her husband arrived at the door with their dinner guest. In the presence of an anger reaction, naturally, one expects to find the antecedent 'should/should not' evaluative cognition (B):

Client: She damn well should have stayed awake and gotten her work done – or set the alarm, if necessary. But one way or another, she should have had dinner on the table when we arrived!

Of course, the client (husband) will recover his composure only as quickly as he accepts his wife's essential fallibility and gives up his imperative tirade about what she *should* have done. To get a better grasp of what the incident was all about, however, the 'what/why?' inquiry is appropriate:

Therapist: *What*, exactly, was the consequence of her having fallen asleep on the job?
Client: Well, there I was at the door with my boss – already knee deep in compliments about the chicken curry I was sure would greet us the moment we walked in. And she was sprawled out on the couch, with her hair still in curlers. The place was a mess, and there was no dinner in sight! (A)
Therapist: So . . . *what* happened?
Client: I could have wrung her neck! (C)
Therapist: *Why?*
Client: Well, by this time my boss was shuffling around, sort of pretending that we'd just dropped in by chance. (A)
Therapist: And *what* happened?
Client: He didn't actually say anything, of course, but I'm sure he was thinking I was a complete idiot to have brought him home to a situation so totally out of control. (A)
Therapist: I see. *What* then?
Client: I couldn't imagine his letting me arrange an office picnic, much less take over the accounting department (A) – I could have killed her! (C)

It should be clear, from the clinical dialogues above, that the client's anger (C) emerged in reaction not simply to the objective reality (A) of a dazed and forgetful wife, messy house and absent chicken curry, but to his mental image (A) of events unseen, as well. The rational-emotive therapeutic procedure, therefore, appropriately addresses the client's irrational evaluations (B) of *both* his objective *and* subjective realities (A). The objective (on camera) realities were: (i) wife on couch/hair in curlers, (ii) messy house and

(iii) no dinner. The client's subjective (cognitive/inferential) realities were: 'boss thought I was an idiot and hardly responsible enough, after this, to take over the accounting department'.

The anger-producing irrational evaluation (B), in whatever event, of course, is a constant – typically a variation on the theme, 'She shouldn't have done it!' The important point here, however, is the fact that what she 'shouldn't have done', the stimulus event (A), is not adequately defined by the *objective* realities of the moment. As the 'what/why?' inquiry reveals: 'That woman cost me my boss's respect and confidence – and sabotaged my promotion to department head!'; that is what he is most angry about – in this instance, a component of his *subjective* reality, an event considerably removed from/wife on couch/hair in curlers, etc. The richness of the rational analysis of almost any emotional upset is found at point A, in the clients' definitions of the circumstances to which they react. The purpose of the 'what/why?' inquiry is simply to insure that the whole picture of those circumstances comes into view.

But how long should a clinical inquiry continue? Or how deeply should one probe, in the definition of A? Some clinical judgement is called for. One would not want to press clients for inferences or predictions they had not made, nor for consequences which they had not originally conceived. Neither would one terminate such an inquiry, simply because clients had generated plausible and popular inferences, predictions or consequences. It works well, instead, to continue to solicit components of the event (A), only until clients either seize upon one of them as *the* key item, or simply run out of original responses to the inquiry. In the case of the clients seizing upon a particular component or aspect of the stimulus situation as key, it is appropriate and wise to validate their reality, by acknowledging the importance to them of that aspect of the A scenario. As in the case of the angry client, above, if he says that jeopardy to his promotion is the key item, then one can let it be the key item. One always has the privilege and can find an opportunity to address some other aspect of the situation – any that seems to have had significant emotional impact, e.g. in the same case as above, perhaps to deal with his feelings about having let his dinner guest go hungry.

In a nutshell: Once the whole of the picture (A) has been solicited with the 'what/why?' inquiry, whichever component is considered most critical by the client is, indeed, most critical to the client, whether it happens to be in the middle or at the end of the inference chain of events (A). What the therapist ultimately will focus attention on, however, may include a number of the other components of the chain (elements of the stimulus situation), selected in accord with clinical judgement, in collaboration with the client.

In the event that the client does not seize upon one or more of his own inferences or predictions as primarily definitive of A, he usually will simply continue until he runs out of original responses to the 'what/why?' inquiry and then either stops responding, or begins to invent new material in the session, i.e. 'I suppose, then, I could wind up on welfare, or maybe die of despair' (said without conviction).

If clients run out of original responses and stop responding, the picture A is complete. One can then collaborate with them in the selection of the principal components and proceed from there to the identification and challenge of B. If they run out of original responses, but *do not* stop responding, it is only necessary to detect the verbal and non-verbal cues that suggest that they have become inventive and have begun to embellish their original picture (perhaps to please the therapist), to know when to end the inquiry and join with them in identifying the key components of the A scenario. And then on to B.

A third indication that the 'what/why?' inquiry has run its course (after: (1) – client stops responding/indicates 'That's all there is'; and (2) – client invents additional A material in session) is sometimes a sudden shift, in inquiry, from the development of A material into a stream of B and C responses. In this instance, they neither bring the inference chain to an end, nor embellish it with new predictions and consequences, but swing spontaneously into persistent, if not urgent statements of evaluation and reaction. For example:

Client:	Now, of course, he'll never promote me. (A)
Therapist:	With *what* consequence?
Client:	I'll just get so depressed. (C)
Therapist:	*Why* is that?
Client:	I couldn't stand it! (B)
Therapist:	How come? ('*Why*' equivalent)
Client:	I just couldn't look myself in the eye. (B)
Therapist:	*Why* not?
Client:	Complete loss of pride, I guess. (C)

At this point, one would appropriately end the 'what/why?' inquiry, so as not to imply to the client that there must be more to the stimulus situation (A), when there isn't.

As mentioned above, one would not deal *only* with the last item in the client's inference chain, simply because it was last. Neither would one deal *only* with the item the client considered the critical item, simply because it was the client's top priority. The complete rational-emotive therapist knows to address the irrational ideation associated with any component of the stimulus situation to which the client has reacted strongly. In the case above, that might mean getting the client to challenge his evaluations of such A components as spotting a messy house, no meal for a guest, wife embarrasses boss, boss increases social distance, as well as no promotion. In point of fact, an incident that consumed no more than 5 minutes, between the time the client and his boss arrived at the door and the boss made his exit, could easily justify half a dozen or more discrete rational analyses – some, of course, more significantly related to the client's major upset than others.

In summary, then, one cannot reasonably well undertake to change, or encourage change in, clients' evaluative cognitions (B) in RET, in the absence of a reasonably robust picture of the event(s) (A) in response to which they report having a disturbance (C). The stimulus event A, moreover, is understood to include components that are purely cognitive in nature, particularly predictions, forecasts, assumptions, interpretations and expectations, some of high and some of low probability. Whether of high probability or low, clients' inference structures and other cognitive components of the stimulus event A are likely to tell the rational-emotive therapist more about what clients are upset about than the purely objective, 'on camera' pictures of A, although the former often must be solicited through appropriate clinical inquiry.

Reference

Ellis, A. (1962). *Reason and emotion in psychotherapy*. Secaucus, N.J.: Lyle Stuart.

Chapter 2

Value judgements and self-evaluation in rational-emotive therapy

Ruth A. Wessler

Rational-emotive therapy (RET) attempts to help people become aware of and then change the cognitions underlying maladaptive emotions. Clients are taught that their emotions (C) are the product of activating events (A) in conjunction with beliefs (B) about these events. It is not A *per se* that leads to C, but A combined with the mediation at B. RET therapists teach that while we may not be able to change A (e.g. a lover deserts you) we can, with thought and effort, change B. A's are not ignored, but in RET the emphasis is on changing B. The foregoing may not be new to most readers. The elegant simplicity of the ABC model is a hallmark of its usefulness, but it also leads to therapeutic errors when literally applied. When literally applied, A stands for some objective stimulus, be it from without or within the person. C is the emotion experienced, and thus B stands for any and all forms of cognitive processing that occurs between the awareness of the stimulus and the emotional consequence.

In 1980, Richard Wessler and I presented an expanded version of the ABC model which we called the emotional episode (Wessler and Wessler, 1980). The major innovation in this model was the expansion of A to four stages, giving a model of types of cognitions that can mediate between the objective stimulus and the emotional response, and highlighting B as evaluative thinking or appraisal following Arnold (1980) and Lazarus (1982). Richard Wessler has added another step to the emotional episode, behaviour (i.e. the behavioural response that accompanies the emotional response).

Briefly,[1] the steps in the emotional episode are these:

---

[1] For a fuller explanation, see Wessler and Wessler (1980) or Wessler (1982).

1. *Objective stimulus (S)*: some stimulus, internal or external, presumably begins the sequence.
2. *Awareness*: for a stimulus to have any impact on a person, the person first needs to become aware of its existence. This, and the next step, are basically perceptual processes.
3. *Definition and description*: the person defines what S is (S').
4. *Interpretation*: the cognitive step, often present, of inferring unobservable aspects of, for example, inferring anger when a person does not speak to you.
5. *Evaluation*: appraising the S' or inference as positive, negative or neutral.
6. *Affect*: given a non-neutral appraisal, autonomic arousal.
7. *Behaviour*: Overt behaviour that may or may not follow the effective arousal.
8. *Reinforcing consequences*: Outcome of the affect and/or behaviour that may be influential in a future episode.

Steps 1 through 4 are A in the ABC model. Step 5 is B. Step 6 is the emotional consequence (C) and step 7 is the behavioural consequence (C).

Although I have been satisfied with the model of an emotional episode in teaching the distinction between A and B, it has a major weakness. It does not make a distinction between the evaluation of 'it' (as in 'it is bad to be rejected') and 'I' (as in 'since I have been rejected, I am bad'). We have pretended as if there is something singular that is the object of evaluation. But when I act there are at least four 'objects' – the action, its intent, the consequence of that action and the actor. Often the evaluative conclusion is singular – awful, good, wonderful, unfortunate. When the evaluation is singular it can mean that all objects are evaluated the same way, or, given the person's particular value system, the evaluation of one object outweighs the evaluation of the others.

Most people come to therapy not because they have evaluated their actions (or consequences) as awful, they have judged their very essence as awful.[2] In RET, we are typically much more concerned with helping a client to change the self-evaluation rather than the evaluation of events or their consequences. In fact, we might say, '*Even if* you did a bad thing, how would that make you a bad person?' In teaching beginning therapists this distinction, I have treated 'it is bad' as an A-type statement by saying that disputing 'it is bad' is akin to disputing A. I have not been satisfied with this approach, since both I and my students know that 'it is bad' is in fact an appraisal.

---

[2] Do note that I said 'most people'. It would be an error to assume that all clients evaluate themselves as 'awful'. However, very many do, and it is the therapist's task to ascertain whether this is the case in any particular instance.

Ruth A. Wessler

Table 1 The emotional episode with cognitive rules

Step	Rules
1. Stimulus	
2. Awareness	
3. Definition	Perceptual rules
4. Interpretation	Inferential rules
5. Evaluation	Evaluative rules
6. Affect	Affective rules
7. Behaviour	Behavioural rules
8. Reinforcing consequences	

Cognitive rules

Thus, missing from the emotional episode is a distinction among the objects of evaluation at step 5. My solution, however, is not to further expand a now greatly expanded version of the ABC model, but to add to it rules for the progression of the episode beginning at awareness (step 2) through the behavioural response (step 7). In my addition of rules, I am borrowing directly from the ideas of Beck (1976). My concern in this chapter is with evaluative rules, however, and Table 1 displays the emotional episode with other rules added as well.

Beck (1976) defines rules as two types: (1) standards and regulations, and (2) equations, formulae and premises. The latter serve to order, classify, and synthesize our observations. Following Table 1, perceptual rules give meaning to sensory impressions; inferential rules allow us to draw conclusions from our experiences; affective rules give definition to our emotions; and behavioural rules direct our actions. Both inferential and behavioural rules have received close attention by cognitive-behavioural therapists. A major emphasis in RET remains on evaluative rules, which are primarily those of standards and regulations.

Evaluative rules

To return to the distinction between 'it is bad' and 'I am bad', there is one type of evaluative rule that leads to the former, a second type that leads to the latter. To begin with the first, Lazarus (1982) asserts that appraisals serve the purpose of promoting survival and well-being. Thus, Lazarus points up the functional value of the cognitive process of appraisal. The basic evaluative rule becomes, 'If X is detrimental to my survival and well-being, then it is bad.' To fill in the X, we need an inferential rule, 'X is in fact, conducive (or not) to my survival and well-being.' Just as a young child might be mistaken in inferring that birds are 'all living things that fly', so might I be mistaken in inferring that 'smoking cigarettes promotes my survival and well-being'. If smoking cigarettes, in fact, does not promote my survival and well-being, and further, is detrimental to my survival and well-being, then this particular inferential rule is mistaken. However, given the fact that I believe that inference, it makes perfectly good sense that I smoke. It is reasonable to do what I evaluate as good. It would be unreasonable or irrational for me to hold that belief and not smoke, not do what I evaluate as beneficial. To take another example, many people hold the evaluative rule: 'Having the approval of certain other people promotes my survival and well-being and is therefore good.' Again, it would be irrational to hold that rule and not attempt to gain and hold the approval of those persons. It does not follow from reason that a person holding that rule would seek to avoid or alienate those significant others. Given this rule, it follows that I desire the approval from certain others, evaluate it as good when I receive it and thus feel good (happy), just as I evaluate it as bad and thus feel sad when I do not receive it. My feelings flow from my determination as to whether approval is present or not (probably determined by inferential rules), and from this particular evaluative rule.

Appraisals are related to our preferences (desires, motives) and to our values (morals, standards). We do not have to make up new rules to derive value judgements. Good and bad, right and wrong are synonymous – there is an extensive literature on moral development (see, particularly, Kohlberg, 1963; Loevinger, 1976). Some of the factors on which we might judge behaviour as right or wrong are survival, whether we can get away with it, other's approval (all basically preferences or motives) and, ultimately, in some cases, internal standards. We derive and internalize values and standards which we judge to be beneficial not only to ourselves, but to others as well – in the broadest sense all of humankind. In this sense, my well-being depends on the well-being of others. The Golden Rule states this clearly. Thus, it is good (right) to treat others well, for such behaviour serves my interests, my survival and well-being. Just as it follows from reason for me to seek what I evaluate as good, it is rational for me to do what I judge as right.

When a person states 'it is wrong to cheat', 'it is wrong to behave callously', or 'it is wrong to have extra-marital affairs', we may agree to disagree with that person's specific value choices, but these evaluative rules themselves are not irrational. To take an example, a client is struggling with feelings of sexual attraction to others of the same sex, and holds the value that homosexuality is bad and immoral. The client is feeling guilty. We might,

during therapy, engage in a discussion of values and try to show this client
that by holding some different criteria by which to judge moral behaviour,
that it is not wrong to engage in homosexual relations. But, if that is the only
way in which we attempt to alleviate the client's guilt, we are not doing RET.
If we could succeed in getting the client to change his or her values about
homosexuality, that particular guilt problem would be solved. However, we
would not have helped the client with his or her guilt problems in general, for
when the client does or feels something else he or she defines as bad or
immoral, guilt will ensue.

In this example, I am using the traditional RET distinction between guilt
and regret. The feeling of regret would flow naturally from behaving in a
way judged bad or immoral by the actor, following from the first evaluative
rule I have been discussing to this point. Guilt derives from a different
evaluative rule which may or may not follow the basic evaluative rule. The
sequence is this:

> If X is detrimental to my survival and well-being, then it is bad. Having
> homosexual relations violates my moral code and, therefore, would not
> promote my survival and well-being, and so is bad. Furthermore, if I
> do such a bad thing, then I am no good.

In this final sentence, we have guilt, and finally an irrational belief (rule).
Essentially, the first rule covers an evaluation of the action or event, the
second an evaluation of the actor. The irrationality of the second is simple –
over-generalization – although we may use a variety of techniques to show it
to a client. If the client can be convinced that he or she is not a bad or
unworthy person, *no matter what*, the client will have a general (rule-based)
solution to this as well as other potential guilt problems. Also, I believe, the
emotional freedom from guilt will allow the client to explore alternative
value formulations, with or without my help.

Implications

Emotional intensity

Thus, there are two types of evaluative rules: (1) if X promotes my survival
and well-being, it is good, and its obverse; (2) if X is good, then I (the actor)
am good, and its obverse. The first leads to a whole variety of human
emotions including joy, sadness, pleasure, regret, frustration, annoyance and
love. The second leads to others including guilt, shame, depression and
imperious pride. These sets of emotions are qualitatively different. Guilt is
not extreme regret, nor is depression profound sadness.

I have presented the basic evaluative rule in its general form as an 'either–or' rule – X does or does not promote my survival and well-being. Values, of course, vary in their extent or importance. I may value my job but value my integrity even more (or vice versa). I like one person better than another. Many examples could be given, for people hold many values, sometimes conflicting and of varying importance. The evaluative continuum ranges from extremely bad through neutral to extremely good. The evaluative rules becomes: 'If X (variable) promotes my survival and well-being, then it is (variable) good.' Insert for 'variable', greatly, a bit, etc. The variable determines the intensity of the emotional response. The problem with the statement sometimes heard in RET that 'it is merely unfortunate', is that people easily interpret 'merely' to be the variable in the above rule, then 'merely' is taken to be either a constant or a part of a dichotomous variable, either awful or merely unfortunate.

Emotional intensity occurs on a continuous scale from zero to maximum. Simply, if we evaluate an occurrence as mildly beneficial, we experience a mild positive emotion. If we evaluate an occurrence as moderately beneficial, we experience a moderate positive emotion. And if we evaluate an occurrence as extremely beneficial, we experience an extreme positive emotion – call it joy. To reiterate, the intensity of an emotion varies directly with the intensity of the evaluation.

Dysfunctional emotions, such as guilt, are typically intense since they require an extreme negative evaluation of oneself. However, since intensity is not a reliable clue to differentiate functional from dysfunctional emotions, we are left with two others. Duration is one, and somewhat more reliable than intensity. An emotion like regret is functional. It signals a disparity between action (or consequence) and standard; an unpleasant reminder to guide future behaviour. Faced with the future, we get on with living. On the other hand, guilt, deriving from the second evaluative rule, is a reminder of, or proof of, one's worthlessness. It leads to dwelling on the past in the dim hope of finding an alibi, to the detriment of getting on with living.

The second clue, admittedly, a tautological one, lies in the evaluative rules used. However, as a therapist, it is ultimately the best clue I know of. In assessing a client's feelings, if I discover no evaluative rule leading to the conclusion 'I am no good', I am fairly confident the emotion in question is a functional one, no matter its intensity.

Appropriate emotions

Some emotions, such as guilt, may be dysfunctional or self-defeating, but any emotion is neither rational nor irrational and is always appropriate to the rules that produced it. By 'appropriate' I mean logically following from premises. However, when the term 'appropriate' is commonly applied to emotions, this is usually a judgement made by others (sometimes oneself) when the emotional reaction seems not to fit the stimulus or seems out of proportion to it; such as I, who care little about insects, may think your grief over your dead tarantula is a bit much. Inappropriate is used in two ways. First, when the behavioural expression of the affect is deemed inappropriate to the setting – laughing at a funeral, crying while taking a test, or displaying anger when turned down for a raise. Secondly, when the behavioural expression of the affect is deemed inappropriate to the stimulus, one of the criteria in the DSM-III for schizophrenia, such as laughing when told a loved one has died or crying (not with joy) when told you have won the lottery.

In the first case, the social rules are not that you should not *feel* happy at a funeral or that you should not *feel* sad during a test or even that you should not *feel* angry with your boss, but you should not *show* it in these settings. These, of course, are examples of some behavioural rules. In the second case it is not the inappropriate *display* of the affect (although we only know it through display), but so we say the person is 'out of touch with reality' is autistic, is psychotic. Even in cases so labelled as inappropriate affect, the affect is no doubt appropriate to the world as derived from the person's perceptual and inferential rules, which may be very idiosyncratic. Certainly, in all other cases, the affect is appropriate to the way in which the evaluative conclusion was derived. It is appropriate to feel sad if I infer that you want to leave me and I evaluate your presence as good. *It*, then, *is* sad. Furthermore, it is appropriate to feel depressed if I also then evaluate myself as worthless. My evaluative rule is irrational, but my feeling of depression, although dysfunctional, is certainly appropriate to that rule.

Therapeutic errors

Understanding the two types of evaluative rules and clearly distinguishing between the evaluation of 'it' and 'I' can serve to reduce certain therapeutic errors. The two most prevalent are minimization of feelings and abdication of responsibility. A therapist responding to a cue word that is evaluative – awful, terrible, very bad – no matter what the object of evaluation, is open to these errors. The message delivered to clients is that nothing is bad or, at most, mildly so. Since good–bad is a bipolar dimension, you cannot eliminate one without eliminating the other. Thus, clients are taught benign neutrality. The message is simple: give up your values and preferences and you will not feel badly (nor, then, will you feel good). Needless to say, this is not the goal of RET, which is to help clients minimize *dysfunctional* emotions.

I do not mean to imply that, as therapists, we never want to help a client examine his or her values. For instance, I have a client whose X and 'X is detrimental to my survival and well-being' includes any and all forms of sexual responsiveness and behaviour. However, doing so is a matter of clinical judgement and not a knee-jerk response to the client's term 'bad'. This client's major problem remains the rule she carries that says if she does *anything* bad, she is a rotten, worthless person and will be punished forever.

A major value in RET is responsibility (Ellis, 1981). To assume responsibility for one's actions requires evaluation, evaluation of one's behaviour against some standard judged desirable. For example: 'It is good to be at work on time, in order to keep my job'; 'it is good to be kind to others, then the chances are they will be kind to me'; 'it is good to be honest, because I value honesty in human relations'. We judge whether our behaviour matches or does not match the standard. Judging that the behaviour falls short (when it does) leads to the evaluation of that behaviour as inadequate, bad or wrong. If I value honesty and if I lie, I evaluate my lying as wrong: 'I have lied. *It* was wrong for me to have done so.' Remember, to feel guilty, as opposed to regretful, I would also have to conclude, 'therefore, I am bad'. If we dissolve the evaluative continuum by asserting 'it's OK', not only do we eliminate functional emotions, but we also eliminate the ability to make the judgements required to take responsibility for our behaviour.

Fortunately, such an endeavour is doomed to failure, since making appraisals is no doubt part of our nature, necessary for survival. The error in focusing, without thinking, on the first evaluative rule, is to waste precious therapy time that could be devoted to helping the client rethink the second evaluative rule. Probably one of the major reasons that many people do not take responsibility for their actions is their adherence to the second rule, 'If I did that, I am no good', and the very painful consequence of guilt. Where there is guilt, there is often rationalization (reinterpretation).

A final error made by some therapists, perhaps particularly RET therapists, is to attempt to teach clients that they are not responsible for how others feel. Typically this is done when a client is presenting a problem of feeling guilty as a result of having done something about which another feels hurt or injured in some way; for instance, telling your lover that you want to leave the relationship, the lover then feeling depressed and anguished. The rules that lead to the guilt are these: 'It is bad for someone to feel hurt. It is bad (wrong) of me to cause that bad event. If I do a bad thing, I am a bad person.' Thus, the approach of trying to convince a client that she is not responsible for her partner's depression is not an attempt to change her values (first rule) or her self-evaluation (second rule) – it is still wrong to do a bad thing and she is still bad if she does so. It is an attempt to change an inferential rule – she simply has not done a bad thing, since even though the emotional reaction of her partner is very unfortunate, she did not cause it. My contention is that if my action is going to set off a chain of events that will end in some unfortunate consequence, then I have some responsibility for that consequence. If I push you out of a window, I would say that I, not gravity, am responsible for your falling. If I insult you, I would say that I, not your inferences and evaluative beliefs, am responsible for your feeling hurt or anger. Using the ABC model, if you and I are in interaction, there is no doubt that I am your A. The approach of trying to teach clients that they are not responsible for other people's feelings does, at least, get the therapist out of the business of attempting to change values, but into one of jurisprudence, for which most therapists are neither well trained nor equipped to deal with. Finally, the more time taken to do so means less time to help the client with her guilt – her belief she is rotten for having hurt someone.

Summary

I have elaborated upon the emotional episode (Wessler and Wessler, 1980) to include rules for progression through the episode. My focus in this Chapter has been on evaluative rules, leading to the evaluative response at step 5 of the episode. This seems to be a solution for the difficulty in conveying the crucial difference between the evaluation of some event, behaviour or consequence versus the evaluation of oneself, the important element in what Ellis (1979) calls ego anxiety. Not considered in this Chapter are how evaluative or other rules can lead to anger, discomfort anxiety, and low frustration tolerance, other targets for change in RET. I intend to pursue these topics in the future and welcome the contributions and critique of anyone interested in this model.

References

Arnold, M.B. (1980). *Emotion and personality*. New York: Columbia University Press.

Beck, A.T. (1976). *Cognitive therapy and the emotional disorders*. New York: Meridian.

Ellis, A. (1979). Discomfort anxiety: A new cognitive-behavioral construct (Part 1). *Rational Living*, **14**(2), 3–8.

Ellis, A. (1981). Is RET ethically untenable or inconsistent? A reply to Paul E. Meehl. *Rational Living*, **16**(1), 10–11, 38–41.

Kohlberg, L. (1963). The development of children's orientation toward a moral order: 1. Sequence in the development of moral thought. *Vita Humana*, **6**, 11–33.

Lazarus, R.S. (1982). Thoughts on the relations between emotion and cognition. *American Psychologist*, **37**, 1019–24.

Loevinger, J. (1976). *Ego development*. San Francisco: Jossey–Bass.

Wessler, R.A. and Wessler, R.L. (1980). *The principles and practice of rational-emotive therapy*. San Francisco: Jossey-Bass.

Wessler, R.L. (1982). Varieties of cognition in the cognitively-oriented psychotherapies. *Rational Living*, **17**(1), 3–10.

Chapter 3

Thinking what to feel

Raymond DiGiuseppe

In the present cognitive therapy zeitgeist, the cognitions seen as most important in determining emotional disturbance by theorists are inferences and evaluations about the self or external world (Beck, 1976; Ellis, 1979). Emotions are usually relegated to the role of dependent variables by cognitive therapists. Feelings are considered the result of cognitions and usually receive little other attention. This Chapter will focus on the emotional aspects of cognitive therapies and will suggest the hypothesis that emotions are often the content of the cognitions that lead to excessive disturbed affect.

People have beliefs about the type and degree of emotions they are *supposed* to feel. People also have beliefs about which emotions are helpful or hurtful to themselves or to others. These cognitions, which I shall call *affective expectancies*, have received little attention in the cognitive therapy literature and as a result no systematic research has been carried out on the topic.

Ellis (1979) has frequently said that emotions, thoughts and behaviours are really interdependent processes. This view was recently restated by Schwartz (1982). However, the artificial division between these processes has persisted in the cognitive therapy literature. Thoughts and feelings are seen as being separate elements. However, they are experienced simultaneously. We do not have feelings as independent elements on a flow chart that come after thoughts. Feelings generate new thoughts that in turn maintain, intensify or change feelings. We evaluate those feelings and decide whether or not we like them and care to experience them again.

The evaluations we have about our emotions do not only arise from the sensory experiences which emotions provide us. Cultural, familial and idiosyncratic attitudes exist which may influence evaluations of affect more than the sensory pain or pleasure they bring. Emotion which is disturbed and which may appear obviously unpleasant to therapists may be ambivalently or positively evaluated by clients. If either of these is the case, clients will not necessarily want to change that emotion. Disputing or challenging the irrational thoughts that elicit emotion is futile until clients recognize the advantages of changing the emotion. The following hypotheses will guide the remainder of this Chapter:

1. Disputing irrational beliefs or automatic thoughts will be ineffective if the client maintains positive evaluations about his/her pathological emotion and is not committed to emotional change.
2. All clients have evaluative cognitions about their disturbed emotional experiences. Depressed clients have thoughts about their depression. They may like it, admire it, hate themselves for having it, or become resigned to it.
3. The evaluations clients have about their emotions are multiple and sometimes inconsistent.
4. Clients will also have expectancies of which emotions people in their situation are *supposed* to have. These expectancies will be based on implicit theories of behaviour that the client holds, which are derived from cultural expectations.
5. Clients who cling to affective states which they label as negative may do so simply because they have difficulty construing alternative, more functional emotions.
6. Clients will not feel an emotion which they cannot conceptualize as an acceptable response to a situation.

Commitment to emotional change

The core element in cognitive therapies is challenging, disputing and changing dysfunctional or irrational thoughts. Disputing rests on three prerequisite assumptions: (1) the affective state being experienced is unpleasant, dysfunctional and a change is desired; (2) there is an alternative for the undesirable affect; and (3) thoughts mainly determine feelings. Clients who fail to share these assumptions are poorly motivated to change.

Rather than assume that clients have the three assumptions mentioned above, I suggest that therapists actively explore these areas and explicitly define the emotions to be changed and the alternatives to replace them.

The notion that beliefs mainly determine feelings is commonly taught to clients by cognitive therapists; assumptions 1 and 2 have received little formal attention in the cognitive therapy literature. Clinical experience suggests that clients' thoughts about their emotions or the alternatives available form the basis of many therapeutic failures. Clients will not be committed to changing their thinking unless they are committed to changing their feelings. A brief case vignette may help illustrate this point.

Joe, a 10-year-old boy, was referred because of his angry outbursts. During one session he reported being punished by his parents because he hit his brother. Since we were working on anger control we decided to analyse this situation. In previous sessions I explained to Joe how thoughts determine feelings and how he could change his feelings by disputing his irrational beliefs. Joe was angry at his brother for breaking his bicycle and independently identified his irrational beliefs. 'My brother should not have broken my bike; I can't stand not having my bike.' He was unresponsive to my challenge of his irrational beliefs, and responded: 'What's the mater with you, you want me to be happy about it?'

Joe knew that by disputing his irrational beliefs I was trying to change his anger. But if he were no longer to feel angry he saw only one alternative – to be happy, and that seemed 'crazy' to him. Joe's anger was maintained by his irrational beliefs but given that he perceived only one unacceptable alternative, Joe was not prepared to be unangry. To Joe, anger was the only *appropriate* emotion. Until Joe's thoughts about his anger could be changed, and a viable alternative emotion considered, disputing made no sense.

Disturbed yet desired emotions

Many cognitive therapists who present cases in supervision are at a loss when they confront clients who do not wish to change their disturbed emotions. Their first move is usually to keep disputing. When that does not work, they frequently attempt to shift to another theory. But it is not necessary to forego the cognitive model when one meets such resistance. Ellis (1983) has outlined many cognitive explanations of resistance. One possibility is that clients might resist disputing because they still believe that the emotion, which causes them so much trouble, is actually desirable in some way. An alternative therapeutic strategy is to discuss with clients their rationale for believing that while the emotion in question is painful, it is beneficial in some way.

Some clients claim that the painful emotions they experience are desirable because they motivate or cue them to behave in a certain way. These clients may hold a false, unverified hypothesis, that their disturbed emotions are necessary to maintain desired behaviours. For example, clients may believe that they must feel guilty in order not to commit some moral or social transgression or that they must feel frightened of failure in order to assure achievement. Such anti-empirical beliefs may have developed from faulty learning, cultural messages or family experiences. Once the rationale is discovered, the stage is set to challenge. Therapists can proceed as they would in disputing any anti-empirical statement which is dysfunctional to clients.

The discussion could focus on gathering empirical evidence for clients' hypotheses that disturbed emotions have provided the motivation for functional behaviour. Reviewing the consequences of clients' behaviours when they experience disturbed emotions will usually bring up much disconfirming evidence. Clients can be shown models of others who behave in the desired manner but who do not experience the disturbed emotion in question. This will help clients believe that less disturbed emotions can lead to desired adaptive behaviour. Clients who give up the ideas which maintain the emotion will be much more willing to dispute the irrational ideas that generate the emotion. Another brief case study may exemplify this point.

Mr X was seen in family therapy with his wife and 15-year-old daughter. The daughter was very distant toward her father. Mr X, however, claimed to love his daughter very much. He was the family disciplinarian. Whenever he played that role, he shouted in a deep loud voice at his children. His daughter interpreted his shouting as proof of his lack of affection for her. Mr X had trained himself to become angry at his children for minor transgressions. He readily admitted that his daughter should be perfect, should not answer back, should study hard, and never come home late. Initial attempts to dispute the irrational 'should' that elicited his anger were fruitless (Ellis, 1977). During these discussions Mr X seemed most uncomfortable. At one point he asked the therapist why it was so important that he give up his anger and his demandingness. Wasn't it good for his daughter to know that he was angry? Mr X was firmly committed to the belief that anger was necessary to convince his children that he disapproved of a transgression. If he were not angry they would think he approved of their actions and they would not change their behaviour. Once this hypothesis was discovered, discussed and changed, Mr X could give himself permission to learn to control his anger. This allowed us to move on to disputing the irrational belief that his daugher must be perfect.

Negative evaluations of emotions

In the ABC's of RET, C's often become A's. As noted above, emotions are not experienced in a vacuum. They often become the source of new cognitions. Humans will almost always evaluate how they feel. This has been noted by Ellis (1978) and by Walen *et al.* (1980), who labelled it symptom stress. Depressed patients can become depressed over their present, past or future depression (Burns, 1980). Many anxious patients become afraid of thier anxiety. In fact, this is believed to be a major element in the case of panic attacks and agoraphobia (Stampler, 1982; see Fig. 1).

Ellis (personal communication) has suggested that clinicians should preferably change the symptom stress, or the emotion about the emotion first. The

Fig. 1. Schematic diagram of symptom stress.

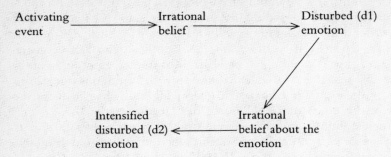

rationale for this is as follows. If clients experience additional depression (d2) whenever they become depressed (d1) about specific events, they will be distracted by the catastrophizing thoughts that lead to d2 whenever they discuss or dispute the thoughts leading to d1. The first goal of treatment is to stop clients from exaggerating the pain of depression by helping them to evaluate it as unpleasant but bearable. Ironically, after one accepts one's emotional upset, one may be more likely to dispute and change the irrational belief that underpins it.

Many but not all clients will hold irrational beliefs about their disturbed emotional states. Rather than wait to have such cognitions interfere with therapy, therapists are advised to ask their clients how they feel about their feelings. Some typical questions might be: 'What do you think about what you feel?', or 'What are you thinking about yourself – for feeling it?' Some clients may even assume that their disturbed emotion is a sign of impending madness, phrenophobia (Walen, 1982).

In disputing the irrational beliefs that determine symptom stress, therapists try to convince clients that the symptom itself is not awful. Phrenophobia and concerns of prolonged incapacity can be alleviated by providing clients with information about the physiology and psychology of the emotion in question. For example, clients experiencing anxiety over divorce will be reassured to know their symptoms need not be the first step to schizophrenia. Clients with reactive depression to true losses will be relieved to find out that their emotional experience is common to individuals with similar activating events.

In addition to symptom stress, an attitude of low frustration tolerance concerning a normal emotional reaction may precipitate a truly pathological response (see Fig. 2). Some clients believe that any kind of unpleasant emotion is 'too much'. Normal apprehension, disappointment, or grieving could become severe disturbance if clients hold beliefs such as:

● My life should be painless.

Fig. 2. Schematic diagram of normal emotion leading to discomfort anxiety.

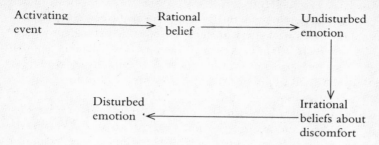

- Unpleasant emotions are unbearable.
- I don't deserve this.

These are all examples of what Ellis (1978) terms discomfort anxiety. It is important to teach clients that everyone experiences negative emotions as part of life. The elimination of these emotions is neither possible nor desirable.

Alternative feelings

Emotional goals are just as important in therapy as behavioural goals. Knowing that one's present disturbed emotion is disadvantageous is one step toward change. The second, equally important step, is choosing an alternative. If a therapist and client have different emotional goals for the client, therapy is thwarted. Consensus concerning the emotional goals of therapy will be difficult to reach if the client has a limited conceptualization of what he/she could feel instead of the emotional pain that prompted the person to seek treatment. It is common knowledge that Ellis (1979) tries to change clients' thinking from believing that activating events are 'terrible' to believing that they are 'unfortunate'. In so doing, clients will no longer experience 'anxiety' but will feel 'concern'. How many clients can conceive of this emotional state when they start treatment? And if they do not understand the concept and experience of 'concern', how can they work to feel an emotion they neither conceptualize or understand? Clients may not know what to experience when they no longer feel depressed. The options are joy, neutrality, or some negative but not disturbed emotion.

Clients who have just experienced the loss of a valued lover may choose joy or neutrality as the goal of therapy to replace the pain of depression. In order to experience joy, they may change their irrational belief to 'I am much better off without that partner.' In order to experience neutrality they may replace the irrational belief with the idea 'It makes no difference that my partner has gone.' Both the joy and neutrality-producing thoughts seem rational, and in some instances may be true. But, if the loss is real, these ideas are mere rationalizations. Such thoughts will most readily be falsified by the person's experiences; and the irrational beliefs are likely to return with the depression. The rational belief which would be recommended by Ellis (1962) is that the event is disadvantageous, bad and painful, but bearable. This idea would be inconsistent with the goals of joy or neutrality. As a result, irrational beliefs would neither be sought nor maintained.

The goal which may be most difficult to conceptualize is a negative but less intense, non-disturbed emotion, e.g. sadness, regret, concern, etc. Rational-emotive therapists strive to help clients experience such emotions in response to negative life events.

Clients will not fully participate in change-producing strategies if they do not conceptualize the alternatives or do not understand why their therapists believe that this is a desirable goal. My belief is that many clients do not conceptualize the emotional goals of RET.

Spivack *et al*. (1976) have presented a different view of cognitive therapy which they call Interpersonal Cognitive Problem Solving Skills (ICPS). Their main thesis is that pathology develops due to a deficit in cognitions which help solve social problems. Two of their ICPS skills are 'alternative solution thinking' (the ability to conceive alternative behavioural responses) and 'consequential thinking' (the ability to evaluate the effectiveness of those behavioural responses).

It is possible that similar skills exist for thinking of alternative emotional reactions to problem situations. I have postulated that such is the case with children (DiGiuseppe, 1981; DiGiuseppe and Bernard, 1983). My clinical experience suggests that adult clients also fail to conceptualize different emotional reactions and they cling to their disturbed emotions because they do not conceptualize an appropriate alternative.

There may be a number of reasons why people fail to conceptualize what to feel. First, they may have poor problem-solving ability for social problems in general. Secondly, the English language may help by failing to have specific words denoting meaning for variations in emotion. Americans, in particular, seem to use words for emotions with no regard for intensity. It would be interesting to see if other languages have more precision in their description of emotions. Thirdly, clients may have had poor role models for the display of emotion in their families, i.e. they may be hard pressed to imagine being annoyed rather than angry at a particular activating event because they have only observed people who have responded with anger. Finally, sex role stereotypes might contribute to what emotions people think they should feel, or what emotions they definitely should not feel in order to be manly or feminine.

Hochschild (1979), a sociologist, has pointed out that culture plays a large role in defining what emotions one can feel and how and when one should express a feeling. It may be most helpful for cognitive therapy to explore how such cultural norms are transmitted and whether pathological populations have failed to receive or incorporate the cultural norms on what to feel.

References

Beck, A. (1976). *Cognitive therapy and the emotional disorders*. New York: International Universities Press.

Burns, D.D. (1980). *Feeling good: The new mood therapy*. New York: Morrow.

DiGiuseppe, R. (1981). Cognitive therapy with children. *In* G. Emery, S. Hollon and R. Bedrosian (Eds), *New directions in cognitive therapy*. New York: Guilford Press.

DiGiuseppe, R. and Bernard, M. (1983). Special considerations in working with children. *In* A. Ellis and M. Bernard (Eds), *Rational-emotive approaches to problems of childhood*. New York: Plenum.

Ellis, A. (1962). *Reason and emotion in psychotherapy*. Secaucus, N.J.: Citadel Press.

Ellis, A. (1977). *How to live with and without anger*. New York: Reader's Digest Press.

Ellis, A. (1978). Discomfort anxiety: A new cognitive behavioral construct. Invited address to the Association for Advancement of Behavior Therapy Annual Meeting.

Ellis, A. (1979). Rational-emotive therapy. *In* R. Corsini (Ed.), *Current psychotherapies*, 2nd edition. Itasca, Ill.: Peacock.

Ellis, A. (1983). Rational-emotive therapy (RET) approaches to overcoming resistance. 1: Common forms of resistance. *British Journal of Cognitive Psychotherapy*, **1**(1), 28–38.

Hochschild, A. (1979). Emotive work, feeling rules, and social structure. *American Journal of Sociology*, **85**, 551–575.

Schwartz, R. (1982). Cognitive-behavior modification: A conceptual review. *Clinical Psychology Review*, **2**(3), 267–294.

Spivack, G., Platt, J. and Shure, M. (1976). *The problem-solving approach to adjustment*. San Francisco: Jossey-Bass.

Stampler, F. (1982). Panic disorder: Description, conceptualization and implications for treatment. *Clinical Psychology Review*, **2**(4), 469–486.

Walen, S. (1982). Phrenophobia. *Cognitive Therapy and Research*, **6**, 399–408.

Walen, S., DiGiuseppe, R. and Wessler, R.L. (1980). *The practitioner's guide to rational-emotive therapy*. New York: Oxford University Press.

Chapter 4

Language and meaning in rational-emotive therapy

Windy Dryden

In this Chapter the issue of language and meaning in rational-emotive therapy will be discussed – a topic which has received scant attention in the RET literature. For example, two of the major texts in rational-emotive therapy, (Walen *et al.*, 1980; Wessler and Wessler, 1980) devote a little over a page to this issue. Wessler and Wessler (1980, p. 179) make the important point which encapsulates the argument that will be made in this Chapter:

> Since all words are abstractions and subject to varying denotations and connotations, it is important that we use a shared vocabulary with a client – specifically, that we define our terms and check out the meanings of the client's terms – and try to keep the dialogue as concrete as possible.

In addition to understanding the client's language, it is equally important that the therapist ensures that the client understands the therapist's use of language. Since therapist language can be best construed as 'A' in the ABC framework, it is likely then to be interpreted idiosyncratically by the client who will then proceed to make evaluations about such interpretations. Thus, the possibilities for misunderstanding are legion. RET is often also miscontrued by fellow professionals given the different meanings that can be attributed to the term 'rational'. Young (1975) has argued that people often construe rational to mean cold, logical and unemotional, whereas in RET rational is defined as 'that which aids and abets our clients' basic goals and purposes'. However, this use of the word 'rational' is not commonly held and, if unexplained, will often lead to wrong impressions being created in the minds of both non-RET therapists and clients.

The language of feeling

RET theory states that when people do not get what they want and do not dogmatically insist that they get what they want, then they are stlll liable to experience negative emotions. To the extent that these emotions stem from rational beliefs and are deemed to motivate people to recover and to set new goals for themselves or to pursue old ones that are blocked, these emotions are deemed to be constructive. In RET terminology specific words exist for these constructive emotions and these are contrasted with emotions that are deemed to be destructive, not only because they stem from absolutistic musturbatory evaluations (musts, shoulds, oughts, have to's, etc.) but also because most of the time they inhibit clients from achieving their basic goals and purposes. Thus in RET, 'anxiety' is considered to be destructive and 'concern' is deemed to be constructive. However, when listening to clients' accounts of their own problems, it is important that RET therapists remember that the ways in which clients use language spontaneously (i.e. before RET), particularly with regard to feeling words, may suggest different meanings to that denoted by RET language.

Thus opportunities for confusion and misunderstanding that arise when we consider the ways in which feeling words are used by clients and RET therapists are many. Consider the term 'anxiety'. Anxiety in RET terminology is deemed to result when there exists a threat to the client's personal domain, a threat which is absolutistically evaluated as 'terrible' or 'awful' and which absolutely *must* not occur. Concern is deemed to result when the client does not evaluate this perceived threat in an absolutistic manner, but instead believes: 'I really don't want this threat to occur but if it does, it does.' Such a belief will result in the person concluding that if the threat does occur it would be unfortunate and bad rather than (absolutistically) awful and terrible. However, clients do not make this distinction spontaneously. They may, for example, report feeling 'concern' when a cognitive analysis reveals that they are, in RET terms, 'anxious'. Conversely, other clients will report feeling 'anxious' when they are, according to RET theory, experiencing strong 'concern', since they do not make absolutistic irrational evaluations. For example, one of my clients consistently used the term anxiety to refer to keenness. Had I assumed that his use of the term anxiety was in fact synonymous with the RET use of the term anxiety, I would have wasted a lot of therapeutic time by seeking to find irrational evaluations which did not exist. I might have also assumed that the client was a D.C. (difficult customer) because he would not admit to such irrational evaluations.

An additional issue needs to be considered when the term 'anxiety' is subjected to an analysis of its meaning. Although a client may agree that his or her feelings of anxiety stem from the irrational belief 'This perceived threat must not occur', the client may not agree with the therapist's position that such feelings are destructive. Indeed, many clients consider that anxiety (in the RET sense) will in fact motivate them to carry out a given task. Whether anxiety will motivate them to better performances is, of course, the issue which needs to be addressed. However, for RET therapists to assume that once anxiety has been elicited the client will necessarily wish to change feelings of anxiety to those of concern, overlooks an important fact, namely that clients make inferences and evaluations about their feelings. As DiGiuseppe (1984) has shown, some people consider that good things might happen or bad things might not happen as a result of experiencing (in RET terms) destructive negative feelings. This is one good reason why it is often helpful to discuss with clients their goals for change (Wessler and Wessler, 1980). To assume that the client wishes to change a destructive negative emotion without checking that this is the case may be a recipe for therapeutic failure.

Depression, according to RET theory, is a destructive negative emotion which occurs when clients evaluate some loss to their personal domain as absolutistically awful or terrible, conclusions which stem from the belief 'This loss must not occur or must not be as bad as it is.' It is contrasted with the constructive negative emotion, sadness, which occurs when such losses are evaluated as bad but without the concomitant 'must'. Again, clients regularly refer to their own feelings of 'sadness' when they are really, in RET terms, 'depressed' and vice versa! Continuing the analysis outlined above covering the implications of destructive negative feelings, some depressed clients construe this painful emotion as a sign of acute sensitivity (in a productive sense) and may view a therapist's attempts to help them to give up their depression as an attempt to make them less sensitive – efforts they would stubbornly resist. Thus, again, it is important for rational–emotive therapists to be aware that some clients create private meanings about their feelings of depression which may refer to positive implications of this emotion rather than the negative implications held by their RET therapists.

Guilt, according to RET theory occurs when clients break their moral or ethical codes and absolutistically insist that this must not have occurred. Such individuals damn themselves as bad individuals for committing such a 'bad' act. The rational alternative to guilt is often expressed in the RET literature as remorse, regret or sorrow. These emotions are deemed to occur when the bad act is viewed as bad but when the person concerned does not demand 'I must not have done this bad thing' or conclude 'I am bad for doing it.' Rather, the person accepts him or herself as a fallible human being without (and this is important) excusing him or herself from acting badly. Clients often misconstrue their therapists' interventions when the emotion of guilt is targeted for change, particularly when therapists do not check out with their clients that this is a troublesome emotion for them. Thus, some clients may accuse the RET therapist of encouraging them to do bad things or, less problematically, not discouraging them from doing bad things because they use the term 'guilt' in a different way from their therapists. In addition, clients often believe that guilt, in the RET use of the word, will actually protect them from doing bad things in the future rather than, as is argued in RET theory, encouraging them to do bad things. In this latter analysis, once one damns oneself and regards oneself as bad, this will lead to the person committing more rather than less bad acts. As Ellis puts it: 'How can a shit be deshitified?'

Anger is a particularly troublesome emotion since it often has several meanings. Anger, according to RET theory, is regarded as being a destructive negative emotion which stems from a absolutistic evaluation that the other person must not break my rule or must not act as badly as they do, in fact, act. It is contrasted with the appropriate feeling alternative – annoyance which is regarded as being constructive and stems from the belief 'I don't like your bad behaviour but there is no reason why you must not act this way and you are not a worm (or any other sub-human term that the client uses) for acting badly.' It is important to realize, as DiGiuseppe (1984) has done, that people often consider that if they are not angry they will, by definition, then allow other people to dominate them. In a sense they believe: 'I have to be angry in order to protect myself from other people's bad influence.' If RET therapists do not clearly distinguish between the RET meanings of anger and annoyance for their clients, then the latter may view therapists' attempts to change their anger to annoyance as (1) advice to act less powerfully in the social arena, or (2) suggestions that they would be wise to experience *less* strong emotions and thus to deny the strength of their rational desires. RET theory holds that annoyance is not necessarily less intense than anger but clients often conclude that it is. This is, of course, not the true intention of RET therapists, but without discussing these distinctions *before* implementing disputing strategies, client 'resistance' is likely to occur, although, of course, it is not resistance but the results of a poorly designed therapeutic intervention.

Ellis (personal communication) has recently advocated that in order to get over these semantic problems with respect to the term 'anger', damning anger (an inappropriate emotion) should be distinguished from non-damning anger (an appropriate emotion). Again, if this distinction is not made then the client who positively values 'anger' will be unlikely to give up his or her 'positive' emotion. However, if the therapist can help the person to realize that there are different types of anger and that non-damning anger is in fact productive, and damning anger is unproductive, then the client is at least liable to listen to the therapist, whereas in the previous scenario the client may well switch off from the therapist who is viewed as a person who is trying to encourage the client to relinquish a 'positive' emotion.

Similar arguments can be used when jealousy is the focus for discussion and the distinction between destructive and constructive jealousy can usefully be introduced to clients who, while experiencing the negative behavioural, emotional and interpersonal consequences of destructive jealousy, nevertheless regard their feelings of jealousy as evidence that they really love their partner. If a therapist encourages such a person to work on giving up feelings of jealousy without making distinctions between its destructive and constructive forms, then the person is likely to 'resist' the therapist, who in their mind is advocating that they relinquish their feelings of love for their partner.

Premise language

Wessler and Wessler (1980) have argued that a person's beliefs can be put in the form of a syllogism which contains both a premise and a conclusion. Thus, 'I must do well' is a premise and 'If I don't do well I would be worthless' would be the conclusion that stems from the premise. It is apparent that semantic confusion can often result when RET therapists refer to such terms as musts, shoulds, oughts, have to's, etc. A major problematic area here concerns the conditionality of these terms. Thus, the term 'I must do well in order to pass my exams' is a conditional phrase and not, therefore, irrational because the person is outlining the conditions which have to be met in order for an outcome to be achieved. Indeed, novice RET therapists who are only so delighted to have identified a 'must' in the client's thinking wrongly assume that all 'musts' are irrational and, therefore, to be targeted for change. This is certainly not the case. It is to be understood at this point that rational–emotive therapists are only interested in targeting for change irrational 'musts' (i.e. those that are absolutistic in nature), especially when these are implicated in feelings that the client wishes to change. This latter point is important. I have often heard RET therapists doing sound RET but not therapeutic RET. Here therapists have in fact identified absolutistic musts and are using correct disputational strategies to help the client to give them up, but the problem is that the client does not want to change his or her destructive negative emotions or dysfunctional behaviour.

The term 'should' is particularly problematic. As Vertes (1971) has shown, the word 'should' has several different semantic meanings. It can mean, of course, I absolutely should. It can also mean, I preferably should. It also has an empirical meaning (e.g. given the conditions that exist in the world at this present time, the sun should come up in the morning). It can also refer to matters of recommendation (e.g. 'You really should go and see *Chariots of Fire*'). I have on more than one occasion heard novice RET therapists challenge such non-absolutistic 'shoulds': 'Why *must* you go and see *Chariots of Fire?*' 'Because I like it' the client replies. 'But why must you have what you like?' retorts the therapist. This elementary therapeutic error would not occur if therapists learn not to confuse the word with its meaning.

A particular problem is encountered when the word 'right' is used in therapy in sentences such as 'He has no right to act that way.' I have sometimes heard RET therapists involve themselves in unproductive discussions with their clients concerning the non-absolutistic meaning of the word 'Right'. 'You have the right to do anything, you have the right to rape and murder if that's your inclination' is an example. While this is theoretically correct (this statement really means that there is no law in the universe to suggest that the person must not rape or pillage), the word 'right' is extremely problematic, and in my experience will often be construed by clients as meaning that the therapist is either actively advocating these activities or refusing to condemn their 'badness'. Such is the confusion about the term 'right', that RET therapists might be well advised to drop this from their vocabulary, at least in therapy.

Similar problems can occur when relative or rational beliefs are considered. Thus RET therapists often teach their clients that the rational form of 'must' is 'I want to' or 'I would prefer to'. While this is correct, it is not the only way of expressing a relative belief. Thus, the term 'It would be better' is also a rational belief, but one which does not indicate that the person may actually *want* to carry out the activity in question. Take, for example, students who believe that they absolutely must pass an exam. A therapist, in trying to help such clients discriminate between their preference and demands correctly, helps them see that they *want* to pass the exam but they do not have to. But what if such clients go on to express an irrational belief about working to pass the exam? The therapist who tries to help them to see that while they do not have to work, they would want to work is likely to be using an unproductive strategy which ignores the notion that a person may not want to do what *would be better*. Rational beliefs can then take the form of a desire and, therefore, a client can be encouraged to undertake an activity because of their desire. But a client can also be encouraged to undertake an undesired activity that would be in their best interests because they want the results of doing this activity. Their desire concerns the outcome of the activity and not the process.

Conclusion language

Semantic problems can occur when the language of conclusions is analysed, particularly when the terms 'horror', 'awful' and 'terrible' are considered. These terms in RET theory are distinguished from terms such as 'catastrophe' and 'tragedy' (as in the phrase, tragedies are not awful). In RET terminology, a tragedy is something that occurs which is rated as very bad. 'Terrible' and related terms in RET theory add to the notion of tragedy. 'Terrible' relates to the belief that this tragedy must not occur or must not be as bad as it is. This distinction needs to be made carefully with clients, otherwise they may assume that their therapists are being insensitive to their tragedies by trying to show them that such bad events are not *that* bad. Such clients may ask: 'Are you trying to argue that it wasn't that bad for me to lose all my possessions and my family in that fire?' Indeed, my experience in working with people who have recently experienced tragedies such as losing a loved one or being raped, has shown me that endeavours to teach the client the difference between tragedy and horror may themselves be viewed as insensitive interventions by clients who regard their destructive negative emotions as highly appropriate to their situation.

Semantic confusion can often arise when the term 'fallible human being' is being discussed in therapy. First, it is important to ascertain that the client actually understands what the term 'fallible' means. One of my clients in Birmingham (UK) thought that it meant 'obese' and was insulted as I tried to encourage her to accept herself as a fallible human being in such circumstances! In addition, clients may construe therapists' attempts to encourage them to accept themselves as fallible, as encouragement for them to condone their bad actions, or as reasons to excuse future bad actions. When clients view the term 'fallible' as having bad connotations, it is hardly surprising when they 'resist' their therapists' attempts to encourage them to accept themselves as fallible human beings. Another problem relating to the attitude 'fallible human being' is that it may not reflect accurately the source of the client's irrationality. More than one client has said to me 'Yes, I can accept myself as a fallible human being' but, shortly after, implied: '. . . who *must not* act badly'. It is therefore important when planning disputing strategies to look at *both* premise and conclusion forms of syllogisms to ensure that irrationalities are being challenged at both levels.

The associated term 'self-acceptance' also has its semantic problems. 'Acceptance' is a particularly difficult word because it can often be viewed in clients' minds as meaning 'resignation'. Thus, by encouraging clients to accept themselves, their resistance may indicate that they perceive that they are being asked to resign themselves to being forever the slob that they think they are. Acceptance, when viewed as meaning resignation, also conjures up images of inaction, whereas in RET, self-acceptance is viewed as encouraging clients towards productive action.

Semantic problems can also arise when issues of self-rating are being discussed with clients. Clients often have their own private ways of rating themselves. It may come as a surprise to most RET therapists that not all clients regard themselves as 'shits'. In supervising a therapy tape, I heard a RET therapist and his client get into a heated argument due to the therapist's insistence that the client was calling himself a 'shit'. The client replied 'Listen, I have never, ever in my whole life considered myself a shit and I really don't like your attempts to persuade me thus.' Here the client was being more rational than the therapist! Thus the terms shit, bad, worthless, less worthy and undeserving are not synonymous and, in fact, I have found it very useful to discover the particular form of negative self-rating that clients use. The resulting shared meaning that I have been able to establish with my client has been facilitative of both therapeutic communication and the therapeutic change programme.

The language of change

The language which therapists use when they attempt to help clients change can also lead to semantic confusion and constitute obstacles to therapeutic progress. For example, clients may construe the therapist's attempt to have them give up their musts as meaning 'Give up your desire.' Clients may often assume that the opposite of crucial is indifference. In planning such disputing strategies and while disputing irrational musts, therapists are recommended to keep in mind the importance of using the language of desire during this entire process. The term 'homework' can also be extremely problematic because in some clients' minds, certainly in Britain, homework is associated wtih school and with negative experiences. I often find it helpful to ask the client to give me a word that would capture the notion of the importance of putting into practice between therapy sessions what has been learned in the sessions. Thus, one client came up with the term 'training assignment', while another client came up with the term 'transfer task' to capture the meaning of the phrase usually referred to as homework.

While urging clients to persist at executing assignments, Ellis often exhorts clients to 'work and practise, work and practise'. This is good advice but can be construed as very negative by clients who already have a high degree of low frustration tolerance. Thus, for some clients, words like persistence or repetition may capture similar meanings but be less negative in connotation. In addition, one of the hidden dangers of urging clients to 'work and practise' and to 'push themselves hard in therapy' is that some clients may actually consider that their therapists believe that they *have to* do the work or that they *have to* change. In these instances therapists serve as a poor role model in the minds of their clients.

It is important to realize that virtually any word that therapists can use when encouraging people to change may have negative connotations for some clients. It is therefore perhaps a good idea for RET therapists to ask clients at the end of a therapy session, whether in this context they are using any words that the clients are viewing as negative (Beck *et al.*, 1979). If I was a client in RET or recognitive therapy I would review the term 'agenda' negatively. This is because my mother used to ask me at the beginning of every day 'What's on your agenda today, son?', a term which has come to have negative connotations for me.

Using words clients do not understand

RET is best viewed as an educational therapy. Since good education depends on effective communication, it is important that the therapist uses words that clients can understand. My 7 years' experience working in a working-class community in East Birmingham has taught me to be aware of using a number of words that are in common usage among RET therapists. I have found the following words to be most problematic among this population: dysfunctional, fallible, evidence, belief, cognition (to be avoided *almost* at all costs), rational, etc. Such clients will in fact rarely say to you 'I'm sorry, I don't understand what that means', but will give various non-verbal cues to non-understanding. Thus, I have detected over the years the following pattern of non-understanding:

1. *The glazed look*: here the client displays a glazed expression often accom-
    panied by a fixed smile.
2. *The automatic head nod*: here clients nod knowingly as if they understand
    their therapists' RET terminology.

If such nodding goes on for longer than 10 seconds without interruption, this is a sign that clients may not understand what is being said. If this is accompanied by the knowing smile then it is almost guaranteed that the client does not understand a word the therapist is saying!

Toward shared meaning in RET

In this concluding section ways in which RET therapists can strive towards adopting shared meaning frameworks with their clients will be outlined. One important method of checking whether a client has understood the meaning of a concept which the therapist is using is to ask the client for clarification of the client's understanding. Questions like 'I am not sure whether I am making myself clear on this point. Can you put into your own words what you think I am saying?', can be used to good effect in that they encourage clients to be active in the therapeutic process and to use their own language rather than just parroting the language of the therapist. It is especially important for the therapist to pay attention to the non-verbal aspects of the client's responses to such questions. When the client uses exactly the same language as the therapist the way in which the client responds can often serve as a guide to whether or not he or she has understood the therapist's communications. When the client uses the same words as the therapist in answer to such enquiries, the therapist can usefully ask 'What do you understand by the words, e.g. awful. What other words in your mind are equivalent to this word?' I have found asking for synonyms particularly revealing of clients' misunderstandings of the rational concepts I have been endeavouring to teach them. For example, a common 'synonym' that clients use for the term 'awful' is 'very bad'. The latter, of course, is not a synonym for the former in RET theory.

A constructive therapeutic strategy for making clear distinctions between constructive and destructive negative emotions, while ensuring that client and therapist have a shared meaning framework while using the same verbal label, is to define terms before implementing disputing strategies. In particular, emotions should be linked with their evaluative beliefs in any exposition of terms. For example, while trying to clarify whether a client is angry (damningly angry) or annoyed (non-damningly angry), I might say something like this:

> OK, so you say that you are angry. Now, when you were experiencing that emotion, what was more likely to be going through your mind? Did you believe, for example, that that person who did that bad thing was no good and absolutely should not have acted that way, or did you believe that although their behaviour was bad, there was no reason why the person must not have acted that way. Also, did you regard *them* as bad or just *their behaviour* as bad?

I have found that my clients can often more reliably distinguish between the two emotional states when I include their cognitive definitions than when such definitions are excluded. Clients rarely know spontaneously the RET theoretical distinction between these two emotional states. Thus, when discussing feeling terms with clients (particularly when one is distinguishing between constructive and destructive emotions), it is advisable to include their cognitive counterparts.

RET therapists have much to learn from the work of George Kelly (1955) and his followers in personal construct therapy (PCT) with respect to discovering the clients' idiosyncratic meaning systems. One such strategy derived from PCT concerns asking clients for polar opposites for their feelings. This is particularly useful when planning and carrying-out disputing strategies, since it may help the therapist to discover why clients may not in reality wish to change an emotion that they claim they wish to change and which, according to RET theory, is a destructive negative emotion. Thus, for example, I once worked with a depressed client who claimed not to want to be depressed but was resisting my attempts to help her feel sad. I asked her what she associated in her mind as being the opposite of sad, to which she replied 'sensitive'. This highly idiosyncratic use of the word 'sad' as being in some way equivalent to being insensitive helped me to understand why my client resisted my attempts to encourage her to experience what RET theory states is a constructive negative emotion.

In conclusion, I wish to emphasize that therapists should preferably be alert to the idiosyncratic ways in which clients use language and the equally idiosyncratic ways in which they may interpret the rational concepts that RET therapists strive to teach them. It is important for RET therapists to internalize the language system of RET but, in doing so, they should not assume that their clients will magically share the meaning structure implicit in rational–emotive terminology.

References

Beck, A.T., Rush, A.J., Shaw, B.F. and Emery, G. (1979). *Cognitive therapy of depression*. New York: Guilford.

DiGiuseppe, R. (1984). Thinking what to feel. *British Journal of Cognitive Psychotherapy*, **2**(1) 27–33.

Kelly, G.A. (1955). *The psychology of personal constructs*, Vols 1 and 2. New York: Norton.

Vertes, R. (1971). The should: A critical analysis. *Rational Living*, **6**(2), 22–25.

Walen, S.R., DiGiuseppe, R. and Wessler, R.L. (1980). *A practitioner's guide to rational-emotive therapy*. New York: Oxford University Press.

Wessler, R.A. and Wessler, R.L. (1980). *The principles and practice of rational-emotive therapy*. San Francisco: Jossey-Bass.

Young, H.S. (1975). Rational thinkers and robots. *Rational Living*, **2**(1), 3–7.

Chapter 5

Thoughts that destroy intimacy: irrational beliefs about relationships and sexuality

Naomi B. McCormick and Theresa J. Jordan

The assessment and disputation of irrational beliefs have long been critical for clinicians engaged in individual psychotherapy. As cognitive therapists have become increasingly involved in treating sexual dysfunctions and in working conjointly with couples and families, the identification and understanding of specific irrationalities regarding relationships and sex have assumed increasing importance. A review of the work to date regarding irrational beliefs about intimacy and sexuality, suggests that the popular culture assumes a major role in reinforcing maladaptive cognitions that interfere with sexual pleasure and affection. Exaggerated emphasis is placed on such notions as romantic love, penis-in-vagina sex, and the demand for flawless sexual performance. Further, gender differences in irrational beliefs regarding intimate relationships are likely to exist given the differential socialization that occurs in most contemporary cultures. The amount of redundancy among irrational beliefs at varying levels of specificity and the extent of gender differentials in these beliefs have received little or no empirical investigation. Implications for research and clinical practice are discussed.

The cognitive model of psychopathology holds that thoughts influence both overt behaviour and emotional response, and that irrational thoughts contribute to emotional disturbance (Bard, 1980; Ellis, 1962b; Ellis and Harper, 1961; Ellis and Whiteley, 1979). A number of controlled studies suggest that cognitive change approaches, such as rational–emotive therapy, alone or in combination with behavioural techniques, are highly effective in reducing disturbed emotions and actions (see reviews by DiGiuseppe and Miller, 1977; Ellis, 1977c). In addition to this general focus, recent research has also begun to indicate that irrational beliefs or expectations influence adjustment in relationships and level of satisfaction with one's sex partners Eidelson and Epstein, 1981, 1982; Epstein and Eidelson, 1981, 1982).

Although each unhappy person's cognitions are to some extent unique, approximately ten irrational beliefs appear to account for much of the psychopathology treated in individual therapy (Bard, 1980; Ellis, 1962b). These beliefs, e.g. that it is a dire necessity to be approved of by everyone and that it is a catastrophe when things are not the way one likes, are identifiable and relatively distinct from one another (Jones, 1968a; Woods, 1983). According to Ellis's more recent theoretical formulations, each of these irrational beliefs can be characterized as reflecting one of three major 'mus-turbatory' ideologies: (1) *I must* do well and win approval; (2) *you must* treat me kindly, considerately, and justly; and (3) *the world must* make life easy and comfortable for me (Ellis, 1977a).

The assessment and disputation of irrational beliefs are relevant to clinicians who conduct individual psychotherapy. Correcting both general irrational cognitions and specific irrationalities regarding relationships has increasingly become a focus for those who conduct conjoint marital and sex therapy (Beck, 1980; Ellis, 1962a, 1971, 1983; Epstein, 1981a,b, 1982; Epstein and Eidelson, 1981; Epstein and Williams, 1981; Epstein *et al.*, 1979; Stuart, 1980). Correspondingly, theorists and researchers have begun to investigate the existence and role of irrational beliefs that are specific to intimate relationships such as marriage and cohabitation. Eidelson and Epstein, for example, have developed a self-report measure of irrational ideas about marriage which is useful for predicting the extent to which individuals are dissatisfied with their relationships (Eidelson and Epstein, 1981, 1982; Epstein and Eidelson, 1981, 1982), and which can serve as a tool for planning and measuring the effectiveness of therapeutic work with troubled couples.

In the context of these investigations, irrational beliefs specific to sex have received some incidental attention. In this regard, the Epstein and Eidelson instrument includes a set of items designed to tap *sexual perfectionism*, the irrational belief that one should be a flawless sexual partner. This, however, reflects only one of several possible sets of irrational beliefs/unrealistic expectations that are likely to prove harmful to sexual intimacy and satisfaction.

A critical review of empirical work and clinical formulations that speculate about the role of irrational beliefs in marital and sexual problems reveals several gaps in currently available knowledge.

Exploration of irrational beliefs specific to intimate relationships is in the embryonic stages of development; the relations among these specific irrationalities and those more general irrational beliefs formulated by Ellis are not clearly understood. Thus, the question of whether irrational beliefs regarding interpersonal relationships constitute a redundant subset of general irrational beliefs has not been resolved, or even clearly addressed. On an even more specific level, the identification and role of irrational beliefs particular to sex, and their utility beyond what can be garnered from focusing on relationship and general irrational beliefs, remain unknown. Gender differences in the predictive value of increasingly specific sets of irrational beliefs might be anticipated, but have also remained an area of minimal investigation.

The following literature review has been designed to identify areas of strength and weakness in available information regarding the roles of irrational cognitions in establishing/maintaining intimate relationships and attaining sexual satisfaction. First, general irrational beliefs and beliefs regarding marriage and other long-term relationships are considered, followed by exploration of sex-specific irrationalities and evidence for possible gender differences in adherence to specific beliefs. Therapeutic strategies addressed to these sets of irrational beliefs are then considered.

General irrational beliefs and their relation to intimacy

In the delicate interplay of an intimate relationship such as marriage, the more egocentric one partner becomes, the more unbalanced and troubled the relationship is likely to be. If both spouses are egocentric and subscribe to irrational beliefs, the marriage is in even greater danger. As Ellis (1964) points out, monogamous mating is exceptionally difficult for those who irrationally demand their cohabiting partner to treat them with the same polite and careful consideration they might receive from a new lover, friend or business associate.

Irrational beliefs, e.g. that a spouse *must* be continually fair, devoted, loving and forgiving, are lethal in long-term relationships. Such absolutistic thinking triggers rage or depression in the individual and fans the flames of interpersonal conflict (Ellis, 1962a,b, 1964, 1976). The lethal quality of these beliefs derives in part from the denial that relationships change with time, and that certain changes represent natural if not unavoidable developments. For example, many married and cohabiting individuals sabotage their relationships by demanding that long-term involvements retain the extreme excitement, novelty and mystery associated with new experiences. Confusing love and romance, they often overlook or discount the different but perhaps more enduring affection associated with a companionate bond, i.e. intimacy that can be generated between two people who are well acquainted with one another's flaws and histories. This perspective renders seemingly minor activating events (e.g. a spouse's failure to send flowers for an anniversary) exaggeratedly significant, while other positive qualities in a relationship (e.g. good parenting skills, sensitive caring by a partner during illness, etc.) are ignored.

Like Ellis, Epstein argues that disturbed marriages result when one or both partners hold irrational beliefs (Epstein, 1981a,b; Epstein and Williams, 1981). Consistent with this model of marital dysfunction, Epstein *et al.* (1979) report that undergraduates with high scores on the Irrational Beliefs Test (Jones, 1968b), a self-report measure assessing adherence to each of a set of general irrational beliefs described by Ellis, held significantly more negative impressions of a disagreeing couple's feelings and relationship than did more rational undergraduates. Since it is likely that individuals with irrational views will bring this perspective into their own cohabiting or marital relationships, disputation of each partner's general irrational beliefs might serve as a useful strategy in couple therapy.

A perspective complementary to the Ellis and Epstein views is presented by Beck (1980) in his discussion of egocentrism in intimate relationships. By egocentric, Beck means that the individual views present, past and future interactions with a partner exclusively in terms of how they relate to the self. For example, the meaning that a particular event has for his wife would not be part of an egocentric husband's phenomenal field. As a result, he would fail to respond adaptively to the relationship; bursts of painful conflict or unhealthy withdrawal would be inevitable, particularly if the wife was equally egocentric.

Beck's concept of egocentricity parallels Ellis' formulations of irrational beliefs in that the irrational person is essentially egocentric. Her unrealistic demands regarding herself reflect the egocentric belief that she must be perfect or all-powerful. The equally impossible demands she imposes on others and the world around her arise from her sense of being special or entitled, i.e. others should do her bidding and view the world from her perspective. She judges any failure to do this as bad, warranting an enduring negative response.

Some research suggests that people tend to be even more critical of their spouses or dating partners than of themselves. When questioned about the causes of their own undesirable behaviour, for example, young adults report that environmental circumstances obliged them to take a particular course of action. In contrast, these same young people attribute their spouse's or dating partner's behaviour to largely negative personality traits such as selfishness, irresponsibility and inadequacy (Orvis *et al.*, 1976). As Beck (1980, p. 8), concludes: 'A major factor producing collision between mates are [the] incompatible perspectives [or constructions] of particular situations.' In this regard, general irrational views of self, others and the world are likely to be implicated in relationship discord.

As may be noted from the literature reviewed above, the associations between general irrational beliefs and relationships have received some empirical attention. On the other hand, the relations between these general irrationalities and sexuality, including sexual dysfunction, have yet to be explored.

Irrational beliefs about relationships

Clinicians who conduct conjoint treatment might discover that challenging irrational beliefs specific to relationships proves more effective than disputing general irrationalities alone. As Epstein (1982, p. 7) suggests:

> A comprehensive assessment of expectations relevant to marital dysfunction should include commonly held irrational beliefs such as those postulated by Ellis . . . and expectations that are more idiosyncratic to the members of a particular couple.

Eidelson and Epstein's (1981, 1982) Relationship Belief Inventory appears to constitute the single attempt at construction of a measure of dysfunctional beliefs about marriage and other intimate relationships. The inventory consists of five sub-scales or sets of items that are identified in terms of the categories of irrational beliefs addressed: disagreement is destructive, mindreading is expected, partners cannot change, sex must be perfect, the sexes are different. Research to date utilizing this instrument suggests that spouses who hold irrational beliefs about relationships are also more likely to subscribe to the more general irrational beliefs that are assessed by the Ellis-inspired Irrational Beliefs Test (Eidelson and Epstein, 1981, 1982). However, the amount of predictive overlap between general and relationship-specific irrationalities in accounting for variance in dyadic adjustment remains relatively unknown.

Additional myths beyond those tapped by the Relationship Belief Inventory are prevalent and even pervasive in our culture. Cultural myths, marketed by Madison Avenue and other media-linked purveyors of popular beliefs, play a major role in socializing people into specific irrationalities regarding relationships. The worship of all things young and new (e.g. lithe, young bodies; new and exciting romantic involvements) are major among these. Exercise and sensible diet not withstanding, it is irrational to expect a partner in his late 40s to present exactly the same appearance as he did in his early 20s. Equally ridiculous is the expectation that a wife of 20 years wear the same girlish dresses and express the same enthusiasm for listening to her mate's rendition of his day at work that characterized her behaviour during their early life together. Similarly irrational is the belief that one is not a worthwhile person unless one has a mate.

Expectations that the spouse will be unchanged, eternally devoted, and unwaveringly passionate defy the reality that relationships and people change with time. Romantic or passionate love of the kind espoused in popular songs appears to be ephemeral: as people live together, they become more cognizant of each other's flaws and shortcomings. This changing life together, with its changing perceptions, can be rich and growth-enhancing, but would hardly be characterized as 'happily ever after' for couples who adhere rigidly to irrational demands.

While passionate romance may diminish with time, friendship may grow. Hatfield's (1983) description of couples in long-term relationships in mid-life and beyond indicates that many experience a great deal of companionate love for their mates. Companionate love or deep friendship is the warm affection that people feel for those with whom they are intimately entwined. Unlike the newly-attached couple in the throes of being romantically or passionately 'in love', partners in a companionate relationship no longer maintain characteristic postures or rapt attention, touch one another constantly, or gaze deeply into one another's eyes (Morris, 1977). Instead, such couples are often able to be together in peaceful silence. They experience less desire to maintain continual good humour and the endless conversation, smiling and nodding of newer and perhaps less secure affectional relationships. Initial attraction has been transformed into strong, bonding attachment.

Just as it is erroneous to assume that love has ended for companionate couples, it is also highly questionable to conclude that the quality of such a couple's sex life has declined. While the frequency of love-making declines over time and with age for most persons (cf. Kinsey *et al.*, 1948, 1953), the quality of sexual experiences may increase. For example, Starr and Weiner (1981, p. 16) cite a 69-year-old woman who indicates:

> Sex is much more enjoyable and satisfying now. It used to be more frequent, and while pleasurable it has now become less frequent, *but* each time lasts longer and has much greater sensory impact during climax for both of us.

Unfortunately, irrational demands that the quality of love be unchanging can function to deprive a couple of these kinds of positive developments in their relationship.

Irrational beliefs about sex

The human desire for sex may be more cognitive and learned than instinctive (Rook and Hammen, 1977). Physical acts alone do not appear to cause sexual arousal; rather, the meaning that people give to these acts largely determines whether sex will occur and be enjoyed (Gagnon and Simon, 1973; McCormick, 1984). For example, some aspects of a gynaecological examination might produce the same stimulation as interactions with a lover, but would be unlikely to arouse the typical woman who would categorize her experience as medical rather than erotic. In such ways, cognitions play a major role in human sexuality.

As alluded to earlier, not all cognitions regarding sex are rational, nor necessarily facilitative of sexual pleasure. Just as people hold irrational beliefs that create disturbances in their relationships and in their lives in general, they may subscribe to specific irrational beliefs that interfere with their enjoyment of sex. Before disputation of these irrational beliefs can occur, the therapist must, of course, assist the client in pinpointing those sexual irrationalities that are operative.

Delineation of irrational beliefs regarding sex in inventory form, for research and clinical assessment, appears to be relatively absent from the literature (Eidelson and Epstein, 1981, 1982; Epstein and Eidelson, 1981, 1982). However, the literature to date provides many anecdotal sources of information and case reports regarding dysfunctional 'myths' and beliefs that can be used as a guide in therapy (cf. Barbach, 1975; Ellis, 1961, 1962a, 1966, 1969, 1972, 1973a,b, 1977b,d, 1981; McCary and McCary, 1982; Wolfe, 1976; Zilbergeld, 1978).

It appears from this literature that irrational beliefs about sex are not necessarily uncommon or idiosyncratic. In fact, most people in a given culture subscribe to many sexual myths. For example, Westerners are preoccupied with the idea that penis-in-vagina sex is superior to all other forms of sexual expression, a belief linked to the traditional Judeo-Christian concept that procreation is the major justification for sex. This value system has created what Ellis (1973a) aptly describes as a *coitus complex*. According to the liberal version of this complex of irrational beliefs, normal sex might include anal, oral and manual stimulation in foreplay, but should culminate in orgasm during coitus. The coitus complex, which influences many sex educators and therapists including Masters and Johnson, can be taken to imply that 'even penile-vaginal copulation, when it does not result in simultaneous mutual orgasm between a male and female partner, is a serious perversion of human sexuality' (Ellis, 1973a, p. 286). An important corollary of the coitus complex is its rigid insistence on heterosexual and genitally oriented sexuality. The lovemaking of gay people, disabled people who are unable to engage in coitus, and even older heterosexuals who have passed their reproductive years, is overlooked or demeaned. Like other 'shoulds' linked to sexuality, the coitus complex is irrational because it is a dogmatic, definitional concept which can be neither supported nor invalidated by clinical and experimental evidence.

In contrast with the dictates of the coitus complex, there is no reason to believe that procreation is the only valid motivation for sexual relationships. In fact, a number of otherwise normal women require direct clitoral stimulation and are unable to achieve orgasm via coitus alone (Kaplan, 1974). Given this information, it is reasonable to question why women and their partners should work toward the sometimes unachievable goals of validating the coitus complex. Further, there is no verifying evidence that the orgasm achieved via sexual intercourse is superior to that achieved by other means (cf. Masters and Johnson, 1966). As Barbach (1975) argues, the only function of the clitoris is sexual pleasure: if procreation were the sole purpose of sexuality, women would not require a clitoris.

Some sexual cognitions, e.g. that a physically attractive person is a more desirable sex partner, appear to be virtually universal (Cook, 1981; Cook and McHenry, 1978). Adherence to such universal expectations is adaptive in that it can assist the individual to optimize his/her chances of obtaining sexual gratification, given the constraints of cultural guidelines/biases. For example, commonly held or shared guidelines provide the individual with direction regarding what will be considered attractive by peers. In our culture, the rational individual might conform to these guidelines by dressing stylishly, being well groomed, and maintaining good muscle tone and slenderness. In this way, the individual is likely to enhance his/her chances of creating a favourable impression on potential sex partners, and will be likely to have more sex partners and perhaps more pleasure within sexual encounters than self-conscious and less attractive individuals. On the other hand, such guidelines can act as barriers to intimacy and pleasure, as in the case of unfounded biases against sexuality in the elderly or disabled.

Ideas such as those described above have been called sexual myths by some writers (cf. Ellis, 1972; McCary and McCary, 1982; Zilbergeld, 1978) and irrational beliefs about sex by others (cf. Barbach, 1975; Ellis, 1971, 1975; Epstein, 1981b). However they are labelled, they are unverifiable expectations that often place unrealistically high demands on the self or a sexual partner. For instance, one of the major reasons certain women fail to experience orgasms or to enjoy sex fully is 'that they are so overdetermined to achieve' these qualities (Ellis, 1973b, p. 452). Instead of focusing their thinking on pleasurable body sensations and sexually exciting ideas, they think 'what an idiot and incompetent person I am for not being able to have an orgasm without any difficulty' (Ellis, 1973b, p. 452). Correspondingly, male erectile failure is frequently linked to the obsessive internal demand that 'I must get an erection and please my partner through intercourse.' Preferring to enjoy sex and to experience orgasms is rational. In contrast, demanding that this occur regardless of circumstances, and linking one's sense of self-worth to sexual achievement, is neither rational nor facilitative of sexual enjoyment (Ellis, 1969, 1971, 1973b, 1975).

Within the cognitive model of psychotherapy, a sexual dysfunction is based in part on the attributes that an individual makes about the cause and nature of sexual problems (Epstein, 1981b). For example, a man with erection problems is likely to blame himself for his sexual dysfunction. Such self-blame would be consistent with the myth that the man must take charge of and orchestrate sex (Zilbergeld, 1978). Therapists can help clients identify irrational beliefs used in interpreting experiences and, through disputation, substitute more realistic, constructive explanations for their sexual problems. For example, the man with erection problems could be encouraged to challenge his belief that he must take charge of and orchestrate sex. As Zilbergeld (1978) indicates, belief in this myth is likely to result in the man being so busy pleasing his partner and discouraging the woman from taking sexual initiative that he is unable to get the stimulation he needs to achieve arousal or erection. The therapist's role in challenging sex-linked irrational beliefs/myths becomes particularly important when cultural biases virtually blind the client to alternative approaches to thinking about and obtaining sexual pleasure.

Gender differences in irrational beliefs relating to relationships and sexuality

Men have generally been stereotyped as more interested in sex and as more independent, interpersonally rigid and assertive than women (Allgeier and McCormick, 1983). In contrast, women have commonly been stereotyped as more romantic or love-oriented than men and as weaker or less competent outside the realm of home and family. While it is highly likely that these stereotyped or expected differences between men and women might influence the development of gender-specific irrational ideas, research in this area is extremely limited and, at best, suggestive.

Members of young dating and cohabiting couples tend to explain their partner's behaviour in terms of traditional sex-role stereotypes (Orvis *et al.*, 1976). Women are described as being influenced by the environment, other people, their own lack of abilities and insecurity about the relationship. In contrast, men are viewed as more insensitive or unyielding, and more likely than women to exercise control over the course of their lives. These findings suggest that women may be expected to be more irrational than men in their demand for approval, anxious over-concern, over-reaction to frustration, dependency, problem avoidance, and emotional irresponsibility. Men, on the other hand, might be more irrational than women in such areas as high self-expectations, perfectionism, blame proneness, and helplessness for change (the belief that the past determines the present and future).

Clinical theory and some research data provide partial evidence for these notions. For instance, rational-emotive therapists point out that women are more likely than men to be 'love-slobs', and whose entire existence is oriented toward pleasing and leaning on partners (Ellis, 1977a; Russianoff, 1981;

Wolfe, 1975, 1976). Consistent with this view, Jones (1968a) reported that women were significantly more irrational than men in their responses to the Irrational Beliefs Test scales measuring demand for approval, over–reaction to frustration, and dependency. Also, Epstein and Eidelson (1982) report that female patients in marital therapy were significantly less likely than their male counterparts to see themselves as responsible for their mood states. In contrast with Epstein and Eidelson's findings, Jones (1968a) found men to be significantly more emotionally irresponsible than women when general rather than relationship-specific beliefs were tapped.

As mentioned earlier, Zilbergeld (1978) has found that men are oppressed by a sexual mythology which depicts sex as a performance with men being responsible for all the orchestration. Consistent with Zilbergeld's ideas, Epstein and Eidelson (1982) indicate that male patients in marital therapy are significantly more perfectionistic about their own behaviour and more likely than female patients to believe that people should be blamed for their mistakes. Male sexual perfectionism might be a subset of more general irrational beliefs: Jones (1968a) found that men score significantly higher than women on blame proneness, perfectionism, and helplessness for change scales. Such unreasonable demands on self and others contribute to male performance anxiety during sex. It is not surprising, then, that researchers report that men with sexual problems are viewed as more responsible for their own or a partner's dysfunction than women (Jayne *et al.*, 1981). Also, males are especially harsh in their judgement of men with sexual problems, attributing greater unhappiness and psychopathology to such individuals than do women (Polyson, 1978).

Summary and conclusions

The literature to date suggests that individuals are likely to subscribe to irrational beliefs that are general in nature, as well as to adhere to some irrationalities that are specific to relationships and sex. While it is fairly evident that irrational cognitions exist at increasing levels of specificity, the appropriate or optimal level for targeting therapeutic efforts remain unclear. For example, little is known about the differential effectiveness of correcting general perfectionistic cognitions versus disputing specific beliefs (e.g. that one must be a perfect lover) when treating a male client whose presenting problem is inability to maintain an erection. A situation-specific focus has been helpful in other areas of research and treatment, e.g. anxiety, self-perceptions, aptitudes. On the other hand, attacking overarching or general irrational tendencies might prove to be the most efficient strategy for promoting emotional health in some individuals. Without empirical investigations of the overlaps among these sets of cognitions, predictions about therapeutic strategies remain at the level of uninformed guesses.

Given present gaps in knowledge, practising therapists might work at developing their awareness of the various levels on which irrational cognitions operate. Recognizing that there are alternative therapeutic strategies to that of disputing general irrational beliefs, provides new methods for attacking a problem that might otherwise appear resistant to change. For example, clients who experience greater difficulty with abstractions and generalizations might profit from disputes geared to very specific irrational beliefs, whereas individuals who are adept at these processes might be best served by disputes geared to more general, overarching cognitions.

To identify adequately the irrational beliefs held by clients, therapists might consider at least three categories or sources of cognitions potentially disruptive to relationships and sexual pleasure:

1. Beliefs that are subscribed to universally or by the general culture, e.g. that attractive people make the best sex partners.
2. Beliefs that are gender-specific, e.g. that men are responsible for providing a good sexual experience.
3. Beliefs that are idiosyncratic to each individual who seeks treatment, or particular to a specific age or geographical cohort.

The alertness of therapists to different sources of irrational cognitions, as well as awareness that these cognitions are likely to exist at varying levels of specificity, will assist in the tasks of comprehensively identifying troublesome thoughts and creatively exploring alternatives. Even in behavioural phases of marital or sex therapy, it is important to maintain an awareness of the effects of irrational beliefs. For example, a couple who had avoided pornography on the basis of a belief that one should be excited only by one's lover were encouraged to dispute this irrational belief and explore the use of this material for their arousal problem. Several weeks later, the therapist recognized that this approach was working as a 'turn off' rather than a 'turn on' for the couple. After having successfully disputed the original belief, the couple decided that since the pornography was so exciting, they should or must be able to perform as well and be as attractive as the people in the films.

Cognitive therapy is likely to be maximally effective when a firm grasp of anthropology, sociology and social psychology complements the therapist's familiarity with the counselling and clinical literatures. As noted throughout this Chapter, many irrational beliefs, including those regarding relationships and sexual intimacy, are socialized by the culture just as are sex-role stereotypes and racial prejudices. Consequently, an effective therapeutic strategy is likely to involve demonstrating to an individual or couple how and where they learned such maladaptive rules, and clarifying that this so-called knowledge is completely arbitrary.

The notion that something is right simply because most people believe or practise it is especially ripe for challenge. This process focuses on disputing the group bias of the culture. An example relevant to this issue involves treatment of a young woman who complained about the absence of sex in her relationship but refused to initiate sex because that is 'her boyfriend's job'. The therapist discussed research suggesting that men are often excited when women make the first pass, although most people adhere to the stereotype that only men should appear to take the sexual initiative. Afterwards, the young woman acknowledged that her partner, a shy and passive lover, disclosed that he had been disappointed in her complete lack of initiative in love-making, and had experienced pleasure when previous women lovers 'attacked him aggressively'. Instead of using this information as a means of improving her sex life, the client interpreted it as a insult regarding her attractiveness, sulking even more than usual. Here, as is probably the case in most real-life clinical situations, there is a combination of general irrationalities (e.g. *I must* have another's approval and *people must* do as I wish), irrationalities specific to relationships (e.g. my *partner should* be able to read my mind and know what I want), and those specific to sexuality (e.g. my *partner should* always be willing to seduce women). Rather than be discouraged regarding the complexity of such interwoven irrationalities, the clinician can share the excitement of untangling these with the client, while the researcher is confronted with the equally complex task of identifying and cataloguing the sources and levels of irrational beliefs that interfere with intimacy and sexual pleasure.

References

Allgeier, E.R. and McCormick, N.B. (Eds)(1983). *Changing boundaries: Gender rules and sexual behavior*. Palo Alto, Calif.: Mayfield.

Barbach, L.G. (1975). *For yourself: The fulfillment of female sexuality*. New York: Signet/New American Library.

Bard, J.A. (1980). *Rational-emotive therapy in practice*. Champaign, Ill.: Research Press.

Beck, A.T. (1980). Cognitive aspects of marital interactions. Paper presented at the meeting of the Association for the Advancement of Behavior Therapy, New York, November 1980.

Cook, M. (1981). Social skills and human sexual attraction. *In* M. Cook (Ed.), *The bases of human sexual attraction*, pp. 145–77. London and San Diego: Academic Press.

Cook, M. and McHenry, R. (1978). *Sexual attraction*. Oxford: Pergamon Press.

DiGiuseppe, R.A. and Miller, N.J. (1977). A review of outcome studies on rational-emotive therapy. *In* A. Ellis and R. Grieger (Eds), *Handbook of rational-emotive therapy*, pp. 72–95. New York: Springer.

Eidelson, R.J. and Epstein, N. (1981). *Relationship belief inventory*. (Available from N. Epstein, Department of Family and Community Development, University of Maryland, College Park, Maryland 20742.)

Eidelson, R.J. and Epstein, N. (1982). Cognition and relationship maladjustment: Development of a measure of dysfunctional relationship beliefs. *Journal of Consulting and Clinical Psychology,* **50,** 715–720.

Ellis, A. (1961). Myths about sex. *Cosmopolitan Magazine,* February, 82–5.

Ellis, A. (1962a). Myths about sex compatibility. *Sexology,* **28,** 652–5.

Ellis, A. (1962b). *Reason and emotion in psychotherapy.* Secaucus, N.J.: Lyle Stuart.

Ellis, A. (1964). *The nature of disturbed marital interaction.* (Pamphlet P255, available from the Institute for Rational-Emotive Therapy, 45 East 65th Street, New York, N.Y. 10021.)

Ellis, A. (1966). *New cures for frigidity.* (Available from the Institute for Rational-Emotive Therapy, 45 East 65th Street, New York, N.Y. 10021.)

Ellis, A. (1969). *Sexual intercourse: Psychological foundations.* (Pamphlet P292, available from the Institute for Rational-Emotive Therapy, 45 East 65th Street, New York, N.Y. 10021.)

Ellis, A. (1971). Rational-emotive treatment of impotence, frigidity, and other sexual problems. *Professional Psychology,* **2,** 346–9.

Ellis, A. (1972). *Myths about spontaneous sex and sensuosity in marriage.* (Reprinted from Forum, 1972. Available from A. Ellis, Institute for Rational-Emotive Therapy, 45 East 65th Street, New York, N.Y. 10021.)

Ellis, A. (1973a). Coitus. *In* A. Ellis and A. Abarbanel (Eds), *The encyclopedia of sexual behavior,* pp. 284–92. New York: Jason Aronson.

Ellis, A. (1973b). Frigidity. *In* A. Ellis and A. Abarbanel (Eds), *The encyclopedia of sexual behavior,* pp. 450–56. New York: Jason Aronson.

Ellis, A. (1975). The rational-emotive approach to sex therapy. *Counseling Psychologist,* **5,** 14–22.

Ellis, A. (1976). Techniques of handling anger in marriage. *Journal of Marriage and Family Counseling,* **2,** 305–16.

Ellis, A. (1977a). The basic clinical theory of rational-emotive therapy. *In* A. Ellis and R. Grieger (Eds), *Handbook of rational-emotive therapy,* pp. 3–34. New York: Springer.

Ellis, A. (Speaker) (1977b). Harmful sexual myths held by men and women and how to exorcise them. (Reel-to-reel recording, available from the Institute for Rational-Emotive Therapy, 45 East 65th Street, New York, N.Y. 10021.)

Ellis, A. (1977c). Research data supporting the clinical and personality hypotheses of RET and other cognitive-behavior therapies. *In* A. Ellis and R. Grieger (Eds), *Handbook of rational-emotive therapy,* pp. 35–71. New York: Springer.

Ellis, A. (1977d). Sex and love problems in women. *In* A. Ellis and R. Grieger (Eds), *Handbook of rational-emotive therapy,* pp. 153–69. New York: Springer.

Ellis, A. (1981). Dr. Albert Ellis's list of 21 irrational beliefs that lead to sex problems and disturbances. *In* A.B. Gerber (Ed.), *The book of sex lists,* pp. 46–8. Secaucus, N.J.: Lyle Stuart.

Ellis, A. (1983). Does sex therapy really have a future? *Rational Living,* **18,** 3–6.

Ellis, A. and Harper, R.A. (1961). *A guide to rational living.* North Hollywood, Calif.: Wilshire Book Company.

Ellis, A. and Whiteley, J.M. (Eds) (1979). *Theoretical and empirical foundations of rational-emotive therapy.* Monterey, Calif.: Brooks/Cole.

Epstein, N. (1981a). Assertiveness training in marital treatment. *In* G.P. Sholevar (Ed.), *The handbook of marriage and marital therapy*, pp. 287–302. New York: Spectrum.

Epstein, N. (1981b). Cognitive-behavior therapy in the treatment of sexual disorders. Paper presented at the meeting of the Society for the Scientific Study of Sex, New York, November 1981.

Epstein, N. (1982). Cognitive therapy with couples. *American Journal of Family Therapy*. **10**, 5–16.

Epstein, N. and Eidelson, R.J. (1981). Unrealistic beliefs of clinical couples: Their relationship to expectations, goals and satisfaction. *American Journal of Family Therapy*, **9**, 13–22.

Epstein, N. and Eidelson, R.J. (1982). Marital dysfunction and depression: Cognitive factors and treatment implications. Paper presented at the meeting of the Association for the Advancement of Behavior Therapy, Los Angeles, November 1982.

Epstein, N. and Williams, A.M. (1981). Behavioral approaches to the treatment of marital discord. *In* G.P. Sholevar (Ed.), *The handbook of marriage and marital therapy*, pp. 219–86. New York: Spectrum.

Epstein, N., Finnegan, D. and Bythell, D. (1979). Irrational beliefs and perceptions of marital conflict. *Journal of Consulting and Clinical Psychology*, **47**, 608–610.

Gagnon, J.H. and Simon, W. (1973). *Sexual conduct: The social sources of human sexuality*. Chicago: Aldine.

Hatfield, E. (1983). What do women and men want from love and sex? *In* E.R. Allgeier and N.B. McCormick (Eds), *Changing boundaries: Gender roles and sexual behavior*, pp. 106–134. Palo Alto, Calif.: Mayfield.

Jayne, C., Epstein, B. and Robinson-Metz, M. (1981). Cognitive appraisals of sexual dysfunction as a function of gender, chronicity, and type of problem. Paper presented at the meeting of the Association for Advancement of Behavior Therapy, Toronto, November 1981.

Jones, R.G. (1968a). A factored measure of Ellis' irrational belief systems with personality and maladjustment correlated. (Available from Test Systems Inc., P.O. Box 18432, Wichita, Kansas 67218.)

Jones, R.G. (1968b). The irrational beliefs test (I.B.T.). (Available from Test Systems Inc., P.O. Box 18432, Wichita, Kansas 67218.)

Kaplan, H.S. (1974). *The new sex therapy: Active treatment of sexual dysfunctions*. New York: Brunner/Mazel.

Kinsey, A.C., Pomeroy, W.B. and Martin, C.E. (1948). *Sexual behavior in the human male*. Philadelphia: Saunders.

Kinsey, A.C., Pomeroy, W.B., Martin, C.E. and Gebhard, P.H. (1953). *Sexual behavior in the human female*. Philadelphia: Saunders.

Masters, W.H. and Johnson, V.E. (1966). *Human sexual response*. Boston: Little, Brown.

McCary, J.L. and McCary, S.P. (1982). Sexual myths and fallacies. *In* J.L. McCary and S.P. McCary, *McCary's human sexuality*, 4th edition, pp. 29–35. Belmont, Calif.: Wadsworth.

McCormick, N.B. (1984). Courtship scripts: Having sex by the rules. Manuscript submitted for publication.

Morris, D. (1977). *Manwatching: A field guide to human behavior.* New York: Abrams.

Orvis, B.R., Kelley, H.H. and Butler, D. (1976). Attributional conflict in young couples. In J.H. Harvey, W.J. Ickes and R.F. Kidd (Eds), *New directions in attribution research,* Vol. 1, pp. 353–86. Hillsdale, N.J.: Lawrence Erlbaum Associates.

Polyson, J.A. (1978). Sexism and sexual problems: Societal censure of the sexually troubled male. *Psychological Reports,* **42,** 843–50.

Rook, K.S. and Hammen, C.L. (1977). A cognitive perspective on the experience of sexual arousal. *Journal of Social Issues,* **33,** 7–29.

Russianoff, P. (1981). *Why do I think I'm nothing without a man?* New York: Bantam.

Starr, B.D. and Weiner, M.B. (1981). *The Starr-Weiner report on sex and sexuality in the mature years.* New York: McGraw-Hill.

Stuart, R.B. (1980). *Helping couples change: A social learning approach to marital therapy.* New York: Guilford Press.

Wolfe, J.L. (1975). Rational-emotive therapy as an effective feminist therapy. (Available from the Institute for Rational-Emotive Therapy, 45 East 65th Street, New York, N.Y. 10021.)

Wolfe, J.L. (1976). How to be sexually assertive. (Available from the Institute for Rational-Emotive Therapy, 45 East 65th Street, New York, N.Y. 10021.)

Woods, P.J. (1983). On the relative independence of irrational beliefs. *Rational Living,* **18,** 23–24.

Zilbergeld, B. (1978). *Male sexuality: A guide to sexual fulfillment.* New York: Bantam Books.

Chapter 6

Irrational beliefs and strength versus inappropriateness of feelings: a debate

Duncan Cramer and Albert Ellis

I. The study: Duncan Cramer

The theory of rational-emotive therapy draws a distinction between appropriate feelings and inappropriate feelings (Ellis, 1973). Rational beliefs lead to appropriate feelings, whereas irrational beliefs lead to inappropriate feelings. Originally, it was implied that the appropriateness of a feeling was characterized by its strength: strong feelings were inappropriate (Ellis and Harper, 1961). In a revised version of the theory, it has been proposed that the appropriateness of a feeling is distinguished by its nature and not by its strength (Ellis and Harper, 1975). Certain feelings such as annoyance, frustration, regret, sadness, sorrow and unhappiness are appropriate, whereas others such as anger, anxiety, depression, despair, guilt, resentment and worthlessness are inappropriate (Ellis, 1973; Ellis and Harper, 1975). In other words, feeling slightly angry is always inappropriate, whereas feeling very annoyed is always appropriate. The aim of this study is to determine which of these two versions is valid. According to the original theory, it was predicted that degree of irrationality would be positively correlated with strength of feeling, regardless of its appropriateness, whereas on the basis of the revised version, it was predicted that degree of irrationality should be positively correlated with strength of inappropriate feeling only. According to the revised version, there should be no relationship between irrationality and appropriate feelings because both rational and irrational thinkers would experience appropriate emotions in a distressing situation, and so there should be no differences between them in terms of these feelings.

Method

Degree of irrationality was measured by Jones' (1968) Irrational Beliefs Test.

To assess strength and appropriateness of feeling, subjects were asked to rate on a 4-point scale (1 = not at all, 2 = a little bit, 3 = quite a bit, 4 = very) how they would feel in terms of four appropriate (annoyed, concerned, disappointed, unhappy) and four inappropriate feelings (angry, anxious, awful, depressed), if they experienced the following five potentially upsetting situations:

1. You realize that you have done badly in an important exam that you had worked hard for.
2. You find that someone you have been going out with and like very much is going out with someone else at the same time without letting you know.
3. You have lost £10 through your own fault.
4. Someone you have been going out with and like very much has told you that they no longer want to go out with you.
5. Someone has stolen your favourite coat.

The appropriate and inappropriate feelings were taken from Ellis' writings (Ellis and Harper, 1975) and were arranged in a different random order for each situation. Both questionnaires were completed by 185 subjects, 157 who described themselves as female (mean age 17.2 years) and 22 who described themselves as male (mean age 18.1 years). Where 10 per cent or more of a subject's data for a variable was missing, the subject's score for that variable was excluded from analysis. Consequently, the significant figures were based on the number of subjects included for any computation.

Results

Pearson product-moment correlation coefficients were calculated between the 10 irrational beliefs, together with a total irrational belief score (TIB) and the four appropriate and inappropriate feelings separately, together with a total appropriate (TAF) and a total inappropriate (TIF) feeling score. Since the number of males was small, only the correlations for the whole sample will be presented. The correlation betwen TIB and TAF and TIF was 0.40 ($p<.001$) and 0.42 ($p<.001$) respectively, thus confirming the prediction from the original version of the theory. The correlations between TIB and each of the eight feelings were all positive and significant, and ranged from 0.25 ($p<.001$) for disappointment to 0.42 ($p<.001$) for anxious. The only two specific irrational beliefs that did not correlate with both TAF and TIF were emotional irresponsibility and problem avoidance. All the other correlations were positive and significant, ranging from 0.14 ($p<.05$) between TAF and blame proneness to 0.41 ($p<.001$) between TIF and anxious over-concern.

Discussion

The results of this study clearly support the original version of the theory which postulated that the appropriateness of a feeling is characterized by its strength, since there was a strong and positive correlation between irrationality and strength of feeling, regardless of its appropriateness. The size of the correlation between irrationality and inappropriate feeling was little different from that between irrationality and appropriate feeling. The revised version of the theory would predict that there should be no relationship between irrationality and appropriate feelings, since both rational and irrational thinkers would experience appropriate feelings in a distressing situation, and so there should be no differences between them in terms of these feelings. These findings are in line with the idea that irrational thinkers tend to 'catastrophize' and to exaggerate their feelings. Consequently, when discussing or assessing the effects of irrational thinking, it is not necessary to distinguish appropriate from inappropriate feelings in the way described in the revised version.

II. A reply: Albert Ellis

Cramer has made an interesting test of one of my major rational-emotive therapy (RET) hypotheses and has come up with results favouring my early view that inappropriate feelings are characterized by their strength (Ellis, 1962, Ellis and Harper, 1961) and disfavouring my latest view that inappropriate or self-defeating feelings are characterized by their nature (Ellis, 1977a,b; Ellis and Harper, 1975). I am not sure, however, that his method of correlating his subjects' degree of irrationality with both the intensity and the nature of their negative feelings provides a good test of my later theory. On the contrary, Cramer's findings may well tend to partially confirm my later view.

Let me first explain what my most recent view on irrationality and inappropriate feelings actually states. I originally thought that just as irrational ideas may be on a continuum, ranging from mild to severe irrational beliefs, so too are disturbed emotions, ranging from mild or moderate negative emotions (such as mild anger), which I identified as appropriate when people are frustrated to extreme emotions (such as rage), which I identified as inappropriate. I later realized, however, that there seem to be two fairly distinct continua of negative emotions when people experience frustration or rejection: (1) mild to severe annoyance at or devaluation of one's own or others' *acts*, and (2) mild to severe anger at and damnation of *oneself* or other *people* who committed the unwanted acts. I hypothesized that the former sets of feelings usually stem from healthy self-statements ('I *prefer* that I and others behave well but we don't *have* to do so and I can stand it if we don't and still find myself and others acceptable as people'); and the latter set of inappropriate feelings stem from grandiose, commanding, musturbatory self-statements ('because I prefer that I and others behave well, we *must* do so, and if we don't do as we *must*, I can't stand it, and I and these others are *rotten damnable people!*'). I theorized – and still do – that the desiring or preferential self-statements lead to annoyance or displeasure (or even anger) at people's *behaviour* and are usually rational and self-helping, while the absolutistic, musturbatory philosophies lead to anger or rage at *people* and are usually irrational and self-defeating (Ellis, 1977b, 1979; Ellis and Harper, 1975).

In differentiating, however, between preferential and musturbatory self-statements and in holding that the former, even when strong, do not *by themselves* usually lead to inappropriate feelings and behaviours while the latter, even when weak, usually do, I never held that people, when disturbed, have *only* irrational beliefs and have *no* rational beliefs, as Cramer seems to imply in his study. Thus, he notes that according to my revised, musturbatory version of RET:

> there should be no relationship between irrationality and appropriate feelings because both rational and irrational thinkers would experience appropriate emotions in a distressing situation and so there should be no difference between them in terms of these feelings (see p. 56).

But this is not at all what I hypothesized.

My view, instead, is that rational thinkers tend to more often stay with rational beliefs (preferences) and therefore experience appropriate feelings, whereas irrational thinkers *start* with preferences and with appropriate feelings and then *add* musts and inappropriate feelings stemming from the musts. If people were *completely* rational (which, of course, they never are) they would *only* have rational beliefs (preferences) and appropriate negative feelings when confronted with undesirable events. Whereas if they were completely irrational (which, again, they never are), they would have *both* rational beliefs *and* irrational beliefs, and would almost invariably have inappropriate *as well as* appropriate feelings about unwanted events.

If I interpret it correctly, Cramer's study first shows that subjects who have what I call appropriate and inappropriate feelings do about equally well on Jones' (1968) Irrational Beliefs Test. It could be argued that the Jones' test is not always valid, as several studies have shown (Baisden, 1980). It could also be argued that the subjects Cramer studied were (consciously or unconsciously) not especially honest either in their responses to Jones' test nor to what kind of appropriate and inappropriate feelings they would actually feel in the five potentially upsetting situations that he presented to them. These are probably good arguments against Cramer's conclusion that subjects with appropriate feelings could not be differentiated from those with inappropriate feelings in terms of irrational beliefs, and I am not sure how he would answer them.

Assuming, however, that Cramer's instruments and his test procedures are unassailable, and that therefore his results are valid, my interpretation would still be that they may merely show that people with irrational beliefs have *both* appropriate and inappropriate feelings, as my revised theory suggests. My view that people who are really irrational (e.g. those who would be diagnosed as being severely neurotic, borderline, or psychotic) have significantly more inappropriate than appropriate negative feelings when actually encountering unfortunate situations has not been tested by Cramer. Nor has my corollary theory that people who have quite inappropriate feelings (e.g. rage and depression) when distressing events occur in their lives are, *at the time they experience these feelings* (and not necessarily later), thinking significantly more irrational thoughts than when they are experiencing appropriate feelings (e.g. those of annoyance and sadness). Cramer has made an interesting start in testing these hypotheses, but I think that considerable more research had better be done to try to test them further.

III. A rejoinder: Duncan Cramer

Ellis, in his comment on my study, begins by making what seems to be a refinement of his revised theory of the distinction between appropriate and inappropriate emotions, which is of considerable interest and which does not appear to have been so explicitly expressed in public before. In this elaboration of this theory, he proposes that appropriate feelings are directed towards specific acts, while inappropriate feelings are directed towards the agents of these acts. While it was always clear that irrational thinking in Ellis' view is characterized by global evaluations of people, it was not so apparent (to the present author at least) that the appropriateness of feelings is also partly determined by the object of these feelings. This clarification of this theoretical position is consistent with other aspects of his theory and is welcomed. However, Ellis begins to cloud this clarification by suggesting, albeit in parentheses, that it may be appropriate to feel anger towards people's behaviour. If it is generally appropriate to express what were previously defined as inappropriate feelings, provided that those feelings are directed towards specific aspects of a person and not towards the person as a whole, then the distinction between appropriate and inappropriate feelings seems to depend on the object rather than the nature of those feelings. At present, it is not clear whether Ellis believes that the appropriateness of a feeling, in terms of his revised theory, depends (1) on its nature, regardless of the object towards which it is directed, (2) on the object towards which it is directed, regardless of its nature, or (3) on its nature and the object towards which it is directed. Further clarification of this point would be of value. The hypothesis that was tested in the study under discussion was implicitly based on the first of the three definitions outlined above, since in this study subjects were asked how *they* would feel under certain circumstances, but no attempt was made to assess the object of their feelings.

With respect to Ellis' second point, it was not intended to imply that irrational thinkers only have irrational beliefs and do not have rational beliefs as well. In fact, the prediction that there should be no relationship between degree of irrationality and strength of appropriate feelings, which was derived from the revised version of his theory concerning the appropriateness of feelings, was based on the recognition that appropriate feelings are determined by rational beliefs and that both rational and irrational thinkers have rational beliefs. If it was thought that only rational thinkers had rational beliefs and that irrational thinkers had no rational beliefs, then it would have been predicted that degree of irrationality would be negatively related to strength of appropriate feelings, since the degree of irrationality would itself be inversely related to the degree of rationality. It was because it was recognized that both rational and irrational thinkers hold rational beliefs to a similar extent that no relationship was predicted between degree of irrationality and strength of appropriate feelings. Perhaps this point should have been made clearer in the study.

Ellis questions the validity of Jones' (1968) Irrational Beliefs Test, although he cites only one of the several studies that he believes supports this assertion. Needless to say, there is other evidence which provides partial support for the validity of this measure. For example, it has been found to correlate with other measures of irrationality (Martin *et al.*, 1977) and with measures of self-acceptance and psychological distress (Daly and Burton, 1983; Goldfried and Sobocinski, 1975; Nelson, 1977). It has also been shown to reflect differences in assertiveness (Lohr and Bonge, 1982) and depression (LaPointe and Crandell, 1980).

It is true that other aspects of Ellis' theory were not tested, such as the hypothesis that people who have inappropriate feelings when actually experiencing distressing events have more irrational thoughts than those who have appropriate feelings under similar circumstances, or the hypothesis that irrational people have more inappropriate feelings than appropriate ones. One of the difficulties in testing this latter hypothesis is that Ellis has not provided a sufficiently comprehensive list of appropriate and inappropriate feelings which could be used to do this. Much further research remains to be carried out to test these and other hypotheses adequately. However, at present, there is some tentative evidence to suggest that degree of irrationality is equally related to the strength of both appropriate and inappropriate feelings.

IV. Concluding comments: Albert Ellis

Cramer, in his rejoinder to my comments on his original critique of my theory of irrational beliefs and inappropriate feelings, rightly asks for more clarity as to whether I believe that appropriateness of a feeling depends (1) on its nature, regardless of the object toward which it is directed, (2) on the object towards which it is directed, regardless of its nature, or (3) on its nature and the object toward which it is directed. Let me try to clarify my views.

1. Usually, but not necessarily *always*, a feeling is appropriate regardless of its nature of intensity. Thus, if I perceive you as treating me unfairly, I can feel displeased about (or hate) your treatment of me mildly, moderately, greatly or overwhelmingly, and any of these feelings would be appropriate, depending on what importance (small or great) I give to fair treatment and how convinced I am that your dealing with me is unfair. I have a *choice* of values (desires) about fairness and about how unfairly (I believe) you treated me, and my chosen values largely determine how intensely I dislike (or hate) your (observed) treatment of me. I can therefore *choose* to feel weakly or strongly about your 'unfair' treatment and no one can tell me that my personal choices of feeling are either appropriate or inappropriate. They simply exist, just because I choose them.

   If, under unusual conditions, I acknowledge (or feel) that you have treated me only a little unfairly and I then feel enormous displeasure (or intense hatred) about your treatment, I may experience inappropriate affect because: (a) I am inconsistent with my own chosen values; (b) my feeling is exceptionally exaggerated, considering what my values are; (c) my feeling probably stems from my absolutely and unrealistically demanding that you *must not* under *any* conditions treat me *at all* unfairly; and (d) my exaggerated feeling of intense displeasure (or hatred) of your treatment will very likely get me into needless trouble with you (and others) and will tend to disrupt my own life.

2. In my view (and that of RET) a feeling is distinctly inappropriate when it is directed toward an entire person (one's self or others) or toward life or the world as a whole. Thus, if I perceive you as treating me very unfairly, I had better not demand that you absolutely *must* not deal with me in this unfair manner and that if you do you have a bad, worthless *person*. If so, I make myself not only displeased at your *behaviour* but also angry at *you* – at your *totality*, your *essence*, your *being*. Instead of striving to get you to change your unfair *acts*, I make myself damn *you* – your *personhood* – and, thereby, I strive to harm or kill *you*.

   Similarly, if I perceive you as treating me as very unfairly, I had better not demand that life or the world absolutely must not allow you (and others) to treat me in this unfair manner and that if life and the world allow this kind of treatment, *they* are wholly bad and therefore *I can't stand* living in this *horrible* existence, and I had better kill myself.

RET states, in other words, that when I command that my desires and values *must* prevail, I damn myself (for not achieving what I *must*), damn others (for not giving me what they *must*,) and damn the world (for not according me what it *has to*), and I thereby make overgeneralized, *global* evaluations which tend to make me *in*appropriately feel anxious, depressed, self-downing, hostile, and self-pitying (Ellis, 1973; Ellis and Grieger, 1977; Ellis and Harper, 1975).

3. If what I have just said is correct, the appropriatenes of a feeling *usually* or *normally* depends on one's *desiring* or *preferring* some kind of accomplishment and/or aproval, therefore evaluating *behaviour* as bad, and consequently in various degrees feeling appropriately concerned, sorry, sad, regretful, annoyed or frustrated when one's desires are thwarted. The inappropriateness of a feeling, by the same token, *usually* depends on one's absolutistically *demanding* or *commanding* some kind of accomplishment and/or approval, therefore evaluating *oneself*, other *people* or the *world* as bad and, therefore, in various degrees, feeling *in*appropriately anxious, depressed, hostile, self-hating or self-pitying when one's demands are thwarted. *Occasionally*, exaggerated or unrealistic preferences without demands may lead to inappropriate or self-defeating feelings; but if so, we had better suspect and look for the implicit or unconscious absolutistic shoulds, oughts and musts that may lie behind them.

Cramer's critiques of my views on appropriate and inappropriate feelings have been quite instructive and have led me to try to clarify my position and to give it more substance. I am sure that the last word on this important subject has yet been said and, sparked by Cramer's study and by relevant additional research to which I hope it will lead, I shall continue to give it more careful thought.

References

Baisden, H.E. (1980). Irrational beliefs: A construct validation study. Unpublished Ph.D. dissertation, University of Minnesota.

Daly, M.J. and Burton, R.L. (1983). Self-esteem and irrational beliefs: An exploratory investigation with implications for counseling. *Journal of Counseling Psychology*, **30**, 361–6.

Ellis, A. (1962). *Reason and emotion in psychotherapy*. Secaucus, N.J.: Lyle Stuart/Citadel Press.

Ellis, A. (1973). *Humanistic psychotherapy: The rational-emotive approach.* New York: Julian Press.

Ellis, A. (1977a). The basic clinical theory of rational–emotive therapy. *In* A. Ellis and R. Grieger (Eds), *Handbook of rational-emotive therapy.* New York: Springer.

Ellis, A. (1977b). *How to live with and without anger.* New York: Readers Digest Press.

Ellis, A. (1979). The theory of rational–emotive therapy. *In* A. Ellis and J.M. Whiteley (Eds), *Theoretical and empirical foundations of rational-emotive therapy.* Monterey, Calif.: Brooks/Cole.

Ellis, A. and Grieger, R. (Eds) (1977). *Handbook of rational-emotive therapy.* New York: Springer.

Ellis, A. and Harper, R.A. (1961). *A guide to rational living.* Englewood Cliffs, N.J.: Prentice-Hall.

Ellis, A. and Harper, R.A. (1975). *A new guide to rational living.* North Hollywood, Calif.: Wilshire Books.

Goldfried, M. and Sobocinski, D. (1975). Effects of irrational beliefs on emotional arousal. *Journal of Consulting and Clinical Psychology*, **45**, 504–510.

Jones, R.G. (1968). A factored measure of Ellis' irrational belief system, with personality and maladjustment correlates. Unplublished Doctoral dissertation, Texas Technical College. Ann Arbor, Michigan: University Microfilms Inc., No. 69–6443.

Lapointe, K.A. and Crandell, C.J. (1980). Relationship of irrational beliefs to self-reported depression. *Cognitive Therapy and Research*, **4**, 247–50.

Lohr, J.M. and Bonge, D. (1982). Relationships between assertiveness and factorially validated measures of irrational beliefs. *Cognitive Therapy and Research*, **6**, 353–6.

Martin, L.M., Dolliver, R.H. and Irvin, J.A. (1977). A construct validity study of five measures of irrational beliefs. *Rational Living*, **12**, 20–24.

Nelson, R. (1977). Irrational beliefs in depression. *Journal of Consulting and Clinical Psychology*, **45**, 1190–91.

Chapter 7

A critical appraisal of therapeutic efficacy studies

Richard L. Wessler

The purpose of this Chapter is to explain my reasons for distrusting much of the research in psychotherapy, especially therapy outcome studies. I hope that my public confession of distrust will at least lead others to read research reports with scepticism, and to influence researchers to conduct better studies.

My therapeutic orientation has been rational–emotive therapy (RET), although my conceptions of it differ in many ways from those of its founder, Albert Ellis. As director of training for the Institute for Rational-Emotive Therapy*, my main activity in recent years has been to train other profession-als in RET, both in North America and Europe. I have co-authored several articles and books on the practice and supervision of RET (Wessler and Ellis, 1980; Walen et al., 1980; Wessler and Wessler, 1980). Since 1974, I have been editor of Rational Living*, a bi-annual journal that publishes theoretical and clinical articles and, of most relevance to this Chapter, research reports.

My experience in training and editing has led me to doubt whether many people who profess to know about RET actually are knowledgeable, and that when they conduct experiments which include RET, they necessarily con-duct poor experiments because of their misunderstanding of the approach. My assumption is that RET does not stand alone. Although I have not verified my assumption, I believe that other approaches are also likely to be misunderstood and misapplied.

The question almost all open-minded counsellors and psychotherapists would like answered is, what works? What can I do to increase my effective-ness, to help a larger proportion of clients with problems of living? One

---

* Editor's note: Richard Wessler no longer holds these positions.

answer comes from one's own experience, as we learn from our successes (which we hope are many), from our failures (which we hope are few), and from the category of persons who seem unaffected by our interventions, often because they choose not to collaborate with us. We can also learn from the experiences of others in the field, either in personal supervision or from reading their books and articles. We can learn from reading research reports, which, because they are presumably examples of objective, scientific investigation, are reliable sources of credible information.

The point is that we need reliable and valid research studies if we are to improve our therapeutic efficacy. However, the research with which I am most familiar suffers in three major ways. First, reseachers misunderstand the therapeutic approach under investigation to the extent that it cannot be reproduced under experimental conditions. Secondly, they select the wrong experimental design, which results in the omission of crucial variables and limits the external validity of the experimental results. Thirdly, outcome studies may err by testing approaches to therapy rather than specific procedures.

Is it RET?

Good psychotherapy research is possible when the psychotherapy under investigation is performed accurately. This demands the involvement of someone expert in the psychotherapy under study to confirm that operations have been performed accurately.

Even people who think they know how to conduct a certain therapy, do not. As an RET trainer, I usually encountered one or more enthusiastic participants on training programmes who told me 'I am so happy to get some training in RET. I've been using it for a long time and I like it very much.' Unfortunately, some of the most enthusiastic were also some of the most misinformed about RET. They were also some of the most difficult people to correct, for they seemed to enjoy what they habitually did. I finished such programmes with the hope that they would either change what they were doing (especially when, in my opinion, it seemed harmful) or at least give their activities some label other than RET.

Common trainee errors are the following:

1. They emulate Albert Ellis' manner of talking, including his well-known use of four-letter vulgarisms but without his sense of appropriateness.
2. They use the basic assumption of RET – that people largely create their emotional experiences through their cognitive interpretations and evaluations of events – to justify and at times encourage people to act unethically (e.g. by saying 'Other people hurt themselves emotionally, you don't have to feel guilty about your actions').

3. They believe that effective therapy consists of exhausting clients with the weight of words and the less clients say the better.
4. They believe that clients are more interested in the therapists' lessons for mental health than in discussing and solving their own problems.
5. They believe that words and meanings are the same, and that every time a client says a sentence with 'should' in it, it is correct to challenge the client (because they know Ellis said there are no shoulds in the universe).

Another set of participants confuse an approach or system of psychotherapy with its typical procedures. They say, 'I'm a (usually, behaviour) therapist, and I want to add RET to my repertoire of techniques.' They equate a specific procedure (e.g. desensitization) with an approach that uses multiple interventions, and do not realize that RET is an assumption about disturbance rather than a prescribed set of procedures for reducing disturbance. This is the same as equating free association with psychoanalysis, talking to empty chairs with gestalt therapy, or keeping a record of automatic thoughts with cognitive therapy. This error is perpetuated by compilations such as Herink's (1980), which:

1. Include specific procedures (e.g. bibliotherapy) used in several approaches along with complex approaches of which, say, bibliotherapy is but one procedure.
2. Treat group and individual forms of the same approach as though they are different.
3. Treat group versions as 'techniques' within the more general approach.

When these errors are carried over into research, it becomes difficult and at times impossible to know precisely what has been done. I recently read an unpublished research report that compared 'behaviour therapy' with 'rational therapy'. Fortunately, the procedures of each were thoroughly described. The 'behaviour therapy' was in fact a form of thought-stoppage, but the 'rational therapy' was a form of cognitive restructuring based not on the work of Ellis but on that of Maultsby (1975). At one time Ellis and Maultsby both claimed that Maultsby's rational behaviour training was synonymous with RET, but no longer do so. They use different procedures and work from a slightly but significantly different theory of disturbance, although both emphasize cognitive factors in disturbance. But the work of Maultsby more closely resembles that of Beck (1976), while the training provided at the Institute for Rational-Emotive Therapy more closely resembles Lazarus's (1981) multi-modal therapy, although it is by no means identical.

These may be seen as petty objections to the way researchers employ labels. However, there is an operational sequence that goes beyond mere labelling. Outcome studies pit one procedure against another or, less frequently, one approach against another. Outcome studies are contests about therapeutic efficacy, and to call the more effective intervention by the wrong name can mislead professionals who depend on results, not to mention clients who depend on professionals. It is as if someone reported that England won the World Cup when, in fact, it was Brazil, except that the consequences are far more serious.

But, even when labels are correctly used, there is no guarantee that the procedures have been implemented correctly. For example, suppose that a study reports that one experimental condition was disputing of irrational beliefs, a procedure most frequently identified with RET. This phrase 'disputing of irrational beliefs' implies two skills: (1) that the therapist knows an irrational belief when he/she hears or sees one; and (2) that he/she knows how to dispute an irrational belief. Based on my experience as an RET trainer, I know that people have a great deal of difficulty learning to identify irrational beliefs. Such beliefs are self-defeating evaluations based on one's personal values, good ideas perverted by exaggeration. They are not simply unrealistic statements or even gross distortions of reality. 'My mother hates me', is not an irrational belief regardless of the facts. 'I'm worthless because my mother hates me' is an irrational belief, because the statement contains an exaggerated evaluation. However, neophyte rational-emotive therapists frequently err by disputing the inferential statement 'How do you know your mother hates you?' rather than focusing on the extreme negative self-evaluation. It is unrealistic to assume that 'therapists' in research studies, who are very frequently graduate students, will not make the same errors as therapists in training.

Even when an irrational belief is correctly identified, it might not be the most important belief to dispute. It might be linked to other, more central beliefs (Moore, 1980) or linked to other, more central emotional processes (Wessler and Wessler, 1980). Furthermore, there are many ways to dispute irrational beliefs, of which the 'Where's the evidence' approach is but one. In addition to such a direct approach, there are more subtle procedures that involve imagery and corrective behavioural experiences. Clinicians and researchers without a thorough grounding in RET principles and practice can easily overlook this fact.

Good research presumes the ability to create independent variables that have some chance of affecting dependent measures. Researchers who lack knowledge of their independent variables cannot be expected to operationalize them correctly. Their knowledge, in the case of RET, comes from books, usually written by Albert Ellis. But Ellis, by his own admission, has written few works for professionals who wish to learn how to practise RET effectively.

While there are now more 'how-to' books for professionals who want to learn how to do RET, the difficulty of learning to do therapy from a book remains. Psychotherapy consists of a set of skills, and skills can be learned best by practice under the corrective supervision of an experienced teacher. As Wessler and Ellis (1980) write, you cannot learn to do psychotherapy by reading books any better than you can learn to play the piano by finding books on musicology.

To summarize the foregoing, psychotherapy research can easily mislabel and otherwise misrepresent its procedures, unknowingly create faulty independent variables, ignore the complexities of existing therapy approaches and, however unwittingly, mislead the unwary reader.

The wrong model

Good psychotherapy, in my opinion, tends to be versatile in its methods but unitary in its theory. It must be versatile because (1) clients' problems differ, sometimes greatly; (2) clients with the same type of problem differ in their responses to certain interventions; and (3) therapists differ in how well they have mastered certain procedures and how well these can be employed with different types of clients. Psychotherapy research, if it is to have external validity, must solve the enormous problem of trying to manage these variables (and others) within a controlled study.

The task of the researcher who studies psychotherapy procedures experimentally is far different than that of the therapist who attempts to help a client. The researcher is obliged to control conditions so that, in the best work, only independent variables vary and only they influence the dependent measures. The therapist, by contrast, is not only free to vary procedures but, in my opinion, is obliged to do so in the best interests of the client. This means that the therapist had better not reproduce the controlled precision of the experiment, but that the experimenter would do well to approximate the flexibility of the therapist.

To my knowledge, this approximation occurs infrequently. Studies fail to account for important differences among clients and among therapists and for the consequent interaction with the independent variables. I do not refer to diagnostic differences among clients nor demographic ones, for these are usually specified in research reports. Instead, I refer to variables that practising therapists discuss among themselves. One example should suffice – client cooperation. Regardless of the name it goes by, cooperation between client and therapist is crucial. Failure to cooperate is sometimes referred to as resistance and lack of motivation. The behavioural outcome we label 'cooperation' depends on other factors, e.g. trusting the therapist, agreeing on therapeutic goals, and working at the tasks of therapy, whether they involve free association, revealing of emotional experiences, following a behavioural programme, or searching one's mind for relevant cognitions. These and other factors that result in cooperation do not exactly defy operational definition, but are certainly elusive – perhaps that is why they are studied so seldomly.

When I read a research report, am I to assume that all subjects cooperated equally, that differences equalled out, that the results apply to my most cooperative clients (the ones I already know how to help) or to the least, average, etc.?

There are additional variables. Were the clients passive, active, hostile, friendly, or combinations of the foregoing? What were their expectations of therapy and therapists' behaviour? In the case of therapies based on learning or educational assumptions, how did clients learn best? In the case of the cognitively-oriented therapies, what conditions led to changes in *this client's* cognitions? Although Bandura (1977) says that self-demonstration via performance is the best way to change cognitions, he apparently does not think this statement is necessarily true for everyone. In my own experience, I have known clients who changed their minds after hearing (disguised) stories about other clients or myself (undisguised), and would not attempt new behaviours to learn new cognitions until they did.

There are therapist variables that are extremely important, in my judgement. Competence, expertise or experience are such variables and probably each comprises several sub-factors. Therapists' attitudes toward clients is another. My intent is not to create a comprehensive list, but to suggest that these variables affect treatment outcomes, regardless of the specific procedures or systems under investigation.

The above issues result from the application of the drug-outcome research model to psychotherapy research. I suggest that this model for evaluating comparative therapy procedures be abandoned. The drug-outcome research model assumes correctly that subjects' knowledge of whether they receive active medication or placebo might affect their symptoms. The double-blind study controls for such expectancy effects. However, the drug-outcome model implicitly assumes that it does not matter who administers the medications or, if it does, this variable will be eliminated by nearly identically dressed nurses dispensing medications from plain envelopes prepared and coded by an unseen pharmacist who alone knows what each subject receives.

But this is hardly the case in psychotherapy-outcome studies, precisely because it is the therapist who is inside the envelopes. The therapist, even if he/she is not the principal investigator, knows whether he/she is doing desensitization or paradoxical intention or is conducting the attention-placebo. And such knowledge coupled with the therapist's belief in its efficacy, can affect the outcome of experiments. Further, partially-trained graduate students will do no better than well-trained therapists who have been given a crash course in some procedures they are not already familiar with, but the latter may be more likely to go beyond the prescribed treatment, albeit unintentionally.

It is especially difficult for experienced therapists to remain faithful to the attention–placebo condition, if my own experiences and those of my close colleagues are representative. In fact, it is difficult to get a good attention-placebo. I once made a set of audio-tapes to instruct clients in RET principles and a set of placebo tapes for comparison. I selected one of Norman Vincent Peale's books, deleted references to God and Peale's endless anecdotes, thinking I had found some non-RET material that sounded plausible. However, the longer I preached into the microphone the more impressed I became with the power of positive thinking. Peale was not saying 'hope for the best', he was teaching a philosophy of forgiveness, tolerance, non-demandingness, patience and other fundamental ideas in RET philosophy. And his positive thinking principle turned out to be something like 'treat people with respect and friendship and they will probably treat you the same way and help you reach your practical goals, and even if you don't you'll feel better'. None the less, placebo groups are worthwhile experimental conditions to retain from the drug-outcome study model, despite the difficulties involved.

But there is another model that seems a closer approximation of psychotherapy than medications. It is the model of surgery, and here I will refer to dental surgery due to my extensive experience as a patient at the hands of these practitioners. Successful outcomes in dentistry depend on both the procedure *and* the practitioner. The same basic mixtures – grinding out decayed enamel, mixing alloyed metal, inserting metal into tooth – can be done skilfully or clumsily, and the results will differ, and shall I praise or fault the procedure or the practitioner or both?

In experimental terms, I suggest that studies include a consideration of the therapists as an independent variable (for I do not see how they can be treated as a constant), and account for therapist–procedure interactions.

Approaches versus procedures

I appreciate flexibility in therapy. I try to fit my procedures to my individual client's characteristics, although I cannot always say how I know or on what basis I do this. I try to match my interpersonal style to that of the client for what I deem therapeutic purposes. I freely use procedures not normally associated with RET, e.g. the empty chair, paradoxical intention, dream interpretation. But I have a theory of disturbance to bind my efforts together: I believe that the majority of neurotic conditions are largely due to rigidity in one's thinking and conflicts among one's personal rules or values.

There is a value in purity, also. Smith *et al.* (1980) conclude their book on psychotherapy research results by saying, in effect, that since we know so little about the superiority of one approach over another, that it is premature to eliminate any on empirical grounds. That is why I first teach 'classical' RET to people who want to learn to do RET, even though I do not ordinarily use it or RET jargon with clients. (I speak of personal rules of living with clients instead of musturbation, awfulizing, shithood, and other Ellisisms; I do not use words like rational or irrational, unless the client already knows them, and I do not teach them the ABC theory.)

Purity in psychotherapy can be approximated by developing and using treatment manuals. The advantages of standardized procedures for research purposes is obvious. However, treatment 'by the book' implies that (1) individual differences are relatively unimportant, and (2) the persons under treatment are monosymptomatic. The first point is difficult to accept for those of us who are steeped in personality theory and have respect for the dignity and uniqueness of the individual. It is rather like my surgeon referring to me as 'an appendix' rather than as a person. The second point also presumes the medical model: that making mutually exclusive diagnoses is not only possible but desirable. In practice, it is a rare client with a single symptom. Some compromise seems necessary if we are to avoid nomethetic rigidity on the one hand and idiographic chaos on the other. However, I predict that no 'pure' form of treatment can survive the test of controlled experimentation.

RET certainly cannot, for it is a point of view about disturbance and treatment, not a series of stepwise procedures. Perhaps the best alternative is a procedure-by-therapist approach in which we test specific procedures against each other, while including therapists as important treatment variables. Thus, we can give up the grand questions such as 'Is RET superior to TA, gestalt, client-centred, and brand X in the treatment of anxiety?' in favour of a different type of question: 'Does counter-phobic activity assignments lessen the severity of social anxiety?' Specific procedures are testable, whereas grand theories are not, and maybe Lazarus (1981) is correct when he urges psychotherapists to do what has been shown to be effective and disregard theories. An experimental attitude on the part of therapists – namely that one procedure can be proved more effective than another – just might be of more help to clients than a my-theory-is-better-than-your-theory programme of research. Both clients and practitioners might benefit from leaving theory to the academic purists and practice to practitioners.

The advantage of studying procedures is that everybody can win, because success can be explained in so many different ways. For example, Watzlawick (1978) reports helping a graduate student overcome his procrastinating about writing his dissertation by having him perform deliberate mistakes to combat his perfectionist tendencies which caused the procrastination. Watzlawick explains the successful outcome in terms of by-passing the logical, digital left-brain hemisphere and altering the client's world view contained within the right-brain hemisphere. In short, the tactic 'worked' because the therapist could 'fool' the client's reasoning and appeal directly to the holistic, non-logical portion of the mind.

What Watzlawick reports is known in RET as a shame-attacking exercise in which one deliberately acts foolishly and risks public ridicule. Its success is explained in RET by theorizing that the client learned to accept himself (as opposed to devalue himself) and thus no longer needed to act perfectly in order to feel worthwhile. Further, the client re-evaluated the situation by proving to himself that criticism is not so unpleasant or horrible that it must not occur.

However, one could argue just as plausibly that re-evaluation occurred due to his learning that public criticism is a low probability event, or that when it is done, it is expressed subtly not obviously. Re-evaluation may occur because the client imagined himself free from shame and embarrassment or reconstrued criticism as a sign that he was making progress toward overcoming his perfectionistic tendencies. Repeated exposure itself might change appraisals in a positive direction. *Any* attempt at mistake-making might prove sufficiently self-regarding to produce new attributions of competence and self-efficacy. Cognitive dissonance principles might be applied to explain an adjustment of attitude: the client concludes that he finds criticism less negative since there is no other explanation for his acting imperfectly; he risks criticism because he does not mind it as much.

A gestalt therapist might conclude that the procedure was successful because of the self-awareness and integration that occurred. A TA specialist might say that the experience allowed a redistribution of energy among ego states. A radical behaviour therapist might explain success in purely operant-reinforcement terms. The point is that a successful therapeutic procedure can have many theoretical explanations.

Pure systems of psychotherapy are not likely to be validated in outcome studies, because systems are theories of disturbance and change. These may be subjected to empirical investigation, but they do not lend themselves to outcome studies, because procedures are not usually deduced from the theories. Procedures usually arise from clinical experience, and a certain intervention can be shared by therapeutic systems which have different theoretical bases.

Therefore, let us have outcome studies which test procedures against one another, regardless of which system first claimed them or now employs them. Let practitioners and their clients benefit from the results of well-designed, accurately performed experiments. Let inter-theoretical warfare be conducted on the benign battlefield of academic research. After the war ends, if it ever does, practitioners and theorists can sit together and exclaim at the results, and then continue on their own separate paths.

References

Bandura, A. (1977). *Social learning theory.* Englewood Cliffs, N.J.: Prentice-Hall.

Beck, A.T. (1976). *Cognitive therapy and the emotional disorders.* New York: International Universities Press.

Herink, R. (Ed.) (1980). *The psychotherapy handbook.* New York: New American Library.

Lazarus, A.A. (1981). *The practice of multimodal therapy.* New York: McGraw-Hill.

Maultsby, M.C. Jr (1975). *Help yourself to happiness.* New York: Institute for Rational Living.

Moore, R.H., (1980). Inference chaining. *In* M.S. Morain (Ed.), *Classroom exercises in general semantics.* San Francisco: International Society for General Semantics.

Smith, M.L., Glass, G.V. and Miller, T.I. (1980). *The benefits of psychotherapy.* Baltimore: The John Hopkins University Press.

Walen, S.R., DiGiuseppe, R. and Wessler, R.L. (1980). *A practitioner's guide to rational-emotive therapy.* New York: Oxford University Press.

Watzlawick, P. (1978). *The language of change.* New York: Basic Books.

Wessler, R.A. and Wessler, R.L. (1980). *The principles and practice of rational-emotive therapy.* San Francisco: Jossey-Bass.

Wessler, R.L. and Ellis, A. (1980). Supervision in rational-emotive therapy. *In* A.K. Hess (Ed.), *Psychotherapy supervision.* New York: Wiley.

Part 2

Practice

Chapter 8

Practising RET with lower-class clients

Howard S. Young

It would appear that psychotherapy has long been the province of the middle and upper socioeconomic classes. According to Halleck (1971), the lower-class individual was usually viewed as too impulsive, too eager for immediate gratification, and too simple-minded for such a sophisticated endeavour. These shortcomings were assumed to interfere with the kind of intense verbal interaction and expansion of awareness that makes psychotherapy a successful enterprise. The same author concludes that, as a result, the mental health needs of the lower-class person have been largely ignored. Further, even when helped, such clients tended to be labelled as hopelessly disturbed, and their treatment tended to be managed with less prestigious, non-verbal measures such as drug or shock therapies.

Despite such pessimism on the part of the mental health establishment toward the treatment potential of the lower classes, it has been my experience that such individuals can respond to and benefit from rational-emotive therapy. This conclusion results from the application of a structured system of clinical strategies that follow from the theoretical principles of RET.

It is the purpose of this Chapter to outline some of the approaches and detail some of the techniques that have enabled me to use this system with lower-class clients who suffer from a wide range of psychological symptoms and disturbances.

The lower classes

Since the 'lower class' can conjure a variety of meanings, I would like to define this social group more precisely. The most widely used instrument for determining socioeconomic status in psychotherapy research (Hollingshead and Redlich, 1958) separates the lower classes into two groups, the working class and the poor, and measures each group according to occupational level, educational background and family structure.

The working classes typically are employed in skilled and semi-skilled jobs and belong to unionized trades or industries. Although some fall below the tenth-grade level in education, most have completed high school or technical training. Their family relationships are usually stable though perhaps less so than those of the upper classes. Coal miners, car workers, truckers, carpenters, and the like are most commonly included in this group.

The poor are usually involved in non-unionized, semi-skilled and unskilled occupations in which irregular employment is common. Education beyond the eighth grade is rare, and family life is marked by frequent separation and divorce. Examples would be individuals who are farm workers, housekeepers, ghetto dwellers, and those supported exclusively by welfare or other marginal subsidy programmes.

In addition to research findings, actual contacts with the lower classes have revealed other endemic characteristics. The most frequently observed include a tendency on the part of the lower-class individual to adhere to strict or extremist religious views, to use alcohol (especially among males) as an exclusive leisure or recreational activity, to express anger and rage spontaneously, to resort to physical punishment or combat to resolve conflicts, and to follow rigid sex-role stereotypes in interpersonal relationships.

The following examples are typical illustrations of the kinds of individuals that might be labelled lower class. The first is a 33-year-old man who sought therapy for periods of panic, as he called them. He is a high-school graduate with some technical school training and is employed as an air conditioner repairman. He has a family of four, including his wife and two young daughters whom he vows will remain virgins until the day they marry. In a recent argument with a neighbour, he used a loaded gun to get his point across. His goal is to make just enough money so that he can retire and move his family to a cabin deep in the woods, far away from hippies, atheists and homosexuals. His weekends are often spent hunting and fishing with close friends, but he actually uses these occasions as an excuse to drink all day and night. He calls himself a redneck hillbilly and says he is proud of it.

The second example is that of a 26-year-old mother of six children who is supported by welfare assistance. She can neither read nor write. She lives in a three-bedroom trailer which is her third home. Her first was destroyed by a flood and her second by a series of shotgun blasts from irate neighbours who claimed this woman had stolen one of the children's bicycles. The husband in this situation claims to suffer from a bad back. He does not receive disability compensation because doctors do not believe there is anything wrong with him. He physically and verbally abuses his wife, but she is a fundamentalist

Christian and was told by her minister that her husband is a cross she must bear. She firmly believes that the more she suffers in this world, the greater will be her reward in the next. She requested therapy for severe depression.

The structured approach

Having introduced the clients, I would like now to move on to the method, that is, the procedures I have found most effective in applying RET to such individuals. Of primary concern is the realization that RET can be practised in a variety of ways. Although basically a cognitive-semantic theory of psychotherapy, RET is multidimensional in application and approach. The creative RET therapist, therefore, can make liberal and appropriate use of empathy, imagery, role-playing, emotional ventilation, operant conditioning, assertiveness training, and other well-established clinical procedures and can consider them an integral part of the total treatment programme.

Recognizing that RET can be put into practice in a broad-spectrum fashion is of particular value if a therapist is attempting to work with the lower classes. Individuals of these strata have been described as the most psychiatrically impaired segment of society (Srole *et al.*, 1962) and often prove extremely difficult to engage and sustain in a therapeutic process. Under these circumstances, an approach is required which will allow for flexibility and diversity while at the same time, staying within the bounds of a structured, well-directed plan of action.

After considerable trial and error, I have developed such an approach, which focuses attention on what I have found to be the most relevant areas of clinical concern with the lower-class client. This framework includes (1) developing a relationship, (2) defining a problem, (3) solving the problem and (4) encouraging change.

These approaches are interdependent and interactive and each is directed toward a particular goal and follows a specialized set of clinical strategies. The remainder of this Chapter will be devoted to discussing the methods and techniques involved.

Developing a relationship

It is my opinion that the purpose of relationship development in RET is to establish the therapist in a position of power and influence over the client. Once such a position has been achieved, the therapist can encourage or persuade the client to change his behaviour. Put another way, the role of therapist is that of a manipulator, and he uses the interpersonal relationship to manoeuvre the client to act in positive and beneficial ways.

Some clinicians may feel uncomfortable about being identified as manipulators. They prefer to view their client contacts in more benign and egalitarian terms. However, I agree strongly with Gillis (1974), who claims that nearly all therapists, whether they want to admit it or not, engage in tactics and strategies that add to their power and influence over their clients. Gillis points out that no matter how benevolent or non-directive one's approach may be, a situation in which one person is allowed to comment on the performance of another presumes a position of control.

It is quite possible, therefore, that the relationship concept so revered in psychotherapy is not, in actual practice, the esoteric sacred entity that some believe it to be. It is more likely that the partnership that exists between therapist and client is no more unique or different than any other kind of social interaction in which one party is influenced to undergo change. When we help our clients, therefore, we are using the same tactics that have been developed over thousands of years in business, law, politics, religion and advertising.

The techniques used to obtain such relationship power may be classified as two main approaches: those aimed at developing command and those aimed at developing friendship. *Command power* results when the therapist gains ascendancy in the relationship through the use of authority, expertise and prestige (importance). The client accepts the therapist's insights, and he changes because he believes the therapist is an expert and knows what is best. The client is influenced by competency and credibility. As you are aware, people will perform previously unthinkable acts if they are ordered to do so by respected authorities. *Friendship power*, on the other hand, results when the therapist gains leverage over the client through the use of non-possessive warmth, positive regard and empathy. The client is influenced by trust and kindness. He accepts the therapist's interpretations, and he changes because he likes the therapist and values the relationship. Your own observations show that people will go to extremes to do things to please someone whose friendship they esteem and want to keep.

Although the use of friendship power is probably more popular among therapists, it has been my experience that command power is the more effective method of relationship manipulation with the lower classes. Such clients tend to be uneasy with and wary of an egalitarian approach because they do not consider themselves the equals of the therapist. Lower-class clients expect the therapist to be an authority and to act like one. There is a high expectation that the therapist be someone who knows what he is doing and is sure of himself.

It is important, however, that an authoritative role not be confused with an authoritarian role. The therapist presents himself as forceful but not demanding and directive but not dictatorial. Although I am recommending that the therapist establish a position of command with the lower-class client, I am not suggesting that the position be carried to extremes, such as conveying the impression of omnipotence and God-like domination. In other words, I am advocating that the therapist maintain a strong position of leadership in the relationship while at the same time remaining empathetic and responsive. There are a number of techniques that can be used to accomplish this end. Command power, for example, may be attained in the following ways.

1. *Use a loud voice.* One of the most effective ways to gain the attention and respect of the lower-class client is through the use of a loud, forceful voice. The lowered or soft voice, although helpful at certain times, is usually non-productive when used on a regular basis to establish authoritative influence over such clients. These individuals tend to lack faith in someone who presumes to be an authority yet sounds unsure of himself. They usually expect an authority to speak in a forthright, powerful, loud-sounding manner. I am not suggesting the therapist yell at the client, but the volume of the voice should be of sufficient intensity and the tone of sufficient quality that the client will listen and, more important, believe what is being said. By modulating one's voice and emphasizing certain points with increased or decreased volume, the therapist can lend authority to his interpretations and insights. The loud, forceful voice connotes a very important message to the lower-class client: I am an expert and I am sure of myself.

2. *Use commanding gestures.* Another effective way to imply you are an authority is to use commanding gestures during the counselling session to indicate that you are the boss. Gestures such as pointing your finger or clenching your fists are effective as long as they are done to imply assurance and not to intimidate the client. For example, while making a point you could hit the desk a few times for emphasis. Such a move would lend drama and impact to your message because only someone that really knows what he is doing usually acts in that manner. Another method that is especially effective when leading groups is to forcefully underline a point made in writing or to tap loudly on a blackboard to emphasize a particular idea or insight. There are, of course, a number of gestures or even postures that imply command and authority, and I suggest that the therapist capitalize on them to convey to the client the distinct impression that he is indeed a person who is in charge of things.

3. *Touch the client.* Along the same lines, another useful way to gain the upper hand in the relationship is to touch clients in some kind of forceful, determined way. I realize that touching usually suggests some kind of intimacy, but this is not what I am referring to here. What I have in mind, for example, is making a point while at the same time vigorously tapping the

client's shoe or maybe reaching over and tightly grabbing a bicep muscle. Such a move is not intended to encourage closeness but to underscore a message in a dramatic way. I believe there is some evidence that touching is a sign of domination, that the 'toucher' is the superior and the 'touchee' the subordinate. My experience seems to suggest that, when done appropriately, touching increases the therapist's authority and influence over the client. Of course, it is important that judgement be exercised and the frequency of such behaviour as well as the sex, age of the client, and the area touched, be taken into consideration.

4. *Establish and exploit a reputation.* In addition to using loudness, gesturing, and touching to assert influence over the client, I would also suggest that the therapist deliberately define himself as an expert. Such a manoeuvre can often go far in giving the therapist powerful advantage with the client. Probably the most common ploy in this regard is a display of diplomas and certificates that attest to one's training and competency. It is, for example, very impressive if you have the title 'doctor' before your name. I see many lower-class clients who think I am a doctor because they first come in contact with me in a doctor's office. I rarely correct this misconception initially, since it often serves the purpose of convincing them that I am an expert.

Other tactics that can enhance the therapist's reputation as an expert include talking to the public on mental health subjects, writing articles for the local newspapers and appearing on radio and television. I appear on a television show monthly, and this has greatly enhanced my reputation as an authority with many clients and would-be clients. Along the same lines, I suggest authoring a brief pamphlet or audio-tape about some mental health subject. Such an effort need not be a great work of literature or published commercially, but it should be given to the client as one means of establishing your expertise. I am constantly amazed at the influence of *A rational counseling primer* (Young, 1974) in establishing my credibility with clients. In my opinion, this booklet is as effective in earning me a reputation as an expert as it has been effective in teaching some of the basic principles of RET.

I realize that some of these approaches may not be feasible for all of you, so let me mention one sure-fire tactic for establishing yourself as a knowledgeable authority. Simply announce in a firm, loud, self-assured voice that you are indeed an expert, and you get results. I clearly state that not only do I know what I am doing, but I am good at it. I have yet to be challenged on this statement, and it often has a profound effect on some clients. For example, I will deliberately tell a client that I teach in a university, publish papers in professional journals, and appear on television. In other words, I advertise my achievements and give myself credit for being an expert. Clients usually respond to such a forthright approach by allowing me to say things and suggest changes in their lives that would probably not be allowed to someone of lesser stature and importance. This kind of power is extremely useful in a learning situation where there is considerable resistance to change.

5. *Display superior wisdom and knowledge.* Another way to attain interpersonal power is to display superior wisdom and knowledge. The therapist can accomplish this end through the use of powerful 'common sense' arguments, esoteric interpretations, psychological jargon, diagnostic labels, and the like. Throwing in some research findings on the topic under consideration can also help the therapist to boost the client's confidence in the therapist's intellectual abilities. Lower-class individuals are often impressed with such tactics and tend to view their therapist as someone who possesses profound wisdom.

This same goal is often achieved when the therapist relates directly to the client the ideational source of his disturbance. Since the monitoring of one's own thought processes is new to most lower-class clients, they are often unable to state readily the ideas that are causing their emotional problems. When this is done easily and effortlessly by the therapist, it can have a striking effect on the client. Such a manoeuvre often encourages respect and admiration for the therapist as a person of extraordinary knowledge. It is my opinion that it is not just the insights that are presented but the way in which the client views the presenter that plays a major role in the therapeutic change process.

I will now comment on some of the techniques that can be used to gain friendship power.

1. *Acknowledge reality constraints.* A first step in promoting oneself with lower-class clients as an understanding caring person is for the therapist to become keenly aware of the reality constraints with which many of these people must deal. The therapist who demonstrates an understanding of authentic environmental pressures will go far in establishing a responsive, empathic relationship. For example, ignoring the reality demands of an eviction notice and showing more eagerness to examine underlying or more dynamic issues not only impairs the relationship but probably the course of therapy itself. Substantial efforts, therefore, would best be directed to exploring fully the current life situation of the client and, where appropriate, to demonstrating genuine interest and concern in reality-based pressures.

2. *Tolerate value differences.* Another requirement in establishing a friendship bond in the relationship involves careful attention to value differences. Often the basic values of the therapist and lower-class client will be different and in conflict. Under such circumstances, it is of paramount importance that the therapist maintain a non-judgemental, objective attitude toward the client's

value orientation. The client who beats his children and steals from his employer, for example, may be acting according to established cultural norms and not necessarily demonstrating psychopathology. What the therapist assumes to be deviant behaviour may well represent an ingrained way of life acceptable within a lower-class context. I strongly suggest, therefore, that the therapist become well-acquainted with the lower-class client's convictions regarding child-rearing, religion, marriage, and the like. Even more important, I suggest that an understanding and acceptance of such values be communicated to the client.

3. *Demonstrate unconditional positive regard.* Closely related to accepting value differences as a method of gaining likeableness, is to convince the client that the therapist accepts him unconditionally. This is usually accomplished by maintaining an understanding facial expression and commenting in a non-judgemental manner when a client mentions objectionable behaviour. However, since RET is a confronting, directive type of therapy, clients sometimes gather the impression that the therapist is attacking or disapproving of them as people. In order to get the point across that it is behaviour or ideas that are under scrutiny and not the whole person, I usually tell the client the following:

> You and I are going to get together and form a partnership. This partnership is going to help you solve your problems. Sometimes we're going to have to get tough with your ideas and some of the things you do, but no matter what we find wrong, it will still be a partnership.

In other words, I try to show him we are going to join forces against 'it' and not against him.

4. *Understand language differences.* Another good method for establishing a trusting relationship with the lower-class client is to gain an understanding of language differences. Many lower-class clients, especially those from rural and ghetto areas, tend to rely heavily on conversational idioms and regionalized jargon to express themselves. It is wise for the therapist to be alert for these language differences, to learn their meaning, and to use them in the therapeutic interchange. Such efforts often improve understanding and communication by helping resistant or threatened clients to identify with the therapist.

Closely related to the use of words familiar to the client is avoiding the use of words or expressions that are taboo to lower-class clients. For example, I cannot think of the last time I used the word 'fuck' with lower-class adults. 'Shit' is close behind, and I once used the word 'ass' and a client walked out on me. Some words possess extremely negative connotations to many lower-class clients, and they will not tolerate their use. In order to enhance communication and facilitate a responsive relationship, therefore, I have learned to avoid the use of words that are objectionable to lower-class clients.

5. *Flatter the client.* It is hard to imagine a technique more powerful in establishing interpersonal power than flattery. I am not referring to positive reinforcement for improved or corrected behaviour, but to the actual complimenting of the client in some way. For example, you might notice and comment favourably on a new hair-do, a new pair of shoes, and the like.

However, the most effective method of flattery I use with lower-class clients is to stress similarities between myself and the client. This is especially productive when such similarities are personal shortcomings or faults. By my admitting that I not only have problems but that these problems are sometimes no different from his, the client often sees me as more approachable and feels more comfortable in my presence. Remember, there is a tendency on the part of clients to see their therapists as gods, as being far above the ordinary problems suffered by mere mortals like themselves. When it seems advisable, I destroy this myth by telling the client how upset I felt when my tyre went flat on a highway or how I slipped and fell while carrying out the garbage the night before. With other clients I might flatter them by telling them that I enjoy spending the session with them, that they seem to have a pretty good way of handling their problems. As long as the remarks are sincere and reflect an honest appraisal of the client's behaviour, they are usually effective.

6. *Write letters.* A technique that is very effective in giving clients the impression that the therapist is a caring person is to write letters to them. For example, when a client misses an appointment, I will sometimes drop him a self-typed letter with a brief personal comment and a time for his next appointment. I believe I once read of a study that indicated that the files of successful therapists contained many such letters. Occasionally, the therapist could send a card or some other kind of remembrance and accomplish the same purpose. This need only be done once in a great while, but the personal touch often gives the client the idea that the therapist is an understanding person who puts a little effort into remembering him.

Problem defining

The purpose of problem defining in RET is to obtain a diagnostic assessment of the client's reality-based and psychologically induced complaints. This procedure helps the therapist and the client gain mutual understanding and agreement about the problems to be discussed and resolved in the corrective process.

Although this might seem an obvious step regardless of socioeconomic standing, it deserves special emphasis in work with the lower classes. Such individuals tend to be quite unsophisticated about the kind of problems suited to verbal therapy. It is not unusual for the lower-class client to request and even demand services beyond the scope of a therapy endeavour. A young mother, for example, insisted that I spank her child because he was using 'bathroom cuss words'. She was convinced that this was my job for, as she put it, 'If you don't punish children, then how can you be of help?'

Because, like this mother, many lower-class clients are often ignorant about what takes place in therapy, it is advised that the client be offered some kind of preliminary instruction about how therapy can work for him. Such an orientation will help prevent misunderstanding and future disappointment. It is my opinion that the closer therapy approximates what the client expects will happen in the experience, the more likely it is that the client will remain in treatment and the greater will be the chance of a positive outcome.

Once the therapist is satisfied that the client has a general idea about what takes place in a therapy encounter, he can then proceed with an exploration of the kind of problem situation that will require such assistance. I have found this is best approached with the lower-class client by a diligent analysis of the problem situation as a whole, in its broad aspects. I do not limit this exploration to irrational thinking but expand it to an investigation of the client's environmental circumstances, the client's value system and, of course, the client's symptoms and disturbances. In other words, I am interested in a thorough examination of the entire ABC spectrum and in any additional information that appears either to contribute to the problem or, even more important, to the solution of the problem.

Some RET therapists might feel impatient with such an approach. They prefer to challenge the first 'awful' or 'should' the client utters, well-satisfied that they have located and zeroed in on the core problems: the client's exaggerated, absolutistic thinking. Although perhaps quite dramatic and certainly accurate from a theoretical point of view, such an approach might prove premature and counterproductive with many lower-class clients.

It has been my experience that lower-class clients disturb themselves with the same irrational thought patterns as does any other class of people. However, the confronting and confuting of these attitudes usually requires a more extensive understanding of the client, his values, his cultural and familiar background, resources available to him, and so on. Without such knowledge even the most brilliant insights will have little value in helping the lower-class client come to grips with his disturbances.

I might add that problem defining is not limited to the first session but is applied to subsequent, on-going sessions as well. The therapist is urged to make each session with the lower-class client a problem-facing endeavour. Otherwise, even though the session may have cathartic value and may help the client feel better, it is unlikely the session will encourage behaviour change and actually help the client get better (Ellis, 1972).

Problem defining with the lower classes, therefore, usually follows a course of action which includes: (1) teaching the client the ground rules of psychotherapy, (2) helping the client identify a problem area suitable to such assistance, and (3) obtaining the necessary details in order to prepare the problem for therapeutic intervention. These goals can be achieved in a number of ways.

1. *Use a biographical data sheet.* One of the most effective and relatively simple ways to gain an idea of how much the client knows about psychotherapy is to have him fill out a brief, one-page, biographical data sheet. This includes the usual name, age, address kind of information, but has, as the last item, a few lines for the client to use to state the problem that brings him to therapy. I usually begin an interview with this questionnaire and use it primarily as an opportunity to explore the lower-class client's understanding of therapy. This kind of approach usually provides a very good idea about what the client views as appropriate for counselling assistance.

2. *Ask the client what he expects from therapy.* Another way to learn how much the client knows about therapy is to ask him what he expects from such an endeavour and in what way he believes counselling might help him. I am not asking what kind of problem the client sees as requiring help but rather what kind of help he thinks he can get. Often this can be quite revealing. I have had answers ranging from a prescription for nerve pills to the removal of warts. This approach usually lends itself to an understanding of the client's misconceptions and often gives a good indication of how much education the client will require before problem defining and problem solving can begin.

3. *Offer an example.* When it is determined that the client does indeed require instruction about the therapeutic process, I have found the best tactic is to offer an example. This is especially effective if the example uses the life of another client. For example, I might say:

> Yesterday, a woman came in to see me because she felt depressed – as if life no longer mattered. It seems all her children are grown, her husband works all the time, and she no longer feels needed. I'm helping her figure out how to cope with the situation.

Usually I take a guess and try to tailor the example to what I believe the client's own problem might be.

4. *Advise the client that therapy is primarily a thinking endeavour.* Another way to help the client understand the ways and means of therapy is to explain that therapy helps you by showing you how to think differently. I tell the client that counselling teaches one to look at problems in another light. This is an especially important concept for lower-class clients to understand, as they almost always want to forget or ignore their problems. I therefore emphasize that the job is not to forget or try to get a problem out of one's mind, but rather to learn how to think about the problem in a different, more sensible way.

5. *Use a client-understood analogy.* Another method I find helpful in explaining to the client what takes place in therapy is to offer an analogy with which he can readily identify. Since, for example, many of my clients are women and housewives, I will frequently use a cooking illustration. I point out that if a particular cake recipe is followed and the cake turns out badly, then no matter how many times the recipe is used, the same poor results will still be produced. This is because, I point out, the receipe is no good. However, the client is told, if a new recipe is tried, the result might be a delicious cake. Therapy, I advise the client, is like learning and using that new recipe-learning as a new way to handle problems.

6. *Help the client understand what therapy cannot provide.* An important part of orienting the client to therapy is to tell him directly not only how therapy can help him but also how therapy cannot help him. I usually approach this subject by trying to advise the client that it is unlikely that therapy will cure all his problems and fix it so he can live happily ever after. I point out that sometimes therapy makes it easier to bear the burden of a problem that cannot be solved. Sometimes I explain it in terms of therapy helping one choose the lesser of two evils and learning to live with the results. It is important that therapy be explained to lower-class clients in this way as, in many cases, the solution to their problems involves choosing between negative alternatives.

7. *Advise the client that therapy will help him feel less miserable.* Along these same lines, I also try to explain the limitations of therapy by helping the client realize that therapy will help him feel less upset as opposed to feeling calm or content. This is another point that is especially important to stress with lower-class clients, as they often believe that 'being normal' means feeling happy all the time or facing hardship and adversity in an indifferent or

care-free manner. I try to explain that therapy will teach them a way to get their emotions under control, to feel less upset but still to have bad feelings, and to be able to solve problems or accept those things that cannot be solved. I usually tell the client that when you have problems you often feel bad but not so bad you cannot handle it. Sometimes I go over the Serenity Prayer with clients to get some of these points across.

8. *Begin each session with a request for a problem.* Once the client has a general idea about the therapeutic process, I usually make a determined effort to get down to business as quickly as possible and to encourage problem defining in order to set the stage for problem-solving interventions. Probably the best way to achieve this goal is to begin each session with a request for a problem. I usually start the session by asking 'What problem would you like to work on?' or 'What kind of problem can I help you with today?' This approach immediately focuses attention on the problem defining and also helps, when necessary, to guide the client back to problem facing when he wanders off into concerns unrelated to therapeutic assistance. Sometimes I might allow such meanderings in the interest of relationship building, but mostly I interrupt the client and say, 'Now let's get back to that problem you wanted help on' or 'I see your point, but let's get back and see if I can help you with that jealous husband of yours'.

9. *Limit the session to one or two problems.* Because lower-class clients often present themselves with a host of problems and disturbances, I suggest you limit the sessions to exploring fully only one or two problem areas and preferably one. Sometimes I will even end a session before the time is up in order to maintain this principle. It is important to bear in mind that it is not necessary to help clients solve every problem that troubles them (Beck, 1976). RET is a problem-solving type of therapy that aims to help the client remedy the present or current problem and, in addition, to learn a general method of handling problems so that future concerns can be resolved independently.

10. *Obtain client agreement on the problem to be resolved.* Most important with the lower-class client is to allow him to choose the problem area to be discussed. I mention what might seem an obvious point to those of you who follow the principle of client self-determination. However, I remind you that lower-class clients share a system of values and standards that usually differs markedly from that of their therapists. As a result, it is easy for the therapist unwittingly to lead the client to work on problems that are maladaptive only according to his standards (which might be quite different from those

followed by the lower-class client). For example, the religiously liberated therapist who glosses over a client's stated concern regarding a religious problem in order to deal with issues the therapist considers more appropriate, is probably missing the point and is offering assistance unrelated to the client's primary concern.

11. *Encourage problem specificity*. Once an ABC understanding of the problem as a whole has been established, I suggest that the therapist help the client define the problem so that the core issue can be identified. What I am referring to here is reducing the problem to a basic concern. I usually find that the problems that bring lower-class clients into therapy can be reduced to the following four categories: (1) those that involve personal failure or shortcomings; (2) those that involve interpersonal rejection or criticism; (3) those that involve loss or deprivation of some kind of major pleasure or satisfaction; and (4) those problems involving a realistic danger to life and limb.

By conceptualizing a problem in this way, I usually find I am quickly able to guide clients into a specific problem-defining framework. From there I can explore the problem in more detail and discover the ideational source of the disturbances or distress. For example, the client who complains about marital problems might be questioned until it is learned that a critical spouse is the central issue. Once criticism is established as the specific problem, the situation might be further reduced by suggesting that attention centre on a recent occasion when such criticism occurred. Further, the actual criticism could then be examined and distilled to learn exactly what it is about the criticism that the client finds so upsetting. This approach not only helps screen out unimportant and irrelevant material but, even more important, it better sets the stage of therapeutic intervention and problem solving.

12. *Assign a problem*. In some cases, certain clients are so confused and believe themselves to be plagued by so many pressures that it is extremely difficult to gain agreement or single out a specific problem. It seems that no matter how much effort is put into problem defining, the client keeps finding more serious problems or is unable to settle on what to work on. The best method I have found to handle this kind of client is literally to assign him a problem. The strategy here is to assign the problem that corrective measures can be initiated as soon as possible. Unless therapeutic measures are taken quickly, these clients will regress and their problems become worse because they are convincing themselves that they are beyond help.

I usually call a halt to this kind of situation by telling the client what the problem is, how we are going to work on it, and that by solving this problem, his other concerns will seem very small by comparison. I then refuse to let him discuss anything else and encourage him to concentrate only on the problem at hand. This is quite effective with chronic complainers and with those who want a pill for every little ache and pain.

Problem solving

Problem solving is the basic goal of the therapeutic interchange in RET and is the place in which the work of therapy actually occurs. Problem solving with the lower-class client usually involves two main areas of endeavour: the examination and remedying of practical problems and the examination and remedying of psychological problems.

Practical problem solving includes those areas in which information, direct advice, referral and similar measures are the most appropriate interventions. My experience has shown that counselling the lower-class client often involves such efforts and does not always require an investigation into the psychological aspects of his complaint. Sometimes, merely informing a client of a specific resource can go far toward alleviating his symptoms. I am well aware that, as clinicians, we usually expect our psychological interventions to serve as the primary method of helping our clients. However, this is not always feasible or appropriate with the lower-class client, and it is sometimes better to offer instruction and guidance rather than interpretation and insight.

I have found that a certain amount of letter writing, telephoning, agency contacting, form completing, and the like, is almost always a part of the counselling process with lower-class clients. This does not mean that if you decide to practise RET with the lower classes you will have to abdicate your role as a clinician. What it usually means is that you had better be prepared to provide some additional assistance beyond the psychological explanations that normally take place within the clinical setting.

Psychological problem solving, on the other hand, includes those areas in which cognitive insight, emotional ventilation, behaviour modification, and the like are the appropriate interventions. The main thrust of an RET approach is to correct conflict-causing misconceptions. This is usually accomplished by teaching the client to think about his thinking, to scan his own thought processes and pick out those ideas and beliefs that create his suffering and unhappiness. In addition to learning how to identify the ideas that cause his upset, the client is also shown how to challenge systematically and correct those ideas until they are more logical and less distress-producing.

It is easy to assume that such an intellectually sophisticated endeavour is beyond the grasp of the average lower-class client. In fact, the initial effort on the part of the client to understand and participate in cognitive restructuring usually does prove unrewarding and can give the impression that the individual is inaccessible to such a process. However, my experience demonstrates that this initial difficulty is usually due to inexperience rather than to incapacity. The lower-class client is simply not accustomed to reflecting about his thoughts and fantasies in any kind of conscious way and then to expressing this information to someone else for analysis. It is not, therefore, that the lower-class client is incapable or unequipped for insight therapy, but rather that he lacks practice and experience.

The lower-class client's potential for psychotherapy, therefore, is as legitimate as that of any other individual. The therapeutic methods employed, as Beck (1976) points out, are merely an extension and refinement of what people have been doing since the early stages of their intellectual development. The particular techniques such as labelling objects and situations, setting up hypotheses, and weeding out and testing hypotheses are basic skills that people normally apply without realizing it. There is nothing about such procedures that would preclude their use by persons of low social standing.

Practising RET with members of the lower classes, therefore, is not a question of the client's innate capacity to participate in a therapeutic process. Rather, it is a question of the therapist's ability to present psychological information in such a way that it is intelligible within a client-understood frame of reference. There are a number of practice-proven, effective techniques in this regard.

1. *Maintain an active-directive dialogue.* Probably the most general requirement for dealing with the psychological problems experienced by lower-class clients is for the therapist to maintain an active-directive dialogue. Since these clients usually have initial difficulty with insightful self-exploration, it is unwise for the therapist to be passive or non-directive in expecting them to confront and confute their irrational ideation. An inactive approach on the therapist's part often decreases client responsiveness because the client simply does not know what to do. It is far better for the clinician to take charge of the interchange and deliberately to direct the client's verbal activity. The more open, straightforward and informative the therapist, the better are his chances of stimulating a free flow of attitudes and ideas from the client. Lower-class clients often respond very well to such an animated though directive approach and are sometimes surprising in their ability to provide therapeutically appropriate material.

2. *Teach the relationship between cognitions and reactions.* An equally important requirement for handling psychological problem solving with lower-class clients is to introduce them to the relationship between cognitions and reactions. This is not always an easy task, as most lower-class clients typically

externalize the source of their emotional problems and often have difficulty believing and accepting that they are responsible for creating and sustaining their own disturbances. I usually find that this information is acceptable to the client if presented in a somewhat simplified, carefully structured manner.

For example, after I gain some idea about the nature of the client's problem, I pause and take time out to teach the ABC principle. Often I do this as a separate instructive experience using examples unrelated to the client's stated complaint. I use this tactic because clients are sometimes too immersed in their own upset and are so convinced that their suffering is caused by outside forces, it is difficult for them to believe that their own thinking is at fault. Once I perceive that the client understands the ABC's, I will show him how to apply the principle to his own problem and upset.

In order for this instructive period to be dramatic and full of impact, I have found the use of visual aids to be a most effective method. I have wall posters, for example, that demonstrate the ABC's, as well as a cartoon character on my wall surrounded by thought bubbles that contain the typical irrational ideas that upset people.

In addition, I use an artist's sketch pad or blackboard and actually draw some illustrations that demonstrate the relationship between thinking and feeling. The therapist need not be an artist to use this tactic successfully. A few stick figures or merely some circles in which you can sketch facial expressions will usually be more than adequate. This kind of teaching manoeuvre usually has more effect on lower-class clients than does trying to talk them into accepting responsibility for their emotional problems.

Another successful way to demonstrate the ABC's with those who believe that either someone can hurt their feelings or that they can hurt the feelings of others is to hand the client a rubber hammer. After he accepts the hammer I ask, 'Who handed you the hammer?' He answers that I did, and I next ask, 'Suppose you hit yourself over the head with the hammer. Who makes you do it – the person who handed you the hammer or you?' The client usually admits that he is responsible in such a case. I then tailor the illustration to fit his particular situation. If the client is upset about criticism, for example, I ask, 'Who criticized you?' The client will tell me the name of the person, and then I will ask, 'Who hit you over the head with the criticism?' This kind of technique can be used in different ways, and clients are able to understand and remember the principle involved much better than with a strict verbal discussion no matter how clear concepts are made.

3. *Explain the difference between rational thinking and positive thinking.* One point requiring clarification among lower-class clients is that rational thinking is often a form of moderate negative thinking and not necessarily positive thinking. Many clients will confidently declare, after a little RET

philosophy, 'I know what you want me to do – just think positively about everything.' I usually explain that in most cases they have decided they are facing a disappointment, and it would be inconsistent to expect them to tell themselves they like the disappointment. I point out that I am trying to help them to be honest with themselves and to think negatively when things do not go their way, but not so negatively that they end up disturbed.

I usually elaborate on this point by explaining that when they believe something is bad, they are not expected to tell themselves that it is good but to stick to what they really believe: the situation is bad. When they do this, I explain further, they will feel bad, and that is the way one is supposed to feel under such circumstances. I tell the client I have no argument with him when he thinks and feels like this. However, when he believes a situation is not just bad but very, very, very, very, very, very bad, then I suspect his thinking may be too negative, and this will result in his feeling upset. I tell the client that I am just trying to help them cut out some of those 'verys' and that is what rational thinking is all about.

4. *Inform about appropriate emotions.* Along with teaching clients to differentiate among negative thinking, positive thinking and extreme negative thinking, it is important to advise them about the kinds of feelings to be expected from rational thinking. Often lower-class clients will readily agree with the wisdom of rational thinking but will complain that I am suggesting they eliminate their feelings. They usually express this point by declaring that I am trying to make them uncaring about a certain problem or situation.

The best way I have found to overcome this misconception is to draw a vertical line on a piece of paper or blackboard, labelling the top of the line 'upset' and the bottom of the line 'indifference' or 'calm'. I then explain that rational thinking will put the client somewhere in the middle of the continuum – a point which might be labelled 'less upset'. I usually stress the word 'less' in front of the feeling that is disturbing the client rather than relabelling that feeling. This is usually less confusing and seems to present a more manageable goal to most lower-class clients. The client, for example, who feels anger, is helped to feel 'less angry' rather than to feel 'annoyed' or 'irritated'.

5. *Explain symptom formation.* Another step in the psychological problem-solving process with lower-class clients involves helping them understand the nature of sympton formation. Many of the lower-class clients I see often display or complain about physical disturbances that accompany emotional upset. Sometimes these symptoms result in actual illness or diseases such as ulcers or colitis, but usually they are experienced as very distressing internal body changes. An accelerated heart beat, rapid breathing, difficulty in swal-

lowing, stomach upset, cold hands, and headaches are common examples.

Often the client has been told by a doctor that his symptoms are caused by his nerves or that 'it's all in his head'. This kind of explanation, although true in a sense, usually means very little to the average lower-class client. As far as he is concerned, he has been told that he has imagined his aches and pains. Clients usually react in a typical fashion, feeling angry, bewildered and anxious, and they frequently end up aggravating their symptoms even more.

I usually help the client to understand the situation by explaining that the nervous system that allows him to feel an emotion also operates other important parts of the body, such as the heart, lungs, stomach and blood vessels. These body parts are sort of on the same electrical circuit, I point out, so when a person 'turns on' an emotion, he 'turns on' other parts of the body as well. I further point out that when the emotions are in an uproar there is a good chance some other part of the body will also be in an uproar.

6. *Provide insight.* Since the confronting and confuting of irrational ideation is a primary goal in an RET endeavour, it is of utmost importance that such a process be introduced to the client in the most effective and efficient manner possible. It has been my experience that the most feasible method of helping the lower-class client to identify and remedy faulty thinking patterns is simply to do some of his thinking and reasoning for him. In this case, the therapist assumes the role of informed teacher and tells the client what the client is thinking, why his thinking will lead to problems, and how to adopt a more realistic point of view. Because the specific irrational attitudes that usually result in specific emotional disorders have been identified (Beck, 1976), the RET therapist has at his disposal an established method for quickly helping the client to locate the cognitive-semantic source of his disturbances.

In addition, the therapist corrects these irrational aberrations according to the principles of rational analysis (Ellis, 1973; Maultsby, 1975). Contrary to what might be expected, clinical experience has shown that directly supplying lower-class clients with such insight actually encourages them eventually to do such reasoning and analysing on their own.

7. *Use appropriate cognitive insights.* Because the insight process with most lower-class clients is to be a therapist-directed activity, it is extremely important that the therapist make sure the insights imparted to the client can be clearly and easily understood. One reason the lower-class client often gives the impression of being unable to benefit from verbal therapy is because such insight is presented in an unintelligible manner that is beyond the client's ability to comprehend. This apparent obstacle can usually be overcome, however, if the therapist makes an effort to tailor psychological insights to the intellectual and educational level of the client.

For example, lower-class clients who see their problems as catastrophes and feel upset, often find it hard to understand that it is their own negative, grossly exaggerated point of view that is causing their disturbance. As far as the client is concerned the situation is awful, because it is awful! Intellectualized discussions which attempt to prove that it is unlikely their situation is a genuine catastrophe, or philosophical debates which challenge their belief that their problem is truly awful, usually fail to make an impact.

However, when their problems are framed in a simplified, visually structured way, lower-class clients are better able to see the difference between authentic misfortune and imagined horrors. I usually accomplish this by using a sheet of paper on which I put two columns. One column I label 'Pain-in-the-Neck HASSLES' and the other column I label 'End-of-the-World HORRORS.'

Next I encourage the client to tell me exactly what is wrong in his problem. Then, after we list all the disadvantages and inconveniences involved, I will ask the client in which column the problem belongs – the hassle column or the horror column. Clients almost always see the point and admit that their problems belong in the hassle column. I ask them how they would feel if they could see their problem as a hassle instead of as a horror. Clients usually admit that they would feel much less upset. I then inform them that the job is constantly to tell themselves the truth, that the problem is a pain-in-the-neck, nothing more and nothing less.

A similar approach can be used to deal with the principle of self-acceptance with lower-class clients. This has consistently proved to be a most frustrating task with this client group. I am often successful, however, by redirecting the client's attention from rating himself to tolerating frustration. The strategy is to get away from the self-concept issue as much as possible and to avoid attempting to convince the client that self-blame is illogical and unnecessary.

Again I use the two-column method on a piece of paper or blackboard. Only this time I label one column 'It's Bad' and the other column 'I'm Bad'. I then encourage a discussion of the problem and try to show the client how it can be understood as a manageable frustration and not as a blow to his pride or his ego. I deliberately shift the emphasis to the 'It's Bad' column because this allows for the introduction of insights and semantic strategies that are more intelligible to the lower-class client.

For example, the disabled client who believes that his inability to work proves he is a worthless, totally incompetent individual and suffers accordingly, is shown 'It's Bad' that his handicap that prevents him from working. 'It's Bad' because he is unable to gain a sense of achievement. 'It's Bad' because he cannot earn as much money as before. 'It's Bad' because he cannot provide for his family as well as before. 'It's Bad' because he will have to settle for less satisfaction from life, and so on. The client is constantly directed to focus on the 'It's Bad' column rather than on 'I'm Bad', even when I recognize that the psychodynamics involved deal with lowered self-esteem.

I emphasize to the client, then, that he is a person 'with less' rather than the more pernicious concept that he is 'less of a person'. This manoeuvre allows for cognitive interventions that deal with frustration tolerance, an issue that is usually more amenable to therapeutic intervention with most lower-class clients than those involving self-value.

8. *Stick to accepted insights.* Once a particular insight has been presented, understood and accepted by the client, it is strongly suggested that this formation be repeated without significant change. In other words, stick to what seems to impress the client as the cognitive source of his distress and use the same words, analogies, visual examples, and the like to reinforce continually the message. Putting clarifications and interpretations into different words or using other but similar analogies may prove stimulating and creative to the therapist but confusing and bewildering to most lower-class clients. Although the repetition may be monotonous at times, it usually proves to be an effective approach in helping lower-class clients to understand and accept the rational concepts presented on their behalf.

9. *Modify self-statements.* Another effective problem-solving tactic with lower-class clients involves the use of self-statement modification. Despite efforts on the part of the therapist, some lower-class clients do not respond to a rational analysis of their problems even when provided with accurate insight and interpretation. Sometimes, detailed and even simplified explanations seem to fall on deaf ears and may be little more than wasted effort. Under these circumstances, it is better to teach the client to modify irrational attitudes and thought patterns through rote learning rather than through insight learning. In other words, instead of using reason and logic to rid the client of his faulty assumptions, the therapist presents him with a different, more realistic set of ideas which the client is told to memorize and to repeat to himself whenever he encounters the circumstances that he claims are upsetting. Although this approach is often not as interesting and challenging for the therapist, it can be very productive with certain clients.

10. *Analyse upset about upset.* One of the most common psychological problems experienced by lower-class clients occurs when they feel upset about feeling upset. In essence, they have become sensitized to their own symptoms and disturbances and are no longer concerned with the original subject of their distress. In other words, they feel anxious about feeling anxious, depressed about feeling depressed, anxious about feeling depressed, guilty about feeling angry, and so on.

It is important for the therapist to be alert to this condition or else effort will be wasted on analysing a situation and accompanying ideation that may well have caused the initial upset, but that is now secondary to the actual or current disturbance. In ABC terms you might put this in an ABCBC perspective. This is sometimes a chronic problem of long standing and is easy to identify, as the client will often not be able to indicate anything other than emotional upset as the complaint. Clients who state their problem as 'bad nerves' are a good example.

I usually inform the client immediately that the source of his problem is his own upset. I tell him that this is a fairly normal condition and although unpleasant it is hardly fatal. Lower-class clients frequently believe the intensity of their symptoms means that something is drastically wrong with them, and they may feel nearly on the verge of a horrible death. I try to illustrate the harmlessness of the situation by explaining that when they have a toothache, they feel pain, sometimes even a lot of pain. I ask the client what would happen if they thought about the pain all the time. Would it get better or worse? Usually they see the point. I reinforce this by telling them it's the same with their emotional problems. The more they preoccupy themselves with their suffering, the worse it will seem, but it will never kill them or harm them any more than will a bad toothache.

Another intervention that can be used in situations of this sort involves informing the client that his upset will not drive him crazy. A very popular misconception among the lower classes is that their emotional problems will cause them to lose their minds and that they will end up in mental hospitals. The most effective way I help clients cope with this idea is to ask, 'How do you feel right now?' Usually they answer, 'Terrible!' Then, in true *Gestalt* fashion, I advise them really to get in touch with their upset. They usually comply without much effort, and then I ask, 'Now how do you feel?', and they usually answer, 'Worse!' Then I say in a convincing voice, 'Well, that's about it – that's about as much of a nervous breakdown as you are going to have. You came through it. Congratulations.' Next I shake their hands and ask them if I am shaking the hands of people who are suffering and who have emotional problems or of people who are crazy and who belong in state hospitals. By my pointing out that a nervous breakdown means suffering and not insanity, lower-class clients will often stop ruminating on their symptoms and allow other problems to be faced and resolved.

For those clients who state that their only problem is bad nerves, which is a common presenting complaint among lower-class individuals, I usually respond that they have good nerves. I point out if they had bad nerves they probably would not be able to feel good or bad. I further inform such clients that they probably have the best nerves in town – all they have to do is to tell themselves one 'awful' or 'terrible' and their nerves get right down to business and make them feel upset. I tell the client that only a very strong set of nerves could cause him so much misery.

11. *Co-ordinate behaviour change with cognitive change.* Although the goal in RET is to correct symptom-producing cognitions, overt behaviour change is also encouraged as part of the problem-solving process. Such behaviour change is sometimes sought for its own sake but, in most cases, it is co-ordinated with basic efforts to correct the client's disturbed thinking. In other words, whenever possible, behaviour modification is used as an adjunct of cognitive restructuring. Lower-class clients tend to cling to certain prejudices and self-defeating attitudes even in the face of admitted contradictory evidence. However, they usually respond well when encouraged to act 'as if' they believed therapist-dictated rationales. Persuading the client to act on rational insights despite his lack of conviction often makes it easier for him to convince himself to modify attitudinal distortions and to adopt more sensible thought patterns regarding the problems and conflicts.

12. *Teach responsible assertive behaviours.* In addition to my encouraging cognitive change by also encouraging related behavioural change, I find the lower-class client responds well to assertiveness training in problem solving. This approach does not necessarily make specific efforts to help the client locate and correct the cognitive source of his problems. What I am referring to here is to an emphasis on teaching the client what to do – actual instruction for overt behavioural change with a minimum of effort put into corrective measures on behalf of the client's thoughts or covert behaviours.

I recognize that when behaviour is corrected at the expense of rational and appropriate cognitions, people often change but for the wrong reasons. In many cases, they maintain their irrational belief systems in spite of their apparent progress or improvement. Unfortunately, we are not always able to direct our clients to resolve their problems in the most elegant manner. Sometimes, with certain clients, especially those from the lower classes, we had better take what we can get as long as it relieves suffering and does not cause further conflict. I think it important that we bear in mind that our goal as therapists is to help our clients solve their problems, and we may not always be able to do this according to 'scripture'.

I usually find that most assertiveness training with lower-class clients falls into two general areas of endeavour. The first includes teaching clients to deal directly with the presenting problem. Usually this is a one-shot deal, and generalization to other areas of concern is neither expected nor encouraged. An example would be a woman whose husband has retired and who moves her, against her silent protests to the contrary, to a trailer in the mountains, where he plans to spend the rest of his life fishing and watching television.

The woman, however, wanted to remain in her community with her grown children and her close friends, whom she visited regularly.

She ends up in the hospital with a diagnosis of depression. The woman had not discussed the situation with her husband because, she says, he was not the type who either talked things over or listened. Instead of examining the cognitive–semantic roots of her depression and her inability to confront her husband, I instructed her on how to assert herself with her spouse. She was rehearsed in exactly what to say to him, how to handle his silences if there were any, and so on. She followed her instructions. Her husband listened to her and agreed to move back to the community and only to 'retire' on weekends.

A second area in which assertiveness training with lower-class clients is the best problem-solving approach, involves teaching such clients how to handle oppressive interpersonal relationships where one partner in the relationship acts in an aggressive way. Married lower-class women are especially unfortunate in this respect, as they are frequently involved in Tarzan–Jane types of interactions. Such women are frequently berated by their husbands and usually require therapeutic assistance beyond an understanding of the cognitive source of their distress. What is usually required is the learning of actual verbal behaviours that can be used to handle manipulative criticism.

The best approach I have found for this kind of situation follows the general pattern of the client's first acknowledging that there may well be some truth to the critic's point of view. This agreement is given regardless of whether the critic is actually right or wrong. Secondly, the client is told to express his opinion and then to repeat these two steps until some kind of compromise opinion or action can be worked out. If the critic is dangerous, the client is instructed to work on agreement only and not to attempt to express his point of view, at least initially.

For example, the woman who is unfairly called lazy by her husband is instructed to inform him that he may well have a point. She is taught to tell her husband, in a sincere manner, that she, in fact, might be very lazy. The goal is to establish the husband in the position of boss and to allow him to believe he is right. In most cases the previous scenario was for the wife to argue the point and for the husband to go to whatever extremes he deemed necessary to prove his point. Usually this meant reducing the wife to tears or, in some cases, beating her.

The husband wants to be boss, so therefore the wife gives him the title without a struggle. Once this is accomplished, she can offer her opinion. She might, in this case, disagree and inform her husband of the many tasks she did complete during the day. If the husband still disagrees and tells her she should be doing more, once again the wife agrees and accepts this opinion. She tells the husband he is probably correct again but expresses her opinion that she is doing about all she can. Usually, the husband just wants to be considered lord and master and once this has been established, he acts more benevolently, is less demanding, and gets off his wife's back.

If the client follows these tactics and the husband remains critical or aggressive, there is a good chance the husband is quite disturbed and nothing will help the situation. In such a case, this is pointed out to the client and therapeutic endeavours shift to a discussion of the client's motives for staying in such a situation.

This method has been justly criticized (Lange and Jakubowski, 1976) because it does not allow for the true expression of one's feelings and, when carried to extremes, may be countermanipulative and could discount valid criticism. It is important to realize that this tactic is not for use with a critic who is generally reasonable and honest but rather with someone who consistently acts in an extremely aggressive, destructive, manipulative manner.

Encouraging effort

With the usual exceptions, in order to grow and to change, the client is expected to put knowledge learned in therapy into practice in concrete and specific life situations. This usually requires hard work and effort on the part of the client and is rarely achieved through passive listening or insight osmosis. Clients who do best in therapy, therefore, are those that commit themselves to change and then work hard to bring this change about.

Encouraging a client to understand and accept such a commitment and the hard work that follows is, of course, no easy task. The lower-class client, in particular, presents a special problem in this area and often requires special help in understanding his part in the change process. This is probably explained by the difficulty the average lower-class person seems to experience in differentiating psychological assistance from general medical treatment. In the medical setting, the problem or illness is not considered the patient's domain, and self-treatment is discouraged lest it interfere with the healing process. When the lower-class person presents himself for psychotherapy, therefore, he expects to be 'doctored' – to have the emotional problem treated or cured with little or no participation on his part.

In addition, the lower-class client shares the same myth about psychotherapy as do other client groups, that change will occur when the therapist uncovers some hidden insight or incites some kind of purifying emotional outburst. In other words, something special is supposed to happen in therapy, and when it does a magical transformation will take place. The client will then have the answers to all his problems and will be able to live happily ever after. The lower-class clients that I see seem particularly prone to this misconception because they are exposed to or believe in religious faiths that promise instant and everlasting happiness if they undergo a sort of spiritual surrender to Christ.

Unfortunately, this myth about the magical powers of therapy is not always limited to clients. Even RET therapists could confuse the sometimes dramatic events that occur within the clinical setting as evidence that change has automatically taken place. It is sometimes easy to believe that a penetrating insight is sufficient to correct a client's disturbances.

It is important to bear in mind that what happens within a therapy session, even an RET session, is for the most part an intellectual endeavour. The wisdom of the therapist's words, regardless of how accurate, will have little consequence unless the client translates those words into action in some way. If the therapist is effective during the session, then the client has probably gained intellectual understanding of his emotional problems. Even though such experiences may appear quite intense, they are in the final analysis, only blueprints for change.

Interpretation and insight about the client's faulty thinking patterns, therefore, is not an end in itself but rather a means toward an end. More to the point, the RET therapist is responsible for more than tracking down and correcting the client's distorted cognitions. The therapist must also direct his attention to the equally important but perhaps less glamorous task of informing and persuading the client to overcome his disturbances by practising his insights in some kind of conscious, self-directed way.

Although I view the client as responsible for putting in the practice and effort to make change possible, I see the therapist as accountable for instructing the client that such effort is indeed required and then encouraging, persuading, and otherwise inspiring the client actually to attempt such efforts. I might mention in this regard that I am often told by my clients that they do not always feel good when they enter or leave my office. They frequently complain that I put pressure on them – that I seem to be pushing them, expecting something from them. When I hear this, in most cases, I know I am doing my job. My clients are quite correct: I do expect something from them and I do push them. I expect them to do their job, to work at change, and I push them to do this.

I will now detail some of the ways in which I educate lower-class clients as to their part in the change process as well as some of the techniques I use to motivate such clients to expend effort and to practise.

1. *Explain that self-directed effort is required.* Since direct instruction is already accepted, the first step toward encouraging the lower-class client to act on insights learned in therapy is simply to tell him that improvement will require work and effort on his part. A client can be given an explanation of the

normal resistance that humans seem to experience when trying to change their actions. If he is advised that emotional and psychological problems are merely bad habits, that they are difficult though hardly impossible obstacles, the client is often willing to put forth the necessary effort to achieve change. Explaining emotional disturbance as a bad habit is an especially valuable tool for getting across the importance of self-effort to lower-class clients. This kind of educational approach often takes the magic out of how psychotherapy is supposed to work and puts behavioural change within a framework the client understands – that of hard work, practice and effort.

2. *Explain that progress will take time.* In addition, it is important to advise the client that progress will take time and will not happen overnight. Because the lower-class client often confuses psychotherapy with medical care and faith healing, he often expects unrealistic results from his therapeutic experiences. Perhaps the most prevalent expectation is that psychotherapy will quickly and permanently cure his emotional problems and that after a few sessions the client will no longer feel upset or experience distressing symptoms. Emphasizing to the client that behavioural change is almost always a long, slow, tedious process rather than a dramatic, sweeping, sudden affair (Harper, 1975), is best done as soon as possible.

It is also better to inform the client that although improvement is likely, a permanent cure that will leave him care-free and unaffected by life's frustrations is highly unlikely. He can be told that the lessons learned in therapy will take some time to put into practice, that progress will be gradual, and that his efforts will probably have to be made on an ongoing, regular basis for the best results to be achieved.

3. *Offer an explanation of what is normal.* I also help clients gain a realistic expectation of therapeutic outcome by offering an explanation of what it is like to feel emotionally normal. A simple explanation is to tell the client that mental health means learning how to handle disappointments without feeling too upset – bad, but not too upset. I make the point that normal means feeling both good and bad, not just good all the time.

Unfortunately, the expectation of feeling good constantly is common among lower-class clients who believe their therapy experiences are supposed to 'heal' them of all their suffering and leave them unaffected or comfortably calm about problems. In order to determine if this expectation exists, I will often ask clients how they believe they are supposed to feel if they think rationally about their problems and follow my suggestions. Often they will report they expect to feel relieved or peaceful. One client whose mother was dying slowly from cancer told me that if she could think the way I had been advising, she could feel as if a huge weight had been lifted from her shoulders and her heart would be full of joy. In other words, she would feel happy because her mother was dying.

If this misconception goes by unchallenged, clients will usually drop out of therapy because the results cannot possibly equal expectations. Clients will believe they have been shortchanged and will quickly lose faith in the therapy process. Once this occurs, even the most skilful interventions and the most brilliant insights will have little impact, because these manoeuvres will not provide the desired effect or produce enjoyable disappointments or comfortable suffering.

I usually attack this problem in two ways. First, I point out to the client that I follow the exact principles I am trying to teach him, and I have yet to feel good about a disappointment. If I am unable to feel cheerful about disappointments, I ask how they expect to be able to do it. I also point out that people who smile or feel calm in the face of adversity are usually not called well-adjusted or normal. They are usually called crazy. Secondly, I tell the client that the goal of our efforts is to help him feel unhappy rather than miserable. Sometimes I will use a continuum illustration to get this concept across. I show him that he belongs somewhere in the middle of the continuum between calm and miserable. I point out that feeling miserable usually prevents him from solving problems because it is a feeling so strong that it controls him. Unhappiness, I explain, is an unpleasant feeling, but it is one that can be controlled and used as a motivation to solve problems.

4. *Teach suffer power*. In addition to helping the client understand what to expect from therapy, I also teach him the principle of suffer power or struggle strength. This principle holds that progress in therapy initially requires that one put in effort while feeling upset. In other words, I instruct clients that they are to force themselves to challenge an idea or change an action even though they feel disturbed. This is an especially important tactic with lower-class clients as they almost always want to wait until they feel better before trying out new behaviours or trying to think things out. I tell them that they have literally got to do the opposite of how they feel, and that this is the secret of getting better – trying to change when they do not feel like changing.

5. *Assign homework tasks*. As you are aware, assigning reading, writing and activity-oriented tasks outside the therapy session can enhance outcome because such efforts often encourage the client to realize that he is expected to use his own efforts to bring about change. Task assignments work well with the lower-class client as long as such assignments are problem-specific and well within the intellectual and achievement level of the individual client.

In the area of reading, I have found that Lembo's (1974) book, *Help yourself,* Hauck's (1973) *Overcoming depression*, and my booklet *A rational counseling primer* (1974) are most effective. Other RET books do not seem to work as well with lower-class clients because they prove too difficult for such clients to read. I might mention that the main purpose of using literature with the lower classes is not necessarily to teach the principles of RET but to establish an expectation of benefit from therapy. Many clients fail to understand what they have read but will declare they are sure it will help them. It is this faith in therapy that I aim for in assigning initial reading experiences.

In the area of writing assignments, I experience considerable difficulty with males. Most lower-class clients have little experience with the skills required for expressing themselves through written communication. I have been able to overcome this obstacle with lower-class females by suggesting they write me letters or keep a diary they can share with me. I will advise them to write about their problems, their thoughts and their feelings, as well as about some solutions. Often this kind of approach helps the client look at his or her problems more objectively and sometimes can be quite potent in encouraging change. On some occasions I will return a letter and ask the client to rewrite it from a more rational perspective.

One tactic that usually gets good results is to direct the client to fill out or complete a form which monitors his behavioural change efforts. I usually design these forms for the client and then have him use them in a check-off fashion between sessions. The forms can be used for simplified cognitive homework or activity homework assignments such as cleaning the house or going for a job interview. Often the completion of these tasks provides the client with evidence that change is actually taking place as a result of his therapy experiences and tends to encourage even further improvement.

The best method I have found to use the ABC homework form is to complete the assignment for the client. I have tried many approaches, including redesigning the form and using cartoon characters, but apparently this kind of endeavour is quite confusing to lower-class individuals. I found I was spending more time trying to explain the mechanics of filling out the form than on actual problem solving, so I have abandoned using this as an independent homework assignment. However, when I do it for them the ABC form seems to be quite productive with clients. What I do is to fill it out while the client is talking and I use his own language. I give the client the form after the session is over and tell him to study it between sessions.

Along these same lines, I often write down on a piece of paper rational thoughts or actions that can be followed until the client's next session. I tell him to hang the paper in some prominent place, such as the refrigerator door or bathroom mirror, and to read it as often as possible. Another good technique is to write the same message on a small piece of paper and to have the client place it inside the cellophane of his cigarette pack and to read it whenever he lights up.

Finally, let me comment briefly on the kinds of activity assignments I usually find most productive with lower-class clients. As I have mentioned, these tasks can complement attempts to restructure cognitions or can be used as attempts to solve problems without corresponding efforts to change thinking. In general, I find that activity assignments work best when they deal with the problem itself rather than serving as exercises designed to build skills that can eventually be applied with the problem situation. The client who is afraid to say no to her mother-in-law, for example, is given direct instruction on how to handle this situation. This method is used in place of having her practise saying 'no' to others until she is more comfortable with this kind of behaviour and then applying it with the mother-in-law. Lower-class clients would view such skill training as creating a problem to solve a problem.

6. *Make liberal use of positive reinforcement.* The principles of contingency reinforcement are well-established procedures that can be used by RET therapists to encourage change through effort and practice. Through the offering of various rewards or penalties, behaviour can be manipulated to increase or decrease in frequency. It is strongly suggested that the RET therapist become familiar with these principles and use them to motivate the lower-class client to change his ways.

Positive reinforcement, for example, can be used to increase behaviour frequency through offering excited verbal praise, gold stars, and with extremely difficult clients, a free therapy session. This can be applied to already improved behaviours or as an anticipated reward. However, one area where such reinforcement is effective is with behaviour that has not been changed, but the client is given credit for change. Sometimes this is called attribution reinforcement, and the principle is to tell the client he already exhibits traits or performs actions he has yet to demonstrate. For example, the client who complains of extreme shyness and is afraid to speak up for himself can be told, 'I really find that hard to believe. In last week's session you gave me a tough time – you really stood up to me more than most people. You really came on as if you were sure of yourself and meant business. I was really impressed.'

7. *Use negative reinforcement or aversive control.* Another method of contingency reinforcement is to arrange negative consequences in order to decrease unwanted behaviour. This can be done by withdrawing a positive outcome or, in some cases, seeing that a penalty follows certain objectionable behaviour. Negative reinforcement can be used, for example, by ignoring or

not offering interest in a particular subject or area you want stopped. For instance, the client who comes in week after week and merely complains and pays little attention to your interventions and efforts, can be handled by remaining silent or perhaps appearing busy with something else while the client is talking. When questioned you can reply: 'Since you only want to complain I really can't be of help to you.' A more direct method is to tell the client you are not going to listen anymore, that you have decided you cannot help them. Often clients will begin to work on things if they realize they are not going to be able use therapy as a confessional and will no longer receive the empathy and attention they want.

Sometimes a client can be convinced to get on the ball and do something about his problems if some kind of penalty is arranged on his behalf. It is advised that the therapist and the client decide together the kind of penalty to be used so that the arrangement will be viewed as a corrective measure instead of a punishment. For example, you might get the unemployed man who claims he is too anxious to sit through an interview to apply for two jobs or else he has to call and talk to his ex-wife whom he claims to hate. However, one of the most potent ploys you can employ to penalize a client for lack of progress is simply to impress upon him that the natural outcome of one who does not work at change is to suffer, and this will continue until the change takes place. Sometimes this information has a dramatic impact on clients, and they will begin to put in more effort outside the therapy.

8. *Combine both positive and negative reinforcements.* One of the most effective methods of motivating behavioural change is to combine both positive and negative reinforcement. This is especially useful with depressed clients who week after week complain of depression and do nothing but sit on their behinds. I will first ask them if they really want to get over their depression. Usually they reply in the affirmative. Since they almost always tell me that the only highlight of their miserable existence is the therapy session, I adhere to the following plan of action: I write down a list of things to do. This list is not a new one, but includes those activities the client has failed to perform for quite some time. Then I tell the client that if he does all the things on the list, I will see him for the whole session and listen to all his woes. However, if he does not do the items on the list, I will see him only for 10 minutes, and all we can talk about is the weather. The charge, I point out, will be the same as for a full session. With selected clients this tactic can sometimes produce immediate results.

9. *Have clients listen to tapes of their sessions.* Encouraging the clients to listen to audio- and video-recordings of their therapy sessions is a well-established method of motivating clients to put in effort in RET. This also works well

with lower-class clients with some important modifications. They usually do not own tape-recorders, so they have to listen in the office immediately after their sessions. The best method I use is to have the client come in well in advance of his appointment. During the time before the session he is instructed to do some kind of written assignment pertaining to his problem. During the session he discusses the written assignment. After the session is over, he is directed to a separate office, where he listens to the recording. I have found this a good way to motivate clients, particularly those who have trouble understanding some of the insights being presented to them.

10.   *Include family members in the counselling session.*   A very effective tactic that frequently encourages behavioural change is the participation of other family members in the counselling process. There is an expression in West Virginia: 'Hit the bark, you hit the tree. Hit my family, you done hit me.' Family ties are close, and this can be used to advantage in attempts to motivate clients to put forth the necessary effort to bring about change. I am not referring to family therapy *per se* but to choosing a particular member of the family and gaining his cooperation in helping the primary client. I have allowed, for example, an understanding and concerned husband to sit in on a few sessions with his wife so that he can see what I am trying to accomplish. Since the husband is not as disturbed as his wife, he usually understands more readily what points are being made and repeats them back to the client between sessions at specific times when the client is having trouble.

This can also be done very effectively with uncooperative family members. In this case, such an approach has to be handled with care, lest the problem member of the family think you are faulting him or her for the client's unhappiness. For example, one very domineering and manipulative husband refused to allow his wife to leave the house unless she was in his company. He was jealous and would fly into a rage if he suspected she was flirting in any way. I knew he resented me because I was a man and because his wife talked to me privately each week. It was important that his wife get out of the house and gain some independence, or she would remain depressed in spite of the cognitive efforts to the contrary. I talked with the husband and told him I knew he wanted his wife to get better. I further told him that after extensive studying of the problem, it had been decided that she would get well if she could get out of the house during the day. Such activities as visiting her older children, shopping, and the like were presented as the kinds of tasks that would be needed on a regular basis to cure her. Then I told the man I had tried everything to get her to do this but, for some reason, I was unable to motivate her to change. I admitted I was failing, and if he could help out and make his wife go out, he would be a better man than I. I also pointed out that the sooner the wife began to be more active, the sooner she could stop seeing me. She was allowed out the next day.

11. *Encourage weekly contacts.* Although few systems of psychotherapy will dispute the value of weekly, or even more frequent client–therapist contacts, the lower classes are often unaccustomed to attending therapy on such a regular basis. They usually view such 'doctoring' as a once-in-a-while, one-shot deal. I have found simple instruction is the best policy for countering this kind of client attitude. If mental health care is described as an educational process involving the same kind of instruction and attendance as did school experiences, clients will usually feel more receptive to regular therapeutic contact.

12. *Use half-hour sessions.* One method I have found that encourages change is to rely on the 30-minute session. The pressure of a shorter time period can often motivate the therapist to get down to business more quickly and to move the client toward change. Although I favour the 30-minute session with clients of all socioeconomic levels, I have found it very productive with the lower-class client. Often therapy with these clients can prove non-productive because the counsellor is trying to solve too many problems in a given session or is trying to approach a particular problem offering too many insights. This tends to confuse the client because it dilutes the potency and impact of the message that the therapist is trying to convey.

For example, I once saw a coal miner for four sessions that totalled about 50 minutes. He was a chronic drinker since the time he claims to have caused the death of a close friend in a mine accident. The first session lasted about 17 minutes. I pointed out the ideation that usually results in guilt, got the client's agreement that this was what he was thinking, and explained how to think more rationally. After I was sure the client understood what was being explained, I wrote down the rational insights on a piece of paper, told him to study them, and promptly ended the session. The man had other problems, but this was his main concern. To discuss other problems or to allow him to ramble on about his guilt feelings would have proven less effective than a short, to-the-point session. The remaining three sessions were used to reinforce what had been learned in the first session.

References

Beck, A.T. (1976). *Cognitive therapy and the emotional disorders.* New York: International Universities Press.

Ellis, A. (1972). Helping people get better rather than merely feel better. *Rational Living,* **7**(2), 2–9.

Ellis, A. (1973). *Humanistic psychotherapy: The rational-emotive approach.* New York: Julian Press.

Gillis, J.S. (1974). Social influence therapy: The therapist as manipulator, *Psychology Today,* **8**, 91–95.

Halleck, S. (1971). *The politics of therapy*. New York: Science House Inc.

Harper, R. (1975). *The new psychotherapies*. Englewood Cliffs, N.J.: Prentice-Hall.

Hauck, P. (1973). *Overcoming depression*. Philadelphia: The Westminster Press.

Hollingshead, A. and Redlich, F. (1958). *Social class and mental illness*. New York: Wiley.

Lange, A. and Jakubowski, P. (1976). *Responsible assertive behavior*. Champaign, Ill.: Research Press.

Lembo, J. (1974). *Help yourself*. Niles, Ill.: Argus Communications.

Maultsby, M.C. Jr (1975). *Help yourself to happiness*. New York: Institute for Rational Living.

Srole, L., Langer, T., Michael, S., Opler, M. and Rennie, T. (1962). *Mental health in the metropolis: The midtown Manhattan study*. New York: McGraw-Hill.

Young, H.S. (1974). *A rational counseling primer*. New York: Institute for Rational Living.

Chapter 9

Practising RET with Bible-Belt Christians

Howard S. Young

Not long ago, an earnest-looking young man handed me a pamphlet entitled 'Five Facts You Need To Know For Eternal Life'. Once he had my attention he thrust at me another pamphlet. This one was called 'The Golden Rule Is Not Enough!' Before I could recover I was holding yet another tract, this one asking: 'Heaven or Hell – What Is For You?' The scene was played out one Saturday afternoon in a grocery store parking lot while I was getting out of my car. I have learned to accept such literature, to thank the giver sincerely, and to go on my way. To protest or do otherwise is to invite a sermon that would put Billy Graham or Oral Roberts to shame. I once kiddingly told such an individual that I followed the teachings of Satan and that I truly believed in the Devil. That was a mistake. I was relentlessly tracked through a shopping centre by a first-class maniac desperately trying to save my soul before it was too late. It was not until I convinced my soul-saver that I was really a Christian and lover of Jesus with all my heart that I was finally again left to my own resources.

In Huntington, West Virginia, where I live, such religious zeal is common-place. As you may or may not be aware, Huntington is in the midst of the Bible Belt, a section of the country reputed to be the stronghold of extreme religious conservatism. It is a place in which the Bible is the best-seller and prayer is considered the answer to all problems. Revival meetings, religious bookstores, 24-hour Christian radio broadcasting, gospel singing, and faith healing are the order of the day. Billboards, flashing neon road signs, and bumper stickers all proclaim the news that 'Christ is the Answer' and 'Only Jesus Saves'.

Who are these God-seekers, these over-religious, devout believers? Although many are probably members of a Protestant church group such as

the Southern Baptist or the United Fundamentalist Church, they really seem
to care little about sectarianism. In fact, most Bible-Belt Christians claim no
main-line religious affiliation. They simply refer to themselves as Christians.

Even though, at first glance, such individuals might appear unlikely
candidates for psychotherapy – especially a logico-empirical system of
psychotherapy developed by a dyed-in-the-wool atheist named Albert Ellis –
it has been my experience that RET can be applied very effectively with
Bible-Belt Christians. It is the purpose of this Chapter to discuss some of the
approaches and techniques I have developed to accomplish this goal. I am
going to assume that many of you are unfamiliar with Bible-Belt Christianity, and I will therefore offer a brief introduction.

Individuals who profess to be Christians are often called Fundamentalists,
but this label correctly applies only to a group of 'God-fearers' who belong at
the ultra-conservative end of the continuum. At the other end are the
'God-lovers', the Evangelicals. Although similar in their adherence to Biblical absolutism, the two groups are divided by important differences.

The *Fundamentalists* focus attention on sin and damnation. They are best
represented by the hell, fire and brimstone preachers who like to denounce
the wicked world with the rhetoric of doom. Fundamentalists are usually
opposed to drinking, smoking, gambling, dancing and public swimming.
Most recently, one of their ministers called for the abolition of rock music
because all such music is 'aswarm with adultery, fornication, uncleanliness,
heresies, and revelings'. Another minister put it this way: 'If I don't understand something, then it's a sin, and I oppose it!' Their formula for family
structure is a simple one: the man is the undisputed head of the house, and the
woman is his obedient wife and servant.

Probably the most noteworthy feature of this devout group is its pre-
occupation with the overwhelming fear of divine wrath. Fundamentalists
might justly – though paradoxically – be called 'Old Testament Christians'.
They believe the closer one comes to God through holy living, the more one
can sense one's sins in the eyes of God. Since the only result of sin is eternal
damnation, this individual feels fear and guilt. These feelings may be relieved
only through repentance. However, this repentance brings one still closer to
God, reminds one again of one's sins, leads to further fear and guilt, demands
additional repentance which in turn brings the sinner once again closer to
God, and so on. According to Biblical scripture, no one is ever free of sin, so
the Fundamentalist believer is forever caught in a kind of *Catch 22* – a vicious
cycle in which the hope is that one's dying words are a request for forgiveness.

For reasons that must be obvious, Fundamentalist preachers are opposed to
psychotherapy and often try to sabotage efforts on the part of their flock to
seek and remain with such help. It is not unusual for my clients to confide that

their ministers have threatened them with the fires of hell for coming to counselling sessions. Psychotherapy – and psychiatry in particular, as one client was warned – is the work of the Devil and is not to be trusted.

The *Evangelicals*, on the other hand, offer a theology that places emphasis on forgiveness and salvation. They are the God lovers and seek an ongoing personal and intimate relationship with Christ. This is a kind of spiritual union in which the individual surrenders his will or independence to God and allows divine inspiration to guide his life. Evangelicals do this because they believe that man is a sinner and is weak and that he cannot overcome these handicaps without Christ's love and guidance.

Once Christ is accepted as a personal saviour, all is possible – literally all. No problem is so large that it cannot be relieved or resolved with Christ's help. The Evangelical message is one of hope, joy and eternal happiness.

Probably the most striking feature of this religious approach, however, is the phenomenon of being 'born again'. During the process of dedicating one's life to Christ, it is claimed that a kind of mystical, intensely emotional experience takes place. The individual who undergoes this spiritual initiation is considered reborn or saved, is relieved of all past sin, and is free to make a fresh start in life. Many converts explain their rebirth as a sensation similar to an electric shock. Some say it is as though a lightning bolt had suddenly struck them and had travelled through their bodies. One 'saved' Christian claimed his salvation felt as though a sudden flow of energy and joy had come over him, a sensation akin to nothing he had ever experienced before. After being saved, these joyful Christians are eager and willing to relate the scenarios of their experience in great detail to anyone who will listen. It appears that the telling and retelling of their testimony strengthens and recharges their faith.

It is Evangelicals who have captured the public attention of the day. Celebrities on television talk-shows rave about their conversions; books written by the reborn are beginning to appear on bestseller lists; and a recent Gallup poll indicates that 94 per cent of Americans now claim they believe in God or a Universal Spirit. However, it was probably the nomination and election of Jimmy Carter as President that gave the Evangelicals their greatest publicity. Mr Carter admitted to being a 'born-again' Christian, and he claimed to read a chapter of the Bible daily.

It would appear that Bible-belt Christianity, whether it surfaces as God-fearing Fundamentalism or God-loving Evangelicalism, is a religious form that is on the rise in the United States. The Southern Baptists, for example, claim a membership of 12.7 million with a growing rate of 250,000 per year. I might add that the population increase in 'that old-time religion' is not limited to the Bible Belt; of even more interest is the change in social-class composition of conservative Christian churches. Some recent research

indicated these churches are no longer the exclusive province of the stereotyped, uneducated red-neck from the Deep South but are now attracting a
country-wide, predominantly well-educated, middle-class participation. It
was suggested that the economic reversals and social changes of the past
decade so disrupted the traditional security of the middle class that a search
for new meaning led to the certainties of the Bible and the Christian promise
of eternal salvation.

It is quite likely, therefore, that whether you practise RET in West Virginia
or not, and whether you like it or not, one of these days you will find yourself
face-to-face with a confirmed fundamentalist Christian. Since it is the
primary purpose of this Chapter to discuss the application of RET with this
client group, let me get down to business and discuss some of the clinical
issues involved. It might prove helpful to approach the subject by dealing
with some of the questions that might well be asked before engaging in such
an endeavour.

1. *How much religious education must a therapist have before he or she attempts to*
   practise RET with fundamentalist Christians?

My answer is very little! I am not well-versed on the Bible. Most of the
religious information I need for my work comes from the clients themselves
or from my occasional viewing of the religious programmes that fill the TV
channels in my area. I watch Billy Graham, Oral Roberts, Rex Humbard and
other media ministers. Their message is repetitive, easily remembered, and
extremely useful for therapeutic interventions.

The way in which the preachers get their message across is especially
noteworthy. I strongly suggest you listen to some of the evangelists on
television or radio. Although they sometimes come across as dogmatic and
authoritarian, they are nevertheless extremely effective speakers, and they
have a remarkable ability to persuade listeners to accept what they have to
say. I have borrowed much from their delivery and style, and I often use their
methods to get my own therapeutic message across to both religious and
non-religious clients.

However, it is not necessary to put even this much effort into a religious
education if you plan to practise RET with Bible-Belt Christians. Merely
become familiar with the principle of forgiveness as found in the New
Testament. It goes like this: when you sin, you confess your sin to God, you
ask for God's forgiveness, you receive God's grace, and then, freed of guilt,
you work hard to avoid further sinning so that you can fulfil God's purpose
for you. In RET terms, this principle might be expressed in the following
way: you make a mistake, you assume responsibility for the mistake, you
accept yourself as a fallible human being, and you then work hard to avoid

further mistakes so that you can strive for maximum happiness.

Both the Bible and RET, therefore, view self-blame as playing an important role in human suffering, and both offer similar approaches to dealing
with the problem. In fact, it might be said that teaching the principle of
acceptance and the tactics employed to put this concept into practice is the
goal of many RET encounters. The therapist who acquaints himself with the
similarities between Biblical forgiveness and rational acceptance has at his
disposal an extremely effective cognitive-philosophic tool for dealing with
most forms of emotional disturbance.

2. *What about the therapist's religious convictions? Can an atheistic or non-religious
   therapist practise RET with Bible-Belt Christians?*

My answer is a definite 'Yes!' I do not believe the therapist need be a
Christian, Catholic, Jew, Buddhist, Hindu, or whatever, to practise
psychotherapy with clients. The question of whether the client and therapist
must share the same religion in order to ensure an effective therapeutic
outcome raises an issue that frequently comes up in therapy. Can the white
therapist work with a black client? Can the male therapist work with a female
client? Can the straight therapist work with the gay client? and so on.

Numerous studies have addressed themselves to this issue. The answer is
usually the same: in some cases, it is important that the therapist and client
share certain common characteristics, but in most cases it is not. It would be
practically impossible for the average therapist who works with a varied
clientele to possess traits similar to those of all his clients. For one thing, he
would have to suffer their disturbances. After all, how could one expect a
therapist to help a psychotic client, an alcoholic client, or a manic-depressive
client, unless he himself suffered or, even better, was presently suffering
from such disorders?

It is important to bear in mind that there is nothing about psychotherapy
that requires the therapist to be anything other than an educator or teacher.
Our job as therapists is to teach clients that alternatives, cognitive or
otherwise, exist, and that chances are very good that if they follow some of
these alternatives, they can either resolve their problems or learn to live with
them better. As long as this information is presented in a responsible,
empathic manner, there is no reason why therapy cannot take place between
people of different religious, social, ethnic, and other varied cultural, intellectual and emotional backgrounds. Although exceptions do exist, it is my
opinion that the non-religious therapist, therefore, can work effectively with
the extremely religious client. The primary requirement for such an endeavour is that the therapist demonstrate an accepting, understanding,
non-judgemental attitude toward the client's religious values and beliefs.

3. *How do you handle questions about your own religious beliefs, or lack of them, if you know that the information may create a serious problem for the client and might possibly result in termination of therapy?*

It is my suggestion that you answer such questions very carefully! Although I am usually a strong believer in answering the personal questions posed by most clients in a direct and honest manner, I have found that this is not always advisable with religious clients. If you are asked a question about your religious convictions, and you believe that an honest but negative reply could interfere with therapy, then I suggest you evade the issue. Try to answer the client and leave the impression you are a believer without really stating things as such.

If you are backed into a corner and nothing less than a straight 'yes' or 'no' answer is acceptable, I strongly suggest you lie and tell the client you are a firm believer. In my opinion, honesty is not always the best policy in these cases, and if the client is really in need of help, and a more acceptable counsellor is not available, it is better to free the client of any doubt he may have about your motives and to tell him what he wants to hear. Otherwise, many clients will suspect you are the Devil himself trying to seduce them away from God. Very little therapy could take place under such circumstances.

4. *Are there any Christian religious beliefs that are off-limits to RET interventions?*

Yes, there are a few. I strongly suggest, for example, that you avoid confronting and confuting (1) the existence of God, Christ or the Holy Spirit; (2) the existence of the Devil, Demons or the Forces of Evil; (3) the infallibility of the Bible; (4) the existence of a heaven that is somewhere in the sky; (5) the existence of hell, a place of unbearable suffering, somewhere down inside the earth; and of course (6) life after death.

For our purposes, these absolutes will have to remain inviolate and beyond the province of psychotherapeutic investigation. To do otherwise – to contradict such notions – will usually bring the therapeutic endeavour to a quick end. Surprisingly, however, the inviolability of these concepts need not interfere with cognitive and semantic efforts to convince Bible-Belt Christians to change their thinking and overcome their disturbances. In fact, it is the very source of these absolutes, the Bible itself, that can provide the ideology for successful RET therapy.

It is important to realize that the Bible contains many sane and rational passages that can easily lend themselves to sound therapeutic interventions. I have already described the similarity between the Biblical principle of divine forgiveness and the RET concept of self-forgiveness. It is hard to imagine an emotionally disturbed client who could not use some assistance in overcoming the tendency to condemn himself and others. In addition, the Bible offers many other ethical principles that are consistent with the tenets of RET and that can be applied very effectively to most forms of emotional disturbance.

However, the method I use most frequently to skirt fundamentalist absolutes and to encourage clients to surrender upset-producing, irrational ideas involves the interpretation and definition of the Scriptures themselves. I usually follow a procedure that first accepts a particular passage as literal truth, then changes the meaning of that passage so that it proves more rational and helpful to the client. Since there is little agreement among Bible-Belt theologians as to the exact meaning of Scripture, this tactic is rarely challenged. Clients often respond dramatically to this approach because my interpretations appear to have the sanction of God himself.

An example may help to illustrate this method more clearly. A 50-year-old coal miner suffered an accident that was caused by the coal company's neglect of proper safety precautions. He was extremely angry and depressed because the company would neither recognize its liability in the matter nor offer him compensation. Since the accident had left him permanently disabled, I asked why he had not sued the company for restitution. The man told me he was a Christian and that the Bible said you are not allowed 'to law against your neighbor'.

I accepted this stricture without question but offered the man a different interpretation. I explained that the passage meant you were not supposed to bring legal action against someone for selfish reasons. I agreed that it was wrong to sue someone so that you could get rich – you are supposed to love your neighbour, not cause him trouble. However, I pointed out that if the man sued the company, he would not be doing it only for himself. Such legal action might be used as a way to force the company to improve its safety standards and might thus save lives. I informed the man that if he used the law against the company, he would likely be helping his neighbours. In other words, I redefined legal action as a virtue and not a sin.

In addition, I asked the man if he believed, as a Christian, that he was the head of his house. He nodded his agreement, and I admonished him for not fulfilling his Christian duty in this regard. I pointed out to him that his failure to sue the company left his wife and family with scant economic support and subjected them to unnecessary hardship. By taking the necessary legal action, I told my client, he would not only be helping his neighbours but his family as well, and that, I emphasized, is what God wants him to do. It's in the Bible! This proved to be the clincher: the man's anger and depression subsided as soon as he learned that he had alternatives that were in keeping with Biblical law. I understand that he later obtained the services of an attorney.

Rather than arguing with the Scripture, I interpreted it differently and showed this client that he was looking at things in the wrong way. I tried to offer an explanation that would allow for the most rational course of action under the circumstances. Combining this strategy with the principles of forgiveness has proved consistently the most effective way of intervening in the disturbances suffered by Bible-Belt Christians. I have received remarkable results using this approach and have been able to convince some of the most rigidly narrow Christians to change their thinking and actions.

I might add that I am not interested in whether or not I am Biblically accurate, nor am I the least bit interested in checking up and finding out if what I have to say or even what the client has to say is actually found in the Bible. In many cases, I take considerable liberty with a particular passage or verse, and it is quite possible that my interpretation would not stand up to ecclesiastical review. My goal is not to provide pastoral counselling consistent with accepted religious dogma, but rather to provide a therapeutic experience that follows the rules of rational analysis. In short, I present the Bible according to RET.

My suggested approach can probably be illustrated by the use of examples. Let us therefore look at some clinical situations that demonstrate those cognitive strategies that I have found most effective with Christian clients.

Forgiveness ploys

This first example is that of a young woman who had to be hospitalized because of extreme guilt and depression. It seems that she had borne a child by a man other than her husband. Her husband was unaware of the situation, and the woman claimed to be so distraught that she could not look the child in the face. Although she was not a regular churchgoer, she was raised in a fundamentalist family and had undoubtedly absorbed their beliefs.

When I met her for the first time, I asked her why she felt so guilty. She claimed she had broken one of God's sacred rules: she had committed adultery and was sure she would end up in hell. I asked her if she knew who Jesus was. She gave me an incredulous look and said, 'Of course I do!' I said with great conviction, 'I doubt that. You may know the name, but you certainly don't know anything about what he had to say.' Now that I had her undivided attention, I told her the story about how Jesus handled this kind of sin. I related that he was once confronted by some religious leaders with a woman who had been charged with adultery. The religious leaders wanted the woman severely punished, and I asked my client 'What do you suppose Jesus recommended?' My client looked blank. I told her that Jesus directed that the woman be forgiven and allowed to go her way. He offered her his grace and an opportunity for a new life.

I then confronted the woman. I asked, 'What do you think Jesus would recommend for you? Do you think he would want you to feel miserable and be shut up in a hospital, or would he want you forgiven so you could be at home taking care of your family and raising that child of yours in a proper Christian manner?' The woman seemed visibly relieved. I gave her the homework assignment of getting down on her knees and asking Jesus to forgive her. I told her all she had to do was to be sincere and to promise Jesus she would try not to commit adultery again and that her sin would be forgiven. The woman received some additional counselling along the same lines and showed a marked improvement at the time of her discharge from the hospital.

Here is another example that uses the same approach. This case involves a young woman who felt extremely guilty over a recent abortion. According to the woman, her act had brought God's wrath upon her and she was undeserving of any happiness.

Therapist: Let me see if I understand you. You killed someone.

Client: No, I didn't do it, but I'm responsible. I arranged for the abortion, and I went through with it.

Therapist: Okay, I got that, and the reason you are so upset and haven't been back to church since the abortion is that you know God hates you?

Client: That's right. I just couldn't go into the church and walk down the aisle knowing what I did and knowing God would judge me.

Therapist: But, why won't he forgive you? I thought Christ was a forgiver. Did you forget that?

Client: For an abortion! That's murder! The Bible says thou shalt not kill!

Therapist: But, it also says that no matter what the sin – you can be forgiven. You can gain grace through Jesus.

Client: But, this is serious; it's not a minor sin. It's killing a person – an unborn child.

Therapist: In other words, you really did it this time. You committed the biggest sin of all – you killed an unborn, innocent child.

Client: Well, what do you think? That it's okay? That I'm not responsible?

Therapist: I think you've been reading the wrong Bible. I thought you said you were a Christian, but I guess you skipped over the part of the Bible I'm thinking about. It's from the New Testament – the Christian part!

Client: What part?

Therapist: Well, let me put it this way. You said you were responsible for killing a person, right? You consider that an unforgivable sin. You think it's the worst thing in the world – the biggest sin of all – and you can't live with yourself because of it.

Client: Yes.

Therapist: Well, I can think of a killing, a death that is worse, and it's in the Bible.

Client: What do you mean?

Therapist: Who died on the cross?

Client: Jesus.

Therapist: Let me ask you this. Do you really believe your sin, your responsibility in the killing of your unborn child is a bigger sin or worse than the killing of Christ? That the world will suffer more from the death of your unborn child than it did from the death of Christ?

Client: No, I guess not.

Therapist: Let me ask you something else. What did Christ say to the people responsible for crucifying him? What did he recommend for them? Did he get angry and hate them? Did he want them punished? What were his last words on the cross?

Client: He said to forgive them.

Therapist: Let me see if I have this right. You can kill Christ, the son of God, and you can not even ask for forgiveness and still be forgiven. But if you have an abortion in an overpopulated, crowded world, you have to go straight to hell.

Client: I never thought of it that way.

Therapist: I know. If I could just get you Christians to practise what's in the Bible, you'd be okay.

I proceeded to use similar arguments and made considerable headway. However, this young woman was in a way testing me to learn what my approach would be, and the next interview revealed some additional information.

Client: I thought about what you said, and I really feel like a load has been taken off my chest, but I really didn't tell you everything.

Therapist: Well, fill me in, and maybe we can put the Bible to work again and clear it up.

Client: Well – that abortion I told you about wasn't the first.

Therapist: You've had another.

Client: Three more! I've four altogether.

Therapist: Wow, you're certainly fertile, but what's the problem?

Client: I can understand what you said about forgiveness for one abortion, but what about four? I should have learned my lesson.

Therapist: You mean you can get one pardon from God, but if you make the same mistake more than once, you're scheduled for a trip to hell.

Client: Well, there's got to be a limit.

Therapist: Really? There you go again! Reading the wrong Bible! I remember something about Christ saying that you can be forgiven seventy-times-seven. That means you could have four hundred and ninety abortions and still be forgiven. God would still have love for you.

Client: You mean I can do whatever I want? I can get pregnant, get an abortion, and just keep going on and on, four and ninety times and I'm still forgiven – it's okay in God's eyes?

Therapist: Yes and No! Yes, you can have four hundred and ninety abortions and still be forgiven. But no, it's not okay. It's still a sin in God's eyes. Jesus would be disappointed in your actions, but he would not condemn you. When you ask for forgiveness you are first of all admitting that you did something wrong, and God expects you to feel sorry and unhappy about breaking the rules. However, instead of blaming yourself, he wants you to accept yourself as someone who made a mistake – just an ordinary human being. God wants you to feel responsible and unhappy but not condemned and guilty. You see, Jesus allows you more than one mistake because he knows you are human and that try as hard as you may, you will still make some mistakes. He offers forgiveness so that you can stop blaming yourself and get to work on trying harder to do things right. He still wants you to feel bad but not so bad that you end up making more mistakes. That's what happened to you. You made one mistake and felt so upset that you stopped going to church and kept right on making the same mistake over and over again.

As you can see, I attempted to blend the RET concept of acceptance with the Biblical principle of forgiveness. My goal was to help the client realize that acceptance or forgiveness does not condone wrongdoing or sinning, but rather encourages the individual to assume responsibility for the error and to work to take corrective measures in the future.

Some Christian clients, however, are so influenced by the Fundamentalist doctrine of punishment that they will not accept forgiveness, no matter what the Bible says. As far as they are concerned, they must suffer some kind of severe penalty for their sin. Left to their own devices, such Christians will torture themselves as much as possible and still believe they have not suffered enough.

This example involves a coal miner who got in a fight in a bar. His brother-in-law came to his defence and, unfortunately, was shot and killed, leaving a wife (the client's sister) and four young children. The coal miner began to drink heavily in order, as he put it, to drown his guilt, a practice he continued for more than 2 years. At the time I saw him he had been out of work for some time as a result of physical problems caused by his drinking.

I explained the principle of forgiveness, but the man insisted his 'crime' deserved punishment, not forgiveness. My approach in this case was to suggest that the man had already suffered enough. I pointed out that the penalty for his crime was that he had saddened his sister, had deprived her of a father, had felt extremely guilty for the past 2 years, and was presently in the hospital facing an operation necessitated by his drinking. I said, 'Suppose God had punished you – could he have come up with anything worse?' This started the client thinking. I further pointed out that not even prison, a beating, or some kind of painful torture could equal the suffering the man had already endured. I asked him if he ever stopped to think that maybe God had called forth all of his misery, and the reason he was talking to me now might be God's way of telling him he had suffered enough for his sins. This concept seemed to make sense to the man, and I reinforced it with other, similar arguments. He stopped drinking and returned to work in the mines.

Here is an example in which the client applies forgiveness not to himself but to someone else. This is a particularly difficult requirement for many Christians. When someone wrongs them, they are supposed to be forgiving and to love that person. Unfortunately, their human tendency is to feel anger and resentment. What usually happens is that the individual suppresses the anger that makes him feel guilty for violating a Biblical injunction.

The client in this case was an elementary school teacher who was having problems with a critical manipulative assistant assigned to her room. Apparently, the teaching assistant would try to take over the class by denigrating my client and the students would laugh at the whole thing. My client did nothing about the situation. Extremely angry, she would have liked to have confronted the woman, but she believed her anger was sinful and felt guilty about it. She therefore withdrew from making any attempt to correct the situation. The teaching assistant took advantage of the client's passivity, and the situation worsened. Finally, the client's hospitalization became necessary. My first goal was to convince the woman that her anger was not a sin and that the standing up to her tormentor would actually be a Christian virtue.

Therapist: When God is in your heart and is directing your life, what happens to you?

Client: You are happy and you do good things.

Therapist: I agree, but what about when you are unhappy and do bad things? Who's directing your life then – God or the Devil?

Client: The Devil, I guess.

Therapist: Okay, now let's see how this applies to your situation. When this woman tries to take over your class and gets the kids to laugh at you, when she does evil things, who is influencing her to act in this way – God or the Devil?

Client: It's the Devil.

Therapist: Good, we've got that important point established. Now, what have you been doing about it?

Client: Nothing.

Therapist: And what are you supposed to do about evil and sin? What's a Christian supposed to do about the Devil?

Client: You're suppose to fight sin and evil. You're not supposed to give in to the Devil's temptation.

Therapist: Yes, and up to now you're been backing away and letting the Devil have his way. The Devil is not only making this woman do bad things, but he's making life miserable for you. And you, a Christian, have been letting things go bad without so much as a word.

Client: But what can I do?

Therapist: You can forgive the woman – she's not in her right mind. It's not all her fault that she treats you the way she does. It is because the Devil is tempting her and is winning. You can be angry and hate what the Devil is making her do. You can become determined to do your Christian duty and fight the Devil. In other words, when she treats you badly, you can undestand the situation and actually feel sorry for the woman, but instead of backing off, you can stand up to her. It's not really the woman you are mad at and standing up to, but the things she is doing because of the Devil. You may have to feel angry, but it's not the

	woman you feel angry toward, but the Devil in her that's making her treat you badly.
Client:	When you put it that way, everything seems different. I couldn't forgive her when I thought she was doing those things because she really wanted to hurt me. I just never thought she was possessed by the Devil.
Therapist:	So you can love and forgive the woman but not her sin. The sin is the work of Satan, and you'd better get tough and try to stop the sin.

You may recognize this as a crude method of separating the person from her actions and deploring the action but accepting or forgiving the person. Once the situation was put in this perspective, the woman was receptive to assertiveness training. In addition, I told the teacher to pray for the woman, to help the woman recognize that the Devil was guiding her life.

These case illustrations give you a general idea of how I rely on the forgiveness principle as a major intervention tactic in practising RET with Christian clients. Now I will offer several other cognitive techniques that demonstrate other rational approaches to Christian dogma.

Self-sacrifice strategies

One of the main and most pernicious tenets of Bible–Belt Christianity is the demand for total self-sacrifice, especially from women. This is a case of a middle-aged woman whose grown children make unfair demands on her. They expect her to babysit at any time, to allow them to drop in for coffee, to listen to their problems over the phone for hours on end, and to entertain them every Sunday when they expect to receive a full-course meal without any help on their parts. The woman is afraid to say no to her children because she believes she has to give of herself without question, since such behaviour is mandated by Scripture. This therapy takes place in the hospital, where the woman is suffering, understandably, from depression.

Therapist:	I feel quite honoured to be talking to you. I've never met anyone so religious.
Client:	I'm not that religious.
Therapist:	You have to be.
Client:	What do you mean?
Therapist:	You're obviously one of Christ's disciples – the thirteenth, I guess.
Client:	(She gives me a puzzled look.)
Therapist:	You see, Christ only expected such total self-sacrifice

from his disciples. He asked them to give up everything – their jobs, family, money, friends and devote themselves totally to him.

Client: I'm not that way.

Therapist: You sure are! You devote yourself completely to your family because you believe it's your Christian duty. You don't dare tell them no or ask them to leave you alone once in a while, because you believe God says you have to do everything for them. You get no rest at all, right?

Client: Well, God comes first, my family second, and me last – it's in the Bible.

Therapist: Yes, that's what God says to do, but you go to extremes. I agree that you are supposed to worship God first, take care of your family second, and finally look after yourself. But you're only doing the first two. You're not looking after yourself at all. And do you see what's happening? You end up in the hospital where you can't go to church and where you can't take care of your family at all. You really can't take care of God and of your family unless you take care of yourself.

This theme was reiterated until the woman realized that she would have to think more of herself and consider her own feelings and desires in order to behave in a proper Christian manner. You may recognize this as an attempt to foster in the woman an enlightened self-interest so that she could consider herself first and others a close second. It was not put this way, because such a concept often smacks of selfishness to many Christians. However, by showing her that you can actually be a better self-sacrifice in the long run if you consider your own self in the short run, the message was rendered more acceptable.

The next case involves a Baptist minister who used the self-sacrifice doctrine to protect and bolster his self-esteem. He would say yes to practically any request made of him, claiming this was the Christian way. The outcome was predictable. The man was overwhelmed by demands for all kinds of assistance to the extent that he neglected his own family and his own health. After a number of sessions, it was apparent that his self-sacrifice was motivated primarily by his fear of lowered self-esteem if he refused to help someone and that person were disappointed with him. He claimed that he was a man of God and, as such, could not turn people down in their time of need. Most recently, he loaned a very unreliable teenager $750 to buy a car, knowing the money would never be repaid. After a responsive relationship had been established between us, I confronted him with the following argument:

I think you use being a Christian as a cop-out. It seems to me that you bend over backwards to give everyone what they want because you are really afraid that if you turn someone down they will dislike you. When this happens, you make yourself feel crummy because you think you are less of a person – a nobody. You're not giving to others for their sakes, so you can think well of yourself. Your motive is not Christian self-sacrifice but good old-fashioned pride. In other words, it seems to me that you do good unto others to glorify yourself, not God.

Let me tell you what I believe Jesus would have done with the young man who wanted to borrow $750. First, he would have viewed the situation as an opportunity to teach a lesson in Christian living instead of as a threat to his pride. In this case I'll bet he would have figured that merely giving money to someone so young and so unreliable would be quite foolish. He would think this way because he would know that being Christian means learning that the world is a tough place in which to live and that you don't always get your way. My guess is that Jesus would have refused the young man and would have taken the young man's disappointment and resentment in stride. Jesus wouldn't put himself down, because he would know that performing your Christian duty is not always pleasant and that not everyone is going to agree with your decisions. Jesus might have suggested that the young man work and save his money or perhaps arrange for a bank loan. Either way, however, he would still feel confident even if the young man hated him because he wouldn't be aiming for man's approval but rather for man's spiritual enrichment.

My goal was to encourage the client, in typical RET fashion, to concentrate on performance and duty rather than on self-rating or pride. Although my expansion might not satisfy some theologians, it nevertheless had a powerful appeal to my client. I often find that Christian clients who experience problems with self-conceptualization and assertiveness respond well if told to emulate Jesus. I usually describe Jesus as a rational, assertive, liberated individual who was not afraid to stand up for what he believed, regardless of the circumstances. Using Jesus as a model in this way is an extremely effective tactic that inspires many clients to make immediate changes in their behaviour because they believe they will be doing what God wants them to do.

Pray for strength

A recently divorced woman was going through the trials and tribulations that frequently accompany a broken marriage. She was a very pious Christian and the situation was a particularly difficult ordeal for her. In addition to the moral problem, her husband, a disturbed alcoholic and the one that initiated the divorce action, would call her frequently. He blamed her for the entire situation, he lied to their children, and he withheld support payments. The following approach proved most effective:

Client: I just don't think I can take another minute of it. I've tried everything. I prayed to God and asked him to help, and not even he answered my prayers. Now I'm losing faith in God!

Therapist: That sounds pretty serious.

Client: I've asked him to relieve me of the burden. I've sincerely put the problem in his hands. I don't even think he's listening.

Therapist: Let me see if I have this right. You prayed that your husband would start acting rationally, that he would stop bothering you, would tell the children the truth, would give you enough money, and would make you feel better. You prayed to have this awful weight lifted from your shoulders.

Client: Yes, that's it exactly, but the Lord has given up on me. I think it's because of the divorce. He's making me suffer because of the divorce.

Therapist: No, he isn't. You didn't get the divorce. Your husband did. You're not responsible, so God won't punish you for something that's not your fault. That's not your problem. I'll tell you what your problem is – you don't know how to pray.

Client: What do you mean?

Therapist: You're making the same mistake that many Christians make. You're asking God for a miracle, for him to do all the work, for him to simply snap his fingers and make all the bad go away and make everything all good. You want God to do everything with no effort on your part. That's not his job. I'll tell you what to pray for.

Client: What?

Therapist: The strength to bear the burden. That's what to pray for! Ask God to help you bear things – put up with things exactly as they are. Pray for the strength to handle the struggle better. I'll bet if you change the words of your prayer you'd feel a lot different. Try this: go home tonight and pray. Only this time ask God to help you merely put

up with a disturbed, mixed up former husband, and see if
things won't get better for you. With the Lord's help,
you'll begin to handle things as they really are instead of
praying to make them the way you think they ought to be.
I hate to say it, but the Lord helps those who help
themselves.

Since it is unlikely that the woman's disturbed husband will stop his
harassment, the client is far better learning to accept things as they are rather
than demanding that they be different. By my putting this concept into a
religious framework, it became more intelligible and acceptable to the client.
I saw her a few more times, but she claims my advice on praying was the key
to her recovery.

Another client, a minister, expected to be granted immunity from life's
problems and frustrations. He believed his faith was supposed to give him
perfect control over his emotions and to protect him from upset of any kind.
Up to the point when I saw him, he had been rather fortunate and had not
experienced any serious problems. As far as he was concerned, there was
nothing in life he could not manage with Christ's help. Suddenly, however,
within a 2-month period his house burned down, one of his children almost
died of an illness, his wife was stricken with a paralysing disease, and he was
unjustly accused of embezzling a large sum of money. Not surprisingly, he
found his way into a psychiatric hospital. The main source of the minister's
distress was his inability to handle his problems alone. He constantly made
matters worse by downing himself for not being able to view his situation
with indifference or Christian cheer. He responded however, when I por-
trayed matters in the following way:

For a minister you've got a funny attitude about suffering. You think
you're immune to it – that because you're a man of God you don't have
to suffer. I've got news for you: the son of God, Christ himself, did a lot
of suffering. You remember that trip to the cross? He fell beneath his
burden quite a few times. And while he was on the cross – do you think
that was fun, that he didn't feel anything? He suffered. You can be sure
of that! Do you know why? Because even though he was the son of
God, he had a human body with all its weaknesses and limitations. It's
my bet that Christ knew this and didn't get sidetracked by his own
suffering. He didn't get down on himself and give up, because he knew
his humanness meant that he couldn't have perfect control over his
emotions. Maybe you ought to follow his example. Recognise you are
only human, and learn to live with your suffering better. If you do this,
you can solve problems in spite of your feelings. That's what Christ did

– his ministry is alive today because he not only accepted his suffering, but he used it to teach a lesson to the world.

My immediate plan was twofold: first, to have the client accept his inability to control his emotions as a normal failing and, secondly, to make him realize that one can still function in spite of emotional distress. Again I used Jesus as an example to be followed. In this case, I pointed out that the client was trying to outdo Christ himself. I attempted to redefine suffering as a Christian virtue rather than as an incapacitating sin.

The unforgiveable sin

I will conclude with a most challenging case involving a young woman who claimed to have committed the unforgiveable sin. The sin is from Matthew (12:31–32) and reads as follows:

All manner of sin and blasphemy shall be forgiven unto men; but the blasphemy against the Holy Ghost shall not be forgiven unto men. Whosoever speaketh aganst the Holy Ghost, it shall not be forgiven him, neither in this world, neither in the world to come.

There are various translations and interpretations as to the exact meaning of the verse, but as far as my client was concerned she had definitely committed a sin of sins. She managed this task by swearing on the Bible to deny a lie. She reasoned the Bible is the word of God and invested with the Holy Ghost or Holy Spirit as she put it. To use the Bible for such an evil purpose, according to my client, was the same as blaspheming the Holy Spirit. Ministers, her family, and even close friends were unable to convince her that her action did not qualify as the unpardonable sin. Regardless of such efforts, my client was adamant; she was doomed for eternity. She was extremely distressed, and I tried a number of different approaches and got nowhere. Finally, the following tactics proved effective:

Therapist: How did you get saved? How did you get reborn and become a Christian in the first place?

Client: It was at Bible Camp. My friends and I went to the altar and we all knelt down for an hour until I felt the Spirit take over me. It was like nothing I ever felt before. It was the happiest time of my life.

Therapist: You mean you did it deliberately. You knew what you were doing and you planned it. You actually tried to be saved – that's what was on your mind when you went to the altar?

Client: Yes!

Therapist: And after you are saved – do you just sit back and let things happen, or are you expected to do something? Is being reborn and allowing the Holy Spirit into your heart enough to make you a Christian?

Client: No, that's just the beginning. You have to go to Church, keep the commandments, read the Bible, and most of all resist Satan.

Therapist: In other words, being saved and accepting the Holy Spirit in your heart is only the first step – you've got to keep working at things, put in a lot of effort after you are saved to keep the faith. First, the commitment and next the effort?

Client: Yes.

Therapist: Then wouldn't the reverse hold true if you wanted to deny the Holy Spirit? Wouldn't you have to deliberately decide to deny and then work hard to make sure you actively and consciously keep denying and blaspheming. If you really wanted to be an atheist, you'd first have to tell yourself you no longer believe in God, and then go about constantly proving this to yourself and to God! Wouldn't you have to be very aware of what you are doing? Wouldn't you have to speak out against Christ and Holy Spirit to really do a good job of blasphemy?

Client: What do you mean?

Therapist: Well, if you have to do certain things – go through a spiritual rebirth to accept the Holy Spirit and then continue to work hard at keeping the Holy Spirit alive in your heart, wouldn't you have to do pretty much the same thing, put in the same kind of effort and give up your belief and deny the Holy Spirit?

Client: I never thought of it that way, but it sort of makes sense.

Therapist: In that case I don't believe you've denied or blasphemed the Holy Spirit!

Client: Why not?

Therapist: For one reason, you didn't lie on the Bible with the deliberate intent to deny the Holy Spirit. You did it so that you could get away from something. You didn't decide, 'I want to give up my faith' and then consciously lie on the Bible to accomplish this goal, did you?

Client: No!

Therapist: You sort of used the Bible to put something over on someone didn't you?

Client: Yes, but it was wrong . . .

Therapist: I know it was wrong. You may have committed a sin – sort of like using the Lord's name in vain, but hardly the unforgiveable sin. You can't deny the Holy Spirit by swearing on the Bible to deny a lie any more than you can be saved by swearing on the Bible to prove the Truth!

Client: I guess you're right!

Therapist: Besides, even if you meant it, even if you deliberately and consciously meant to deny and blaspheme the Holy Spirit, I doubt if God would accept your decision as final. I doubt if your denial really counts in God's eyes. Do you know why?

Client: Why?

Therapist: Because you didn't keep it up – you haven't put in any effort to keep proving you've really turned away from God and you are really a confirmed non-believer. In fact, you're proving quite the opposite – that you really do believe in God. Your guilt proves you're still a believer and you still have the Holy Spirit in your heart. You wouldn't feel so guilty unless you believed in God and thought you'd done something wrong in His eyes. In order to feel the way you do, to go through all the suffering you've been going through, you have to first believe in God and the Holy Spirit and then believe you've broken some of the sacred laws, and ought to be punished accordingly. If you were a confirmed atheist, you wouldn't have this problem on your mind because you'd believe that speaking out against God and the Holy Spirit was right. You'd feel good about your sin. As long as you feel guilty about what you did, it proves you still have the Holy Spirit alive in your heart.

My goal was to show this client that considerable effort is usually required to either adopt or oppose a particular belief system. I tried to help her realize that she neither directly nor continually put in this kind of effort and, therefore, her act could not qualify as a conscious, deliberate denial of the Holy Spirit. Once again, as in the other examples, I challenged exaggerated, absolutistic thinking through the use of rational arguments that were in keeping with the client's religious values.

Chapter 10

Teaching rational self–value concepts to tough customers

Howard S. Young

RET has been subjected to considerable revision and refinement since its inception nearly 25 years ago. In spite of any changes, however, RET theory still maintains that a good deal of emotional disturbance and dysfunctional behaviour is firmly rooted in negative self-image (Ellis, 1962, 1971, 1974, 1975a,b; Ellis and Grieger, 1977). According to RET theory, many of the symptoms we witness in our clients result from the derogatory ways in which they think about themselves.

Recognizing low self-value as a controlling dynamic in the creation of psychopathology is not unique to RET. Many other theoreticians and practitioners also consider ego hang-ups the critical variable in human emotional misery and suffering. What sets RET apart from other systems of psychotherapy is the approach it adopts to the resolution of self-value conflicts.

Instead of teaching a client to overcome his problems by achieving a positive self-image, building his ego, or gaining self-confidence, RET has long taken the position that the client would better rid himself of both self-upping and self-downing. RET steadfastly dismisses self-rating in any way, shape or form as absurd, philosophically untenable, and nearly always self-defeating.

This Chapter will discuss putting the RET approach to self-value into practice with TC's. T and C are initials that stand for 'tough customer'. The term has become an idiom or diagnostic label that describes clients who often have difficulty understanding RET concepts and putting them into practice. The TC's I have in mind are those who have traditionally been a challenge to therapists, RET or otherwise. They include individuals from lower socio-economic classes, uncooperative adolescents, Fundamentalist Christians, and those with limited intelligence.

Before moving to a discussion of the techniques I have found most effective in getting self-value concepts across to TC's, let us review briefly the theoretical model involved. An understanding of how RET views and handles problems with identity, ego, self-worth, and the like is essential to helping clients get at the fundamental cause of their disturbance.

A self is complex

People, according to the RET perspective, are infinitely complex creatures made up of innumerable different and constantly changing traits and abilities that continue through a lifetime. An individual is a conglomeration of on-going characteristics, mannerisms and behaviours.

In addition, each trait and ability can be rated or judged as good or bad, important or unimportant, valued or valueless. The rating depends on how well or how poorly the trait or ability serves one's personal goals and desires. The self, therefore, contains a myriad of positive and negative features.

This means that the person's identity or overall worth is probably not reducible to a single definitive label or grade that would make any sense. The average person fulfils too many roles with varying degrees of competency or incompetency to be legitimately labelled or rated in any one way. Put another way, one can have a good or a bad trait but not a good or a bad self.

The RET therapist tries to help clients view themselves in a very detailed and itemized, though utterly sensible, way. Clients are typically taught to evaluate their performances and actions one at a time and to avoid using this appraisal to calculate their overall worth as human beings.

The client, for example, who is successful or admired by others, is advised to view these virtues as rewards and satisfactions and not as proof that he is all good, worthwhile, or godlike. If this Chapter is rated as good by myself or others, then it is only the Chapter and my abilities to produce it that can be rated as good. The rating does not carry over to my personality or general worth. My enjoyment, if I am to think and act rationally, would come from a good job rather than from a good ego.

The client who fails or is rejected, on the other hand, is helped to understand that such adversities are disappointments and frustrations rather than evidence that he is all bad, worthless or damnable. Again, if this Chapter is rated as bad by myself or others, I would feel understandably unhappy because I had lost satisfaction but not because I had lost value as a human being.

Uncovering low self-esteem

Although this outline of the RET outlook on self-value has been necessarily brief, it nevertheless covers most of the salient points. In addition to understanding theory, it is also important for the counsellor to realize that ego hang-ups are not always apparent in clients. Although some people do seek therapy specifically for low self-esteem or for a loss of self-confidence, most clients, especially TC's, are not aware of the role self-rating plays in their suffering. In fact, many such clients need to be questioned carefully before this role can be ascertained.

An example of how one tracks down this ideational dynamic might help. This is the case of a young mother of preschool children who lives in proximity to her husband's relatives. These relatives drop in at will, discuss their problems, gossip about anything and everything, drink cup after cup of coffee and, in general, make it practically impossible for her to do her housework and mothering. She has never said anything to them, and her presenting problem is depression. She claims her depression is the result of 'too many in-laws'.

Therapist: Why don't you ask them to leave once in a while? You don't have to be nasty about it. You could explain you've got housework to finish, children to dress, clothes to launder, lots of work.

Client: They wouldn't pay any attention. They'd just keep talking and drinking coffee.

Therapist: How many times have you asked?

Client: I guess never.

Therapist: No wonder they hang around all the time. They probably don't even know it bothers you. Is that right? Is it possible they don't even know they bother you, that they interfere with your housework?

Client: They ought to know.

Therapist: They really have no way of knowing what's in your mind unless you tell them. So why don't you ask them nicely to leave?

Client: They wouldn't understand.

Therapist: That may be true. After all, they're used to being around all the time. There are no rules for them to follow. They can just sort of drop in when they want and leave when they want. So you're right. They probably wouldn't understand if you suddenly wanted them to leave or to visit only at certain times. But let's make sure: do you really want them to leave you alone some of the time?

Client: Yes, I do. I don't mind some visiting but not all the time.

	If they didn't come around so much, I wouldn't feel so bad.
Therapist:	So why don't you ask them to leave, even if they don't understand?
Client:	I'm just afraid. I've never done it before.
Therapist:	What do you think you're afraid of? What would be the worst that could happen if you asked your relatives to leave or only come around once in a while?
Client:	They'd be hateful.
Therapist:	They'd be mad at you? You're afraid to tell your relatives to leave you alone so you can get your work done and take care of your children because you're afraid they'll dislike or hate you? Is that right?
Client:	Yes, that's it. I've always been afraid to speak up. Even when I was in school, I was always afraid the other person would be hateful.

At this point it may appear that I have uncovered the ideational source of the woman's reluctance to assert herself with her relatives: fear of disapproval. However, only part of the job has been accomplished. It is now necessary to learn what it is about disapproval that is so frightening.

Therapist:	Let's suppose you are right. If you speak up and tell them how you really feel, they'll be hateful. Why do you think this is so bad?
Client:	I don't know. It just seems terrible. I feel my throat getting tight just talking about it.
Therapist:	Okay, close your eyes for a minute. Now try to think out loud for me. Let's pretend you've just told your mother-in-law to leave so that you can vacuum the floor. She acts mad and hateful. In fact she storms out of your house and slams the door as she leaves. What are you thinking?
Client:	Oh, I'd just feel like trash, like garbage. I'd feel like the meanest person in the world.
Therapist:	Like the lowest person on earth?
Client:	Even worst than that. I wouldn't even feel human.

From this exchange we've learned that the unassertive mother suffers not from fear of rejection but from fear of lowered self-esteem. A poor self-image is at the heart of her inability to speak up to her relatives. The next step is to help the woman recognize this as her problem and to show her how to think more rationally about herself.

A diagnostic framework

To accomplish this task, I have developed a diagnostic model, which has proved effective in helping TC's overcome their self-image and self-value problems. I have discovered that those with ego problems seem to fit into one of the following three categories:

1. Those who define themselves according to what they do or to what someone else thinks of them. If this type of client does something he defines as bad or if someone has a bad opinion of him, he believes this proves he is all bad. I call this kind of self-appraisal 'Bad Me' thinking.
2. A second category includes those who deprecate or down themselves as the result of disappointments, particularly those concerned with failure or disapproval. I usually refer to those who consider themselves devalued or worthless as 'Less Me' thinkers.
3. Finally, there are those who denigrate or blame themselves for their faults or shortcomings. Probably the most common symptom resulting from this thinking pattern is guilt. I label clients who think in this way as 'Damn Me' thinkers.

I have found that almost all self-value problems, regardless of the misery they cause, are due to 'Bad Me', 'Less Me' or 'Damn Me' thinking in one form or other. Although many clients think of themselves in all three ways, it has been my experience that many others seem to favour one form of negative self-rating over another. It is not unusual, for example, for a client to confide that he is worthless and inferior because of a mistake and in the same breath to claim that he would never damn or blame himself for the mistake, because, after all, he's only human.

Examined closely, each of the three categories I've described actually presents the same kind of over-generalized, dichotomous reasoning. Clients, however, do not necessarily see the similarities. A different set of cognitive–semantic techniques are usually required, therefore, for clients who see themselves in one category but not in another. Methods you would apply, for example, to someone who is primarily a guilt-ridden Damn Me thinker would not work with someone who admits to being a worthless Less Me thinker, and vice versa.

To help you use and apply this framework to better advantage, I will detail each category more carefully and offer some of the strategies I have found most effective in dealing with each. The goal in working with all the categories is to help clients surrender their negative self-ratings.

Bad Me thinking

The Bad Me thinker unwittingly adheres to the philosophy that you are what you do. If you do something such as goofing up on the job, failing a test in school, or blowing a relationship, this means you are bad. In other words, bad acts can turn you into a bad person. Bad Me thinkers also apply this kind of wisdom to what others think about them. If they are the subject of criticism or rejection, they are convinced that bad opinion turns them into a bad person.

Bad Me thinkers can be identified by such statements as, 'If I fail, that makes me a failure'. 'If I am rejected, that makes me a reject.' 'If I lose someone's love or approval, that turns me into a loser.' 'If I do something stupid, that makes me stupid.'

When faced with this kind of thinking hang–up, the therapist must first help the client understand that although people may well be responsible for their actions or characteristics, they are not necessarily equivalent to them. I often point out to my clients that if they bark like dogs, they may well be liable for such actions, but they are hardly transformed into fox terriers.

By the same token, I try to emphasize that the opinions of others cannot magically transform people. If someone thinks my clients are dogs, this assessment does not qualify them for membership in the American Kennel Club. Criticism and rejection, as I frequently explain to my clients, may mean bad experiences but not bad selves.

The goal is to get clients to evaluate their bad performances or bad traits as separate and distinct from their whole or complete beings. This is a some-what difficult concept to get across to even the most capable clients, so it should come as no surprise that TC's have trouble understanding that a person and a person's traits are not the same.

Bad Me challenges

1. One approach that is often successful in demonstrating the difference between performance and self is to use a visual aid. I draw a circle which I label 'self'. Next I put a series of smaller circles like bubbles inside the 'self' circle. These represent the individual's traits and characteristics. I use pluses and minuses to show which of these represent success or failure. From here I show that when one circle or trait goes bad, it does not make the whole circle bad. This visual aid can be used in many different ways and can be tailored to almost any client. The more often that abstract concepts can be illustrated graphically or simplified, the more likely that TC's will understand and benefit from RET insights.

2. Many examples can illustrate the illogic of over-generalizing, but one that helps particularly is to tell the client to imagine that he returns to his car after the interview and finds a flat tyre. I ask the client whether he would junk the whole car because it has a flat. Most clients say that would be silly, because the whole car is not ruined on account of a tyre. I then point out that this is exactly what they have been doing: junking themselves because of a particular fault.

3. This analogy often makes a dramatic impression on clients. Others, however, will pick it apart, insisting that because a car is not human it bears no relation to them. With clients who are so literal, I use a different analogy. I try to show them how their physical bodies are made up of many parts, none of which represents or equals the whole. Here is a brief example of this approach from my practice.

The client is a mother of two and is supported by welfare assistance. She is enrolled in nurse training at a local community college. She presents a number of symptoms and complaints, all of which revolve around her tendency to think of herself as all bad. She is convinced that you are what you do. When she decides for example, that yelling at her children is awful, it proves *she* is awful.

Therapist:	Maybe I can show you a better way to think about yourself. [I pointed at her hand.] Is that your hand?
Client:	[Laughing] Yes!
Therapist:	It is important to you?
Client:	Yes.
Therapist:	Tell me why. Suppose you didn't have that hand?
Client:	It would handicap me. There would be lots of things I couldn't do. It would be pretty bad for me.
Therapist:	So your hand's important! Now let me ask you this: is that hand part of you or is it you? Now really think for me. Does that important hand equal you? Could you describe yourself simply as a hand?
Client:	No.
Therapist:	Why not? You gave the right answer. Now tell me why it is the right answer.
Client:	Because my hand is only part of me.
Therapist:	Do you have any other part, such as your eyes, ears, nose, or big toe that is your whole self? Is there any part of your body, inside or out, that you could say is you?
Client:	No, I guess I'm made up of a lot of parts.

I then went on to show her how she could view her mothering as just one of her many behavioural parts. As a consequence, she would not have to consider herself all bad just because she had this bad behavioural part. Another tactic would be to explain that mothering itself is made up of many different activities. From here it could be explained that yelling at children is just one behaviour and does not represent one's total or only behaviour as a parent. In other words, the client could be shown that one act does not a mother make and, further, that if such an act is bad it does not make the client all bad as a mother.

4. Another way to get across the multifarious nature of a person is to have people carefully label themselves. Once you get them to view themselves in this way, they often recognize that they wear many labels. They can usually see the futility of trying to choose one label that truly represents them as a whole. A client who worked as a secretary was able to label herself as a secretary, mother, wife, ex-wife, shopper, friend and book-keeper. What really astonished her was that she was able to function in all these roles within an hour's time. An even more dramatic way to show people all the labels they wear is actually to use stick-on labels. Write the different roles on the labels and affix them to the client. Within a few minutes, the client may be covered with labels.

5. Teaching clients to say 'It's bad' rather than 'I'm bad' when they are faced with failure or criticism is another method I use. I advise them that this is my own way of separating my traits and abilities from my overall self. I point out that we can find proof of why some fault is bad (inconvenient, disadvantageous, frustrating, etc.), but we really cannot prove that this same fault transforms us into anything good, bad or indifferent. This semantic device often gets people to focus on dealing with their disappointments rather than on saving their egos.

Less Me thinking

A Less Me thinker believes in two basic ideas. The first is that people have some kind of built-in value and, secondly, that disappointments, usually in the form of failure or disapproval, somehow lessen or decrease that built-in value. It's like thinking you are born with a worth of $1000 and after a mistake or two you are worth only a nickel.

This kind of thinking equates failure or rejection with inferiority and worthlessness. When faced with his faults the Less Me thinker puts his whole self down. Less Me thinkers typically devalue and degrade themselves by claiming they are half human, lower than snakes, small enough to fit through keyholes, and not worth a shit. They can be identified by the way they hold their fingers an inch or so apart to describe how small they feel. As far as the self-downer is concerned, he does not even belong to the human race: he is a subhuman creature.

This kind of self-defeating thinking is most readily overcome by helping the client recognize that humans have no intrinsic or in-born value or worth. As a result, they cannot lose something they do not possess in the first place. I am not suggesting a philosophical discussion of whether humans possess worth or value. This might have merit with certain clients but would have very little impact with TC's. I do suggest helping the client to realize that although his behaviour or the impression he creates may be worthwhile or worthless, this does not mean that he himself is worthwhile or worthless.

Less Me challenges

1. Probably the most effective way to show those who down themselves that such thinking is irrational is to help them understand the important difference between 'a person with less' and someone who is 'less of a person'. Let me illustrate this principle in action.

A 25-year-old auto mechanic was hospitalized for depression. During the course of therapy which centred around a number of problems, he admitted with much anguish that he had been sexually impotent for a year. Apparently, this was his major concern, but he had been holding off discussing it because he was ashamed to reveal a sex problem.

Therapist:	How come you didn't mention this before?
Client:	I was too embarrassed. Even now I can feel my face getting red.
Therapist:	What do you think is so bad about having a sex problem? So you can't get it up. Why do you think that's so bad?
Client:	I don't know. It's just embarrassing.
Therapist:	Give it a try. Do some thinking for me. What's so embarrassing about having 'it'?
Client:	Well, you know. I don't feel like a man anymore.
Therapist:	Oh, you mean because you can't get a hard-on and screw your girl, it means you've lost your manhood?
Client:	Yeah. I just think of myself as a nothing – not even a man.
Therapist:	Is that what you think before you start having sex? I mean, do you think, 'I'm gonna screw her ass off', or do you think, 'Shit, if I don't make it, I'm not a man anymore?'

Client:	That I'm not a man.
Therapist:	No wonder you're having trouble. I guess just about anyone would if he believed failure meant he would be robbed of his manhood. Maybe I can't get you to see things in another way so you can get over the problem.
Client:	Like how? I know it's all in my head, but I can't make it go away. I can't stop thinking about it. I've tried.
Therapist:	The goal will be to think about it differently and more sensibly but not to forget about it or try to get it off your mind.
Client:	How?
Therapist:	Well, let me ask you something. Were you born a man?
Client:	Yeah!
Therapist:	You mean you've got a birth certificate and it says male on it?
Client:	[Laughing] Yeah!
Therapist:	Now someday you're going to die. I hope it's at a ripe old age, but someday it's gonna happen, right?
Client:	Yeah!
Therapist:	What will be on your death certificate, male or female?
Client:	[Laughing] Male!
Therapist:	Is there anything that could happen from the day you are born to the day you die that could change that fact? Are you going to remain a man no matter what happens to you between birth and death?
Client:	Yeah, I guess so.
Therapist:	Even if you can't get a hard-on and screw your girl?
Client:	Yeah, I see what you mean, I'm a man whether I can make it with a woman or not; just feels like I'm not a man.
Therapist:	But that's all it would be – a feeling – it wouldn't prove anything. But let's work on it a little more and see what we come up with. If hard-ons and screwing don't make or break you as a man, what would you really lose if you couldn't perform sexually.
Client:	What do you mean?
Therapist:	Do you like sex?
Client:	Yeah, of course!
Therapist:	A lot?
Client:	Yeah!
Therapist:	It's a big deal – a big pleasure, to you?
Client:	Damn right!

Therapist: So what do you really lose if you can't get a hard–on and
                   screw your girl? Your manhood or a big pleasure?

At this point, I wrote on a large sheet of paper the phrase 'Loss of Pleasure'
and just under it the phrase 'Loss of Manhood' to help drive this point home.
The reasoning plus the illustration had a dramatic effect. Within a few more
sessions, the client was able to resume normal sexual relationships with his
partner.

2. Sometimes I can get across the futility of putting oneself down by taking
something from a client. It could be a ring, a watch, money, a purse, or the
like. I try to make sure it has some value, and then ask, 'Are you less of a
person or are you a person with less?' After they see the wisdom of viewing
their loss as merely a lack of an object and the satisfaction they feel owning
that object rather than as a lack of intrinsic value or worth, I return to their
problem and suggest that they handle it in the same way.

3. Less Me thinkers, especially those who have been criticized or rejected, are
often helped by asking them to liken their problems to soda machines. I ask
them what they would think about themselves if they put their money into
the machines and nothing came out. Would they, I ask, believe they are
worthless and inferior because the machines turn them down? Usually, they
are able to admit they suffered deprivations and not loss of value. Once they
get the point, I advise them to try and think about their problems in the same
way.
   Sometimes the brighter clients argue that being rejected by a person is
different from being rejected by a machine. I agree, but I also point out that
the principle is the same: you are still a whole 100 per cent human whether
you get turned down by a soda machine or by a person. You may lose a
bigger or more important pleasure if it is a loss of love, but your self remains
unchanged.

4. Using a client's preference for a particular food is still another way to
illustrate that loss of success or approval does not equal loss of personal
worth. Let's say the favourite food is ice cream. I ask the client, 'If you went
to an ice cream store and they were out of ice cream, would that prove you
were inferior?' Clients can usually see clearly that such thinking would be
idiotic, since all that has really happened is that they were deprived of a
favourite food or delight. I then substitute the client's problem for the
ice–cream, or I ask him to remember the next time he fails or is rejected to say
to himself, 'So too bad, I didn't get my ice cream cone!'

5. Another technique that helps a self-downer is going over a list of his

favourite pleasures or satisfactions. Usually, he equates only one or two with his self-worth. I then ask why he failed to think less of himself when deprived of the other pleasures on the list. This tactic helps the client realize that self-value is an idea created in his head and is not inherent in a particular disappointment. It also helps inform clients with ego hang-ups that life is better viewed as a gain–loss enterprise than as a pride–shame confrontation.

I used this approach with another case of impotency. Besides sex, the client mentioned gambling as a major source of satisfaction in his life. In fact, he was an avid gambler and devoted a lot of time and energy to this activity. He agreed, however, than an inability to participate in gambling would cost him not his manhood but only a great deal of satisfaction. With a little effort on his part, he was able to see how this same line of reasoning could be applied to his sex problem.

Damn Me thinking

Now let's turn our attention to Damn Me thinkers. This category includes those who blame and hate themselves and believe they deserve the severest, harshest punishment for their faults. They think that mistakes and shortcomings prove a person to be so wicked and evil that he or she must be made to suffer in the most cruel way possible. Such thinking may force them into all kinds of self-inflicted punishment, including actually hurting themselves. In extreme cases, Damn Me thinkers have been known to burn, cut, maim and kill themselves as reparation for their failings.

However, it is mental abuse that is by far the most common punishment of those who practice self-hate. Self-damners think of themselves in the most despicable ways they can imagine. They may call themselves names, the more repulsive and obscene the better. Self-damners, therefore, spend a good deal of time cursing and insulting themselves. Identifying such a client is easy: his most common symptom is guilt!

The job of a therapist confronted with a self-blamer is to help him understand that it makes little sense to punish oneself no matter how serious the mistake or crime. Clients are advised, though, to admit to their mistakes and faults, for only in this way can one's failings be either corrected or accepted. They are further advised that brutally blaming themselves goes beyond either correcting or accepting. Such an approach is overdoing it, like demanding brain surgery for a headache when an aspirin will do. When a client makes an error, he is helped first to assume responsibility for his wrongdoing, and then, most important, to avoid blaming or damning himself.

Damn Me challenges

1. Perhaps the best way to help clients accomplish this task is to show them that mistakes and failings often create their own penalties. In other words, clients are shown that most faults already have a built-in punishment. The mother, for example, who is opposed to spanking yet loses her temper and beats her child is taught that she automatically suffers two penalties. First, she fails to live up to her own standards and thereby loses a sense of achievement and, secondly, she will likely have to witness the unpleasant consequences of her actions: her children's tears, maybe their fear and, perhaps, their bruises. Additional punishment in the form of self-denigration, I would point out to her, is both unnecessary and excessive. The goal is to help the client understand that one's faults usually cause enough inconvenience and suffering in and of themselves to make correction or change attractive.

This approach can be demonstrated in the following way. A 28-year-old coal miner was in a serious automobile accident. He had been drinking, and the accident caused the death of his 8-year-old son. Shortly thereafter, his wife divorced him. They had been having marital problems for some years, and the accident was the 'straw that broke the camel's back'. Extremely depressed, the client was convinced he had committed the most heinous crime imaginable and deserved to be dead. I met him in the hospital where he had been admitted for a suicide attempt through a drug overdose.

Therapist: The reasons you OD'd is because you lost your son and wife?

Client: I might as well be dead. I deserve to die!

Therapist: That's a pretty severe punishment for what you did. Why do you deserve to die?

Client: I killed my boy and made my wife divorce me!

Therapist: You actually killed him – you did it deliberately?

Client: No, but it was because of the drinking. I didn't know what I was doing, and I hit another car. It was my fault.

Therapist: I agree it was your fault, but you didn't deliberately do it, did you? I mean you didn't take the drink with the idea in mind that it would lead to the death of your son. It was an accident that resulted from your drinking, right?

Client: Yeah, but it was still my fault.

Therapist: Okay, I'm not trying to talk you out of your fault. Isn't it also true that your wife left because of the accident? I mean you didn't arrange the accident so your wife would divorce you, did you?

Client: No, that's the last thing I wanted!

Therapist:	Okay, what we've got is someone who had too much to drink and as a result got into an accident that caused the death of his son, which in turn caused his wife to leave him. Does that about describe it?
Client:	Yeah. You hit the nail on the head!
Therapist:	But that's not your main problem! Your main problem is that you've been blaming yourself, believing you have to die for your mistake. You've got two problems: one, you've lost a wife and child; two, you're blaming yourself for that loss.
Client:	But I caused it. It's my fault. I'm the one to blame.
Therapist:	Part of what you're saying makes sense. It is your fault. You were responsible, but I'm not sure that means you have to blame yourself. You're kind of doing two things; one makes sense and the other doesn't. First, you're correctly finding fault with yourself, but then you're automatically believing that you have to hate yourself. You seem to think that facing up to a fault and damning yourself have to go together.
Client:	What do you mean?
Therapist:	You admit to your fault and you recognise that it caused the death of your son and divorce from your wife. Your fault, therefore, cost you a son and a wife. That's quite a punishment for what you did. But you add to it. You also hate yourself and try to kill yourself. You think you're so bad and so evil you have to die. That's the second punishment. Don't you think contributing to the death of your son and divorce from your wife is plenty to suffer about? Don't you think that your mistake – the accident – had a built-in punishment?
Client:	Do you mean that I've suffered enough already just missing my wife and son – that that's all I should get for what I did?
Therapist:	Yeah, that's what I mean! If you went before a judge and admitted you were guilty of drunken driving and an accident and he said your sentence would be a dead son and a divorce, would you ask for more?
Client:	No, I guess not. I see what you mean. It's really a different way to think, but it makes sense.

2. The use of an analogy is another effective way to help clients understand that most faults carry a built-in penalty and usually do not require a

self-administered punishment. An analogy I often use is to ask:

> Suppose you are driving your car and it runs out of gas because you
> forgot to check the gauge. It's your fault, and you've got to walk to the
> nearest station, get a can of gas, and trudge back to the car. Would you
> consider hitting yourself over the head with the gas can on the way back
> as punishment, or would you figure that all you had to go through to
> get the car going would be enough of a penalty?

Usually this helps clients get the point. I then suggest that they view their
own mistakes and their consequences in the same way.

3. Another method involves encouraging the client to describe thoroughly
his particular wrongdoing. After his description, I hand him a rubber
hammer I keep on my desk. I ask him to beat himself until he feels he's
suffered enough for his failing. Almost always, the client says, 'That's silly.
That's not going to prove anything.' I then point out that this is exactly what
they have been doing to themselves. They have been beating themselves not
necessarily with real hammers but with negative attitudes about themselves.
Often I advise clients to remember the hammer the next time they feel guilty.
I ask them to imagine they have been hitting themselves over the head and to
stop it.

4. Some clients who damn themselves can understand the wisdom of what I
am trying to tell them, but still they have difficulty accepting the natural
consequences of their actions. They tend to overlook or minimize the effects
of their mistakes or faults and, as a result, believe they have gone unpunished.
In working with these hardheaded types, I often write on a 3 × 5 card the
problems they have caused themselves due to their mistakes and then in big
letters write 'PAID IN FULL!' They are instructed to read the card each time
they begin to feel guilty. It reminds them that their penalty is already set and
that there is no use adding to an already existing consequence.

5. Often there is no obvious penalty or natural consequence for a client's
mistaken behaviour. In such cases it is explained to the client that his penalty
is disappointing himself. In other words, he has failed to live up to his own
standards. Failure to achieve in some important area and the lack of satisfaction that comes with it is a very painful consequence. In other words, I
suggest to clients that they feel responsible and regretful rather than guilty
and damned. One can still feel bad but not be miserable.

   This was put into practice with a woman who committed adultery. Her
husband never found out, so essentially she got away with it. She was able to

realize that damning herself was unnecessary because her built-in penalty was knowing she had broken one of her own important rules. The fact that she could no longer consider herself the faithful wife was, I pointed out, a disappointment. There was no need to condemn herself also.

Elegant and inelegant RET

In these examples we have analysed self-value problems and applied appropriate counselling strategies according to the Bad Me, Less Me and Damn Me framework. Our primary goal was profound philosophical change in the client's irrational assumptions. The specific focus of my interventions was the client's extremely negative, reality-distorted views of themselves. In other words, I have been describing what Ellis calls elegant or preferential RET (Ellis, 1977).

Unfortunately, not all clients and especially not all TC's can benefit from this kind of specialized approach. Other methods, still considered part of the RET system, are sometimes more useful. They are, in practice, similar to other cognitive therapies. Ellis refers to their use as a form of inelegant or general RET. My method is to attempt the elegant version first; if it fails to make an impact, I quickly switch to general RET.

Here is a case example that illustrates the difference in these two versions of RET. A 14-year-old was referred to me because of depression. He was underdeveloped for his age, had severe acne on his face, and was somewhat effeminate in his appearance. He was reportedly ridiculed by schoolmates who called him the class queer and class weirdo. He lived with his highly critical grandmother, who had cared for him since his parents abandoned him as a baby.

The client had an extremely low self-image: he called himself 'unwanted trash'. Since he was quite bright, my initial efforts were designed to help him realize that he was not totally worthless in spite of his shortcomings and the criticism directed at him. Unfortunately, even though I greatly simplified my approach and used a number of the techniques already described, my message fell on deaf ears.

I changed my strategy and concentrated on manipulating the client's environment. In the ABC scheme of things I focused on changing A (the activating event) instead of B (his belief system). The client was enrolled in a small religious school which was devoted to loving one's fellow students; a big brother was arranged for him, he was enrolled in karate classes, and an appointment was made with a doctor for his complexion problems.

Although the client continued to come in for regular sessions, little change was made in his conviction that the approval of others was necessary and that without such acceptance he would have to consider himself inferior. He still believed that personal worth not only existed but that it could be attained through the admiration and approval of others. He articulated this message quite clearly in his last interview when he declared that this improvement, which was remarkable, was due to having friends and people who cared about him. This, he claimed, made him feel important and superior. My own endeavours, by the way, supported this message, as my approach was to show him interest, warmth, empathy, and much positive regard.

In the light of the results obtained with this client, one might ask, why even bother with elegant RET? Why even try to have the client understand and apply abstract philosophical concepts as a solution to his problems? After all, his suffering was relieved and he seemed to be doing much better.

I would criticize the inelegant approach only if it were used without even considering or attempting the more elegant form of RET. The latter is preferred because it aims at correcting the essence of emotional disturbance. Perhaps I am an old-timer in this respect (or downright stubborn), for I still believe that cognitions, especially those that are grossly unrealistic, demanding and absolutistic are the primary sources of dysfunctional behaviour. Even more important, I believe that correcting these irrational cognitions is the best way to help clients achieve pervasive, lasting improvement.

What was accomplished with the 14-year-old client was merely to give a potential loveaholic a big dose of love. In other words, he was not really helped to live in a world which might eventually be a poor source of continued love and approval. Instead, he was helped, by his own admission, to believe that love and approval were necessary, that they could easily be arranged when the going was tough and, more perniciously, that generous supplies of love made one important and worthwhile. In other words, the fundamental philosophies that created the client's disturbance were not only left unchanged but they were actually supported.

Before you conclude that inelegant or general RET is not recommended or is synonymous with malpractice, let me clarify something. I suggest that such an approach is merely less desirable than is elegant RET. The inelegant approach is better used when a client, like the 14-year-old, is unable or willing to benefit from the more preferred and philosophically sound form of RET. In fact, the two versions probably overlap and are often used together in many RET ventures. Further, my experience has proven that with many TC's, inelegant RET is the only version that will produce change or improvement. Finally, I had better be honest and inform you that Ellis (1977) has declared that it has not yet been shown that the elegant forms of RET work better than the inelegant forms.

The religious client

One group that seems receptive to general RET is Fundamentalist Christians or extremely religious clients (Young, 1977). I have found that staying within a Biblical framework offers the best chance at helping such individuals with their problems. A typical example involves a young woman who had sex before marriage. She told her minister, and although she vowed never to do it again, he openly condemned her during a church service and told her never to come back to his church.

She was understandably overwhelmed with feelings of guilt and was sure she was a totally evil person deserving of hell. I talked to her in this way.

Jesus sees you not as a total sinner, but as a person with potential – potential to change your ways. If he believed that once you committed a sin it made a sinner forever, why would he offer his love and forgiveness? Jesus is not as narrow-minded as your minister. He knows you're human and that making mistakes is part of your nature. He created you that way, and he knows that you are made up of both good and bad traits.

'Jesus', I further pointed out to her, 'doesn't label people. He loves them.'
Along similar lines, the following approach proved effective with a guilt-ridden, Damn Me thinker.

Therapist:	Why do you feel God doesn't want you back in church?
Client:	Because of the divorce – it's a sin. You're not supposed to divorce. It's in the Bible.
Therapist:	I thought Jesus forgave people for their sins.
Client:	Yeah, I know. But it was wrong in the first place. I did it knowing it was a sin.
Therapist:	You mean Jesus reserves grace only for people who accidently make mistakes and hell for those who make them deliberately?
Client:	I don't know. I just know it's wrong!
Therapist:	It *was* wrong! You'll get no argument from Jesus on that issue. Just because you did something wrong, though, does that mean you are damned for the rest of your life?
Client:	I know what you're saying, but I just know I sinned. I can't get that thought out of my mind.
Therapist:	I know you sinned, Jesus knows you sinned, your minister knows you sinned, everybody in your church knows you sinned, but what's that got to do with staying away from church and feeling so guilty?

Client: There ought to be *some* punishment.

Therapist: There is!!! You disappointed Jesus. Your punishment is
to disappoint, to let down, your Saviour – to make things
unpleasant and uncomfortable between the two of you.
But Jesus is only unhappy, not condemning of you. Jesus
probably thinks about your sin the same as you do about
your children when they misbehave. You feel unhappy
toward them, don't you?

Client: Yeah!

Therapist: But you still love them in spite of their naughty behaviour. You wouldn't want them to feel guilty for the
rest of their lives and leave home, would you?

Client: Oh no, I'd want them to feel loved – but to stop what
they were doing.

Therapist: Well that's how Jesus probably views your sin. He wants
you to feel responsible and to recognize that you did
something wrong. But that doesn't mean he wants you
condemned and feeling guilty. He certainly doesn't want
you to leave the church because of your mistake any
more than you'd want your kids to leave home when
they misbehave.

In yet another case, a woman was depressed because her husband left her
for a younger, more attractive woman. She considered herself completely
unloveable and totally worthless as a result. I was able to convince her to
surrender her depression by pointing out that even though she did not get her
husband's love, she was still loved by Jesus. I suggested that the love of Jesus
was the more important love because it could lead to eternal salvation, an
important goal for most Christians, whereas her husband's love was only an
earthly, temporary experience. More important, I asked her to consider the
possibility that Jesus's love for her proved she had value and was not inferior.
In other words, she was important in spite of her husband's rejection because
God loved her.

In each of these examples my interventions were on a cognitive level. I
hesitate to consider them as elegant RET because they left untouched some
important philosophical issues: the idea that love is necessary; the idea that
one needs God's forgiveness rather than one's own forgiveness; and, of
course, the idea of the existence of a supernatural power that one must be
dependent on and subservient to. While all these topics might well be subjects
of concern and challenge in the preferred elegant approach, they would likely
be non-therapeutic if not downright damaging if raised with the religious
clients in the examples I have presented.

The disabled client

Other clients who often suffer the agonies of low-self esteem and who respond well to general RET are those handicapped or disabled in some way. Lower-class males are especially vulnerable to self-value problems when unable to work due to injury or disabling illness.

Recently, I counselled a coal miner disabled in a mining accident. Although he received sufficient compensation and was not in serious financial jeopardy, he believed he was no longer a man because he could not work. He was especially troubled because he thought the fact that he stayed at home provided a poor role model for his two sons.

Logically explaining to this man that he need not down himself because he was deprived of a particular satisfaction was to no avail. This argument, no matter how I framed it, meant little to him. I was able to help, however, by showing him how to redefine his manhood. I suggested that learning to live with a handicap was, in effect, a man–sized job. In addition, I suggested that his sons would probably learn an important lesson about manhood if he could show how to cope successfully with adversity. It takes a big man, I told him, to handle a big problem. Anyone can handle things when they're going well, but the real man is the one who stands up to disappointment.

In another case a partially disabled coal miner was allowed to work on a part-time basis because his special skills as a mechanic–electrician were essential to his company. Despite this situation he had a low opinion of himself because he believed that working anything less than a 60-hour week proved him a weakling. After discovering he was an avid baseball fan, I used the following tactic:

Therapist: Who's your favourite baseball player?

Client: Pete Rose! He's number one!

Therapist: Why!

Client: He's Charlie Hustle. He gives it his all and never quits. You can depend on him when the chips are down.

Therapist: Let me ask you something. Suppose Pete Rose, while sliding into third base, hurt his back so bad he could never play full-time again. He stays in baseball, but only as a pitch hitter. He never plays a complete game innings. Would you think less of him and consider him a weakling?

Client: No! He'd be doing what you'd expect: playing until they rip his uniform off.

Therapist: But not full-time – he'd be a part-time player, right?

Client: Yeah.

Therapist:	And you'd still respect him as a man even though he was part-time?
Client:	Yeah, he'd still be valuable and important to his team but in a different way.
Therapist:	So why can't you see yourself in the same way? You were once a full-time worker, but now, because of an injury, you gotta pitch hit. You're still pretty valuable, or the company wouldn't want you around. So why consider yourself a weakling?
Client:	Yeah, I see what you mean – that's a good way to look at it. I'm still in the game, only now it's as a pitch hitter. I never thought of it that way, comparing myself to Pete Rose and baseball. When you put it that way, it seems kind of silly to get down on myself.

In this example, as with religious clients, I still worked toward cognitive or philosophical change, but the 'Pete Rose' approach is inelegant. I allowed that manhood or self-value exists and is dependent on special circumstances. What I did in both of these examples with disabled clients was make the conditions for intrinsic worth less restrictive and once again attainable. In other words, I helped both men to figure out positive ways of viewing themselves in spite of their handicaps.

The guilty client

An approach that is sometimes effective with those who damn themselves and feel excessively guilty is to have them question the wrongness of their actions. Often people who blame themselves have incorrectly found fault with an act that actually could be considered a virtue or at least advisable under the circusmtances. The following example involves a client who feels guilty because she broke up with her boyfriend who, as a result, attempted suicide by an overdose of drugs.

Therapist:	I don't understand why you feel so guilty over your boyfriend.
Client:	I broke up with him, and because of it he OD'd and almost died. It's probably a miracle he's still alive. They pronounced him dead when he first got to the hospital.
Therapist:	What is it that you did wrong then?
Client:	Breaking up with him, because it made him almost kill himself.
Therapist:	It seems like you believe you did two things wrong.

First, you think it was wrong to break up, and second, you believe you made him try to kill himself.

Client: It's the same. If I hadn't broken up with him, he wouldn't have tried it.

Therapist: No, there are two separate points here, and they're not the same. You broke up and that's one thing, and then he apparently decided he might as well be dead – that's another thing altogether. You're responsible for one but not necessarily for the other. Let me see if I can help you figure out how wrong you really were. Did you break up with your boyfriend so you could deliberately hurt him – so he'd try to kill himself?

Client: No, it was because he'd been treating me so rotten: going out with other girls, lying to me, and hitting me all the time. He broke my nose one time. He'd promise to change a million times, but it was the same old thing – for a week he'd be okay, then back to the same old thing.

Therapist: Then is it wrong to end such a relationship?

Client: No, that wasn't wrong. I believe I did right to break up.

Therapist: Then why do you feel guilty? People only feel guilty when they do something wrong. I've never met anyone who said, 'I did the right thing and I feel guilty.' What exactly did you do wrong?

Client: I made him try to kill himself!

Therapist: You did? How?

Client: I just told you by breaking up with him.

Therapist: Wait a minute, you just said that was right. Now it's wrong?

Client: Well it was wrong – I mean right. You're twisting my words.

Therapist: Don't you mean it was right to break up with him, but you believe it was your fault he tried to kill himself?

Client: Yeah, it is my fault.

Therapist: It was your decision to break up. It was his decision to kill himself. It was his fault he tried to kill himself, not yours.

Client: But I'm the one who broke up. If I hadn't done that, he wouldn't have taken the pills.

Therapist: Let me suggest another, and I think more sensible, way of looking at it. Here, take this hammer. [I hand her a rubber hammer I keep on my desk.] Now suppose you hit yourself over the head with it and really hurt yourself. In fact, you end up in the hospital with a fractured skull.

	Whose fault would that be, mine or yours?
Client:	It would be mine, that'd be dumb!
Therapist:	You mean that even though I handed you the hammer, even though I decided to give it to you, it would still be your fault if you hurt yourself with it.
Client:	Yeah, I would be at fault.
Therapist:	Isn't it the same thing as with your boyfriend.
Client:	What do you mean?
Therapist:	You handed him some information, that you wanted to break up. He hit himself over the head with it. Sure you contributed, but he's the one that did the damage to himself by the way he thought about your information.
Client:	I guess that makes sense. I feel better when you put it that way. I guess that's true, because I didn't know what he was going to do. I knew he wouldn't like it, but I had no idea he would take it the way he did.
Therapist:	Yeah, I guess that's the key to getting over the guilt – realizing that his suicide attempt was the result not of your rejection but of how he took things in his head. So I guess you are not as much at fault as you thought.

By reinforcing my client's belief that she was correct to break up and, even more important, by helping her to realize she was not the sole cause of her boyfriend's actions, I was able to dissipate her guilt feelings considerably. This approach failed to investigate how she could have avoided blaming herself even if she had known he might attempt suicide if she broke up with him. However, she was not particularly bright, and I got the impression I would see her only for a session or two, so I opted from the start for a less elegant approach. The issue of self-value was avoided by showing the client that self-value was not at stake in her situation.

The hostile client

Another common emotional disorder that sometimes yields to an inelegant approach is hostility. Although anger is often rooted in low frustration tolerance, it may also have its source in low self-esteem. Many clients feel anger because they believe some action on the part of another has insulted their pride or put them down. 'He made me feel low', or 'She made an ass out of me' are common expressions that illustrate this point.

Clients from a lower socioeconomic background are especially vulnerable in this respect. Anger to this kind of individual is often viewed as a badge of courage or pride. Often they feel that if they have nothing else, at least they have their righteous indignation. I have found that attempts to rid such clients of their anger is often wasted effort, because they believe you are trying to rob them of their self-respect and honour.

In a typical situation, a young welfare mother with five children lived in public housing. The next-door neighbour was probably mentally ill and was in constant conflict with my client. A favourite trick of this woman was to cut my client's clothes-line, allowing the clothes to fall to the ground and get dirty.

Instead of viewing this behaviour as the product of a deranged mind – consider the source, so to speak – my client read this action as a direct attack on her pride as a woman. She told me that the neighbour was trying to tell her that she was a 'big nothing'. She planned to get her boyfriend, a rather dangerous character, to beat this woman up. In this way, my client explained to me, she could once again hold her head up in the neighbourhood.

Philosophically-oriented counselling would make no dent, so I suggested that my client contact child welfare and have them investigate her neighbour's care of her children. This was a legitimate referral since, in the course of the client's therapy, it was revealed that the neighbour's mothering left much to be desired. I told my client that this would disgrace the neighbour and cause her a lot of problems with the authorities. My client agreed that this would be a proper punishment, and once the welfare workers arrived, the score would be considered settled.

In another, somewhat similar situation, a member of a group I ran reported that he had recently kicked out someone's teeth for insulting his honour. It seems the victim had accused my client of running around on his wife, a blind woman. As my client put it, 'I had to show him I don't stand for that kind of talk. If I let everyone say what they want about me, they'd all think I was yellow.' It made no difference, by the way, that the accusation was true. What was my approach? Much to the surprise of some student therapists who were observing my group. I congratulated my client on his restraint and applauded his actions!

I had been working with him for some time and no amount of cognitive restructuring attempts had convinced him that honour and pride were illusions. He had already spent 8 years in prison for killing a man. He carried a gun in his car and lived in an area where it was not unusual to take a shot at someone who trespassed on your property. My counselling efforts, therefore, were designed to convince him that beating, as opposed to killing, could prove his manhood. He seemed to buy this explanation and often credited me with keeping him out of jail with my 'rational counselling'.

Mr Perfect

I will finish this venture into the use of inelegant RET with an example of a client who could be diagnosed as psychotic, paranoid, borderline, psychopathic, or whatever. He was a huge, muscular man who was a former gang leader in a large city. There is no doubt that he had actually killed people to maintain his authority in this role. He was referred to me by his employer in a drug treatment facility. It appeared that the client, whom I called Mr Perfect, was a therapist in the programme and often resorted to beating patients when they disagreed with him.

In talking to Mr Perfect, I found that his fighting was designed to protect his ego. He viewed any questioning of his authority as a direct threat to his pride. However, he refused to admit the possibility that his self-value was ever in question. 'There is nothing wrong with me', he would state 'I'm perfect'. And he really meant it! Clients like this present a special problem. In order to help them overcome their ego problems, the ego problems would better be discussed. However, since any fault, including an ego problem, is denied by the client to maintain self-esteem, the very source of the client's problem is off-limits to therapeutic intervention.

I was able to work around this obstacle by acknowledging Mr Perfect's grandiosity and then chiding him for not being more benevolent toward the rest of humanity, especially the drug patients. I admitted he was God, but suggested he could be a more understanding God. In addition, I suggested to him that in spite of all his strong-armed tactics, Mr Perfect still let himself be provoked by the patients. I told him this was because the patients saw his temper as a weakness, as a flaw in his character. Since he would have no part of a weakness, Mr Perfect quickly showed great control over his temper at the drug treatment centre. What I got him to do was to defend his pride by allowing others to ridicule and disobey him. From the point of view of elegant RET this approach was a failure, but from the point of view of correcting the client's job problems it was a success.

The best laid plans

I would like to finish this presentation by discussing a phenomenon that exists in psychotherapy, especially in a cognitive–semantic approach like RET, and that is that our clients often change, actually get better, but for the wrong reasons. We give them the right messages – the correct insights – but somehow they manage to distort the wisdom of our words and come up with irrational attitudes. Yet they show marked improvement. I find this occurs quite often with TC's, and my suggestion is that in most situations, you leave well enough alone.

One case that comes to mind involved a diabetic male who was unable to achieve an erection. Doctors had determined that the cause was physical and that it would be unlikely he would ever be sexually potent. As a result, the client was convinced he was no longer a man. He responded well to an elegant approach that stressed that a loss in sex function does not equal a loss in overall manhood.

This made sense to him, and he showed immediate improvement. He also appeared able to see how this kind of thinking could be applied to other areas of failure. It seemed as though he was using RET in a most elegant fashion not only to cure his presenting problem but to ward off or minimize future problems as well. I later asked him what he believed caused his remarkable improvement. He said he knew that sex had nothing to do with his manhood. However, he proudly added that he knew he could 'beat the shit out of any man twice my size' and this, he stated with great conviction, proved he was still a man. So much for my elegant cure!

In another example, I was apparently successful in helping a young woman deal with jealousy and depression over her husband's frequent extramarital affairs. I encouraged her to see herself as a woman with less of what she wanted rather than as less of a woman. At the time I explained this insight to her, her face showed visible relief, and when this message was reinforced in subsequent counselling sessions and homework assignments, her improvement continued.

Her progress was noted by others, and she openly credited me with helping her by showing her how to think about herself more rationally. I met her socially sometime later and asked her what she felt I had done for her. I fully expected to hear her praise the RET approach to self-acceptance and the futility of trying to rate oneself. Instead she commented, 'You gave me the confidence and courage to get a breast enlargement! Now that I have big boobs, I feel more secure about myself, more like a real woman, and I don't care what my husband does.'

Finally, I worked with a woman who downed herself severely whenever she was rejected or imagined she was rejected. I used the soda machine analogy, pointing out that if a Coke machine turned her down and if this did not make her worthless, then perhaps the same might be true about turn-downs by people. She listened carefully, asked some very thoughtful questions, seemed to ponder what I was saying, and then began a 10-minute diatribe against Coke. Royal Crown Cola was fine, she said, with Dr Pepper next, and maybe 7-Up, but never Coke or Pepsi. In spite of what seemed to be a very literal way of taking my insights, this woman got better, and she frequently mentioned the Coke machine analogy as the source of her improvement. How this could be I will never know!

References

Ellis, A. (1962). *Reason and emotion in psychotherapy*. Secaucus, N.J.: Lyle Stuart.

Ellis, A. (1971). *Growth through reason*. North Hollywood, Calif.: Wilshire Books.

Ellis, A. (1974). *Humanistic psychotherapy: The rational-emotive approach*. New York: Julian Press/ McGraw-Hill.

Ellis, A. (1975a). *How to live with a neurotic*. New York: Crown.

Ellis, A. (1975b). RET abolishes most of the human ego. Paper presented at the American Psychological Association National Convention, Chicago, September 1975.

Ellis, A (1977). Rejoinder: Elegant and inelegant RET. *The Counseling Psychologist*, 7(1), 73–81.

Ellis, A. and Grieger, R. (Eds) (1977). *Handbook of rational-emotive therapy*. New York: Springer.

Young, H.S. (1977). RET with Bible-Belt Christians. Paper presented at the Second National Conference on Rational-Emotive Therapy, Chicago, June 1977.

Chapter 11

Rural RET: rational–emotive therapy in non–metropolitan communities

Naomi B. McCormick

It is no longer appropriate for mental health professionals to limit services to the traditional, psychologically minded client. Emotional distress is not the exclusive property of those who share their therapists' values: highly educated, liberal, sophisticated urbanites from the middle and upper socioeconomic classes. While it may be true that psychodynamic therapy is unsuitable for a broad variety of clients, cognitive–behavioural approaches such as rational–emotive therapy (RET) are adaptive enough to be appropriate for many types of problems and individuals (DiGiuseppe *et al.*, 1979). For example, Howard Young (1984a,b,c) adapted RET so as to make it maximally effective with adolescent, uneducated, poor and highly religious individuals.

In both North America and the United Kingdom, rural life is changing rapidly. Some rural areas have undergone a substantial decrease in population, whereas others have experienced greater population growth than urban areas (Cloke, 1983; Wilkinson, 1982). Numerous young, single people from rural families are leaving the countryside for the economic and educational opportunities of the city, often leaving the poorest and least well-adjusted members of their families behind (Cloke, 1983; Keller and Murray, 1982; Murray and Kupinsky, 1982). At the same time, increasing numbers of married and older people are leaving urban areas and migrating to rural ones (Christenson *et al.*, 1983; Cloke, 1983; Clout, 1976). Some rural areas now include substantial numbers of affluent professionals who live in the country but commute to urban jobs or are employed in industries that have replaced traditional rural occupations such as farming and mining. For example, many new rural residents manage recreational complexes, whereas others are employed in high-technology industries such as oil refining or government institutions such as colleges and prisons. A burgeoning part of the urban to rural migration is accounted for by the elderly who have relocated to the countryside after retirement (Cloke, 1983). There are a number of reasons for an influx of people into rural areas among which are economic decentralization, improvements in transportation and communications, and residential preferences. Be that as it may, rural clinicians are called upon to serve a broad spectrum of people.

Mental health professionals who serve rural communities are in fact seeing two highly different types of clients: new and long-term residents. New residents, highly educated, liberal and affluent individuals, are similar to urban candidates for private psychotherapy. In this respect, these individuals pose little therapeutic challenge for the practitioner. Long-term residents, often poor, highly religious, conservative, and cut-off from the natural support systems that they had relied on previously, differ greatly from the typical therapy client. Ironically, these individuals are least likely to seek out a therapist's help at the same time that they suffer from the highest levels of social and emotional upheaval. Building on Howard Young's (1984a,b,c) pioneering work, this Chapter describes some adaptations of RET that are likely to be beneficial in working with long-term, rural residents.

RET, like other systems of psychotherapy, has an urban bias. This is related to the disproportionate distribution of psychiatrists, psychologists and social workers in metropolitan areas (Keller and Murray, 1982; Mazer, 1982). Low population density poses another challenge. Often, those few mental health professionals who practise in rural areas are obliged to commute to satellite clinics which provide limited services a few days per week. Home visits, indirect services to clients by consulting with individuals from natural support systems, such as ministers, priests and teachers, and other treatment innovations are recommended in rural areas. Limited resources and uncertain client motivation challenge therapists to develop short-term, community-oriented approaches. RET is well-suited to such a model of service delivery. However, a few alterations in some typical RET practices are advisable to enhance the therapist's acceptance in rural communities. In addition, as most therapists are trained in urban areas, it is important for them to gain a greater understanding of the realities of rural life before treating rural clients.

First, this Chapter debunks the myths about rural life and provides a realistic picture of the environmental stresses and assets found in non-metropolitan communities. Next, adaptations in RET that will enhance its acceptance by rural people are described. Focusing on the therapist's language style, stand on moral and religious issues, and strategies for disputing irrational beliefs, the major part of this article expands on some of Howard Young's (1984a,b,c) ideas to provide a working model of cognitive–behavioural therapy in non-metropolitan settings.

Debunking romantic myths about rural life

In Western culture, the city has always been juxtaposed with the country in a negative way (Wagenfeld, 1982). According to our romantic myths, cities are dirty, decaying places which expose residents to stress and danger, whereas the countryside is clean, healthy, safe and secure. This same mythology characterizes urban relationships as formal, segmented and impersonal, whereas rural relationships are seen as more genuine, real and involving. Like any set of myths, there are underlying elements of truth. However, it is important to remember that rural people have fewer economic and political resources than their urban counterparts. Equally important, a large proportion of substandard housing exists in rural areas despite greater housing improvements in rural as opposed to urban areas and appearances to the contrary (Cloke, 1983; Keller and Murray, 1982).

Crime, mental illness and loneliness are far from non-existent in nonmetropolitan communities. Rather, the illusion that this is the case may come from low population density which minimizes the probability of encountering a disturbed or violent person. In addition, the casual and trusting way that rural people relate to others, including strangers, may belie the stressful realities of their lives. In contrast with the rosy picture of rural life presented by romanticists, a more complex reality emerges. Rural people are subjected to a variety of noxious activating events, some different and some surprisingly similar to those affecting urban individuals.

Emotional disturbance and violence

Epidemiologists, who compare the extent to which people in a given community are emotionally disturbed or commit acts of violence, disagree as to which environment is more pathogenic – urban or rural (cf. Husaini and Neff, 1982; Wagenfeld, 1982). However, there is strong evidence that rural life is far from ideal. Because rural people are less assertive and local adolescents who have better personality integration tend to migrate to cities after high school, various studies have suggested that rural people experience many life crises as more stressful than do urban people (Mazer, 1982). In New Zealand, rural people use stress-alleviative drugs more than those who reside in larger communities (Wilkinson, 1982). Excessive use of such drugs may in part be due to the irrational belief that one cannot stand boredom or familiar routine. However, the poor quality or relative unavailability of public services such as mental health agencies in many rural communities probably exacerbates the problem. Suffice to say that rural men are rejected from the United States Selective Service for appearing emotionally disturbed at higher rates than urban men (Wagenfeld, 1982). There are remarkably higher overall rates of suicide in rural as opposed to urban counties, especially among older men and the poor (Frederick, 1982; Segal, 1976). Reported increases in child abuse and neglect in rural areas resemble those reported in cities. With the exception of murder, violent behaviour in rural communities parallels that of metropolitan areas (Frederick, 1982). Apparently, rural people are subjected to many of the same stressful activating events that affect city dwellers. In addition, they may experience some unique stresses which are of equal importance to the clinician or community mental health planner who serves this population.

Sources of stress and support

Rural families engaged in traditional occupations such as farming are decreasingly able to compete against corporate agriculture and encroaching manufacturing plants and service industries. At the same time, they remain prey to their old enemies: weather, falling prices and high interest rates. This tears people between the desire to remain next to nature and the home where generations of their family have resided, on the one hand, and the desire to move into urban areas where they might earn a more dependable income, on the other (Murray and Kupinsky, 1982). Recently, these problems have become well-publicized in the United States, as a large number of family farms and agricultural businesses have become threatened with bankruptcy an foreclosure.

Sensitive to the dangers of isolation, rural people often go out of their way to help others. I have seen strangers, casual acquaintances and friends rally to the support of a family whose home was destroyed by flood or fire or who lost a loved one through death by donating food, clothing, money and furniture, and by providing emotional support. Unfortunately, local support systems have been deteriorating in rural areas. This has been in part due to modernization, which has diminished reliance on personal contacts in the community to obtain news and has decreased residents' involvement in churches, local government, volunteer ambulance corps and fire departments, civic groups and agricultural advocacy groups (Keller and Murray, 1982; Murray and Kupinsky, 1982). Meanwhile, the extended family has been dispersed. In many cases, the best functioning young people seek jobs and educational opportunities outside their home communities. If they are replaced, it is by highly educated professionals, equally cut off from their own extended families. These new migrants may not be responsive to the original residents of a rural community due to social class barriers and mutual distrust. Furthermore, a number of rural areas are burdened economically with large, retired populations surviving on limited incomes, because elderly people either remain in their small communities or relocate there after retirement.

Advantages of rural life

Clearly, rural communities have lost some of their original advantages while gaining many of the social problems plaguing metropolitan areas. None the less, it would be unfair to paint an overly bleak picture of rural life. Deteriorating or not, local support systems function better in rural than in urban areas. For this reason, formerly hospitalized mental patients make a better adjustment when returning to a small community than when returning to a large city (Segal, 1976). When they perceive the problematic behaviour as being outside of an individual's control, rural people are often more tolerant of deviant behaviour than their urban counterparts. They are less likely to complain to community mental health professionals that a psychotic individual is 'causing' distress in the family. In small communities, a certain number of individuals are allowed to be 'characters' whose very familiarity makes them unlikely to be the objects of fear or hostility.

Certain characteristics of rural areas may facilitate mental health. With their smaller populations, people have a better chance to know one another in rural as opposed to urban communities. When such a community is well integrated or fosters numerous voluntary organizations that can function as supportive structures for those in crisis, long-term emotional disturbance is less likely than in an urban area (Mazer, 1982). Also, the simpler economic and political organization of small communities may enhance residents' intellectual grasp of the resources which are available to them, thereby indirectly increasing their coping strategies. Relevant to this, I feel more confident about the referrals I have made in rural communities. Unlike my experience in major cities, I have access to fairly accurate information about the professional competence of nearly every available psychotherapist, lawyer, health care provider and social agency in my own and some neighbouring counties.

RET in rural settings

In addition to having a firm grasp of the realities of rural life, a few alternatives in some typical RET practices are advisable to enhance therapists' acceptance in rural communities. Specifically, it is wise for therapists to alter their language, their stand on moral and religious issues, and their strategies for disputing rational beliefs in order to be maximally effective with long-term, rural residents.

Communication and values in therapy

Because people commonly catastrophize in four-letter expletives, RET therapists often use obscenities to build rapport, loosen people up, and increase the emotive and motivating aspects of the therapy session (Walen *et al.*, 1980). Clearly, the 'sprightly use of obscenity' may be a useful therapeutic adjunct. However, it is wise to be cautious about one's language with rural clients who tend to have more conservative values than their urban counterparts (cf. Keller and Murray, 1982; Wilkinson, 1982). Profanity has extremely negative connotations for such clients, especially those from the lower socioeconomic classes (Young, 1984c). This was brought home to me when several female adolescent clients, with histories of conduct disorder problems and vocabularies that would make a sailor blush, have criticized my occasional use of popular slang and the word 'fuck'. Ignoring inconsistencies with their own behaviour, these young girls still had high and moralistic standards for others in their small community.

Alternative avenues are open for using language to capture a client's attention. Rural psychotherapists, for example, could make liberal use of colloquial expressions which in my community include such charmers as 'Jezzum Crow!' for Jesus Christ and 'the whole nine yards' for describing an irritating event that has consumed many resources. Therapeutic communication is most effective when the clinician is alert to conversational idioms and regionalized jargon and uses these in the therapeutic interchange (Young, 1984c).

Because they are opposed to dogmatism, RET therapists may take strong stands against some of the less rational things people were exposed to during religious or moral instruction. Rural therapists are wise to be very cautious about appearing to be opposed to religious teachings or conventional morality, however. In comparison with residents of large cities, rural people hold substantially more conservative values in a variety of areas including sexual conduct, politics and religion. 'Greater proportions of rural people rate themselves as very religious, report that they attend church regularly and indicate a faith in the value of religion for dealing with modern problems' (Wilkinson, 1982, p. 24). With this in mind, it would be destructive to ask clients to overhaul their entire value system. Instead of opposing a client's moral beliefs or religious group, the therapist can use these as treatment allies. Some excellent strategies for using religious values to dispute irrational beliefs are suggested in Young's (1984b) article 'Practising RET with Bible-Belt Christians' (see Chapter 9, this volume). The creative clinician can adapt Young's strategies for a variety of religious individuals including the devout Catholics who predominate in my own rural community.

Clergy and religious congregations are an important source of social support in rural areas. I have had very positive experiences treating a married couple with their clergyman as my co-therapist, referring devout Catholics with sexual guilt to a warm and accepting priest in the area, and helping a young mother overcome *post partum* depression by encouraging her to take an increasingly active role in her church.

Disputing irrational beliefs

As Ellis points out, nearly all the irrational beliefs that people oppress themselves and others with can be summarized succinctly in terms of three basic musturbatory ideologies (Ellis, 1977, 1979). The ideology of obsession, anxiety, and depression dictates: 'I must do well and win approval' (Ellis, 1977, p. 12). The anger ideology dictates: 'Others must treat me . . . the way I want them to treat me' (p. 12). The ideology of low frustration tolerance dictates: 'I must gratify my desires easily and immediately, without having to deal with too many difficulties or hassles' (Ellis, 1979, p. 4). In general, disturbed people of all varieties share the same irrational beliefs. However, the unique circumstances of rural life, described earlier, differentiate the way in which a particular irrationality is translated into maladaptive behaviour. Moreover, these same circumstances contribute to rural people being more or less susceptible than city dwellers in particular musturbatory ideologies. When disputing irrational beliefs, the effective RET practitioner avoids discounting the realistic barriers faced by clients attempting to realize their potential. With this in mind, I shall discuss the impact of each of the three musturbatory ideologies on rural people.

I must do well and win approval

Rural people know each other well in a variety of different roles and contexts. For example, on one day, an elementary school teacher might collaborate on some research with me or be a host for my guest lecture; on the next, he might seek my help as a psychotherapist regarding a conflict with his own children. When I go out for half an hour or more, I am certain to see at least one person or family I know from work, my social life, or through others. I cannot present one facade to one set of people and a contrasting one to others. My community is so small that through chance alone, people will see me playing different roles and, if not, they will hear about them from others.

There are some advantages to being known in a variety of roles and contexts. Rural people are less locked into proving their worth via high achievements than those in the city. I treat far fewer workaholics in my rural practice than when I practised in cities. Rural people know that if they fail in one area, they might be competent in another, and that this will be no secret to those around them. The mediocre lawyer, for example, might be admired for his excellent carpentry skills. True too, social skills may be more valued than achievement *per se*. The most personable, but not necessarily the most competent individual, might become president of the garden club or parent–teacher association. Where people come into contact with one another repetitively, cleverness is less advantageous than the ability to reduce inter-personal friction.

Urban people sometimes think that not much happens in little towns. They are right in one way; there are fewer outside diversions such as cultural and sporting events. None the less, the small community is far from a vacuum; the action is taken up by a fascination with interpersonal relationships. People know about others, sometimes as gossips and sometimes as caring individuals. They guess that a friend is in psychotherapy because her car is parked in front of a building in which a particular psychiatrist works. They discuss the possibilities that a neighbour is having an affair because he has lunch with the same attractive woman every Tuesday, or they notice two unrelated adults gaze into one another's eyes for more than a few seconds at their children's soft-ball game. They anticipate divorces or occupational relocations by noticing the 'For Sale' sign in front of particular homes. Anonymity, as it exists in large cities, does not occur in rural settings. For these reasons, rural people are more susceptible to anxiety and depression regarding other people's approval of their behaviour. They are not entirely irrational in this sense. Other people have greater control over them than would be possible in a major metropolitan area. In the city, a conflict with a supervisor could at worst result in the loss of one's job and a poor letter of recommendation. In a small town, this same supervisor could also sabotage a person's social life.

The forced intimacy of rural relationships creates a complex web of emotional 'fallout'. Legal problems cause fallout even when the suspected perpetrator is a family member and not the individual herself. Bail arrangements and court appearances, both minor and major, may be printed in the local newspaper or broadcast over the radio. Given the conservative values of small-town people, they may be more likely to stigmatize someone for having legal problems. As a result, they would be less likely to frequent that person's business or welcome her into their social lives.

Extramarital affairs, suspected or real, are especially problematic. To clarify why this is so, I will describe one couple I worked with who were caught in the rural, social web. The husband was having an affair with a co-worker. After hearing gossip regarding this, his wife saw her husband's car parked next to the co-worker's in front of a local bar. To confirm her suspicions, she entered the bar and surprised the couple having an intimate conversation. Soon, co-workers and neighbours of both spouses were deeply involved in giving advice, much of it contradictory. Meanwhile, the children of the couple and those of the man's lover, a divorced woman, were the best of friends and were puzzled by their parents' tension with one another. After working on their relationship, this particular couple moved out of the area. Sometimes, that kind of practical solution is not realistic, however. Then, the RET therapist is advised to teach people the most elegant dispute possible. It is important to avoid wording one's dispute so as to appear to minimize the complex social net that is woven around the client(s). I commonly say something like:

> You are right; it is a very difficult and painful situation. Your problem in itself is a great burden; it is worse still to live in a fish bowl with everybody talking about it. However, are you being realistic when you say that you can't stand it, that you could never be happy again in this town? Is the gossip about you so hot that everyone will continue to talk about you for years to come – that no new gossip will replace that about you? Even if they do talk about you, how does that make you the cad or patsy they accuse you of being? Must you soak in their poison and believe it? You know, you can't stop them from mixing up poison concoctions, but you can stop yourself from drinking them!

Risk-taking and shame-attacking exercises

Given rural people's greater susceptibility to the demand that others approve of them, it is appropriate to evaluate behavioural exercises that therapists might use to help clients with this issue. The unique characteristics of rural life make it more advisable to give risk-taking homework than to assign shame-attacking exercises. To clarify why this is true, I will describe each exercise in general, first. Then, I will indicate why it would be advantageous or problematic to give such an exercise to rural clients.

Risk-taking assignment challenge maladaptive social anxiety by asking clients to push themselves repetitively to take particular interpersonal risks they have been avoiding (Walen *et al.*, 1980). Typically, the risk involves going after a goal that the client has wanted for a long time (e.g. to be more assertive with a pushy friend or relative). However, until doing the exercise, the client had propagandized himself with either or both of these irrational ideas: (1) 'I can't change even if I want to', and (2) 'It would be terrible to try and fail.' These self-defeating ideas are behaviourally disputed when the client sees that even unsuccessful risk-taking *is* a form of change. Furthermore, the paradoxical suggestion that it is *okay to fail* and that failure is to be encouraged so as to avoid catastrophizing about it is equally therapeutic. Because they challenge dependency needs in a realistic context, risk-taking assignments are very advantageous with rural clients. I have found them especially useful with shy, unassertive, overly 'nice' individuals. When friends and neighbours start criticizing their newly 'gutsy' companion, I help my client dispute her irrational fears of being ostracized by saying:

> It will take people a while to get used to the *new* you. However, if they are never able to accept you this way, must you go back to being their

doormat? Is the relationship with them so wonderful that it is worth being a slave to preserve it?

Shame-attacking exercises ask clients to perform a silly or foolish act in public so as to improve their ability to discriminate between their *behaviour* and their *worth* as people (Ellis, 1979; Walen *et al.*, 1980). Yelling out the stops on subways or the time at a large department store are common shame-attacking assignments. In all cases, a client is encouraged to do something that might be unconventional but that is also perfectly legal and unlikely to create problems for them with people they know. Shame-attacking is a powerful way to overcome the belief that doing something foolish or making a single mistake makes a person a complete fool or failure. However, it is dangerous to assign shame-attacking in rural settings. As discussed previously, small communities do not have anonymity. There are no subways in small communities, and often there are no bus systems. The person calling out the time in a rural shopping mall, even one in an adjoining county, is likely to be seen by his customers or neighbours. It is not worth the risk to be the object of their gossip for such an exercise. Instead, it might be pointed out that life in a rural community has implicit, shame-attacking qualities.

In place of shame-attacking, conventional disputation and REI (Rational-Emotive Imagery) could be used to help clients change the profound disturbance they do experience when 'caught in the act' by their neighbours or friends (cf. Maultsby and Ellis, 1974). At this point, it is helpful to return to my example of the couple in which one partner has had an extramarital affair. Via REI, I could ask them to imagine the affair being written about in the local newspaper. Next, they would be asked to fully experience whatever disturbed emotion would occur naturally (e.g. rage, despair, shame, etc.). Finally, they would be asked to change their emotion for however briefly to one that would be less incapacitating such as annoyance or disappointment. With the therapeutic goal of teaching clients how they could dispute disturbed emotions in the future, they would be asked to recollect what they said to themselves to change their feelings during REI and to use these thoughts the next time a 'well-meaning' neighbour told them how they should evaluate their marriage.

Others must treat me the way I want

My clinical experiences suggest that rural and urban people are equally susceptible to the anger ideology: 'Others must treat me the way I want.' However, the targets of their anger may vary in some cases. Typically, rural people *know* all the people who anger them. Thanks to metropolitan anonymity, urban people have the luxury of becoming enraged at inconsiderate strangers, such as the drunk on the bus, the careless driver and the impersonal clerk. In contrast, the careless driver in a small town may also be the hockey coach of a client's sons. At the same time, this same individual might interact with the client in a variety of other contexts, e.g. in a fraternal organization, on the school board, in church, etc. The mutually dependent relationships that characterize rural life can give therapists an edge in disputing anger. Becoming angry at someone from one's small community can be likened to shipwreck victims starting a fist-fight in a lifeboat. The *lifeboat dispute* goes something like this:

> Okay, he hit your car and is a lousy driver. I'm not arguing with that. Nor am I disputing your experience of this guy as inconsiderate and a big mouth at your American Legion meetings. What I am arguing is this – you are stuck with this guy as long as the two of you live in this town. He isn't about to move away or quit the organizations both of you have joined. You are likely to run into him at least a couple of times a week. Now, how is it helping you to stay angry at him? How is your anger going to change his behaviour or force him to make it all up to you?

Life should be easy

People who have low frustration tolerance tell themselves that it should be easy to gratify their desires in the absence of difficult hassles. As Ellis and Harper (1975, p. 200) point out, such individuals refuse to abandon 'the notion that people and things should happen differently from the way they do and that life turns awful and horrible if good solutions to its grim realities don't quickly appear'. At first glance, rural people appear less susceptible to this irrational ideology than urban people. Rural people are much more fatalistic (Keller and Murray, 1982; Murray and Kupinsky, 1982). Their greater dependency on the whims of nature (e.g. poor weather could destroy a crop) and one another argues against the notion that life could be easy. If one digs deeper, however, it is apparent that rural people do have tremendous difficulties with frustration tolerance. Instead of whining or striking out in anger as an urban person would, however, they withdraw into a kind of learned helplessness.

Cabin fever, a depression experienced by isolated and typically poor rural people, exemplifies the learned helplessness of some rural people. With symptoms ranging from intense irritability to hallucinations (cf. Segal, 1976), suicide rates and admissions to mental hospitals rise in late winter and early spring as people who are stuck indoors become sick of themselves and one another. In such cases, behavioural prescriptions, such as the purchase of a snowmobile or a vacation in Florida, may be more useful than disputation. However, if a family is poor enough, these practical solutions are not viable. Then, the therapist has the challenging situation of teaching the client that it is possible to feel bored without being despondent, of disputing her belief that she cannot stand another minute stuck inside.

Because of their learned helplessness, rural people may take unnecessary risks with their lives. In the United States, for example, there is a higher tornado-related death rate in the South than in the North:

> Although Northerners may have a statistically greater chance of being killed by a tornado, Southerners are killed more often . . . [because of their] . . . greater fatalism and less reliance on technological means to avoid getting hurt (Murray and Kupinsky, 1982, p. 69).

The chronic powerlessness of some rural groups, such as the poor in Appalachia and native Americans on Indian reservations, exemplifies the self-destructive impact of fatalistic philosophy. To handle such cases, the effective RET therapist works at shaking up the client's belief that his life is hopeless. As Ellis and Harper (1975, p. 199) suggest, it would be valuable for such clients to: 'Reject the hypothesis that human misery gets externally caused and that [they] have little or no ability to control [their] depression or self-pity.' In some cases, political activism would be an excellent behavioural prescription to accompany this dispute. For example the impoverished, despondent and lonely rural homemaker could be asked to organize other women in her community into a craft's cooperative. Similarly, the parents of unruly and unemployed teenagers might press their local government for a summer-job programme or recreational facilities.

Summary

Therapists who practise RET, like most clinicians, share an urban bias. This Chapter has attempted to address this problem by describing sources of stress and support in rural communities and indicating how life in rural communities differs from that in major metropolitan areas. Next, some modifications of standard RET practices are suggested for rural practitioners. Rural psychotherapists are advised to avoid using profanity and seeming to take a strong stand against their clients' traditional religious and moral values. Finally, suggestions for disputation are provided which take into account rural-urban differences in susceptibility to the three, basic musturbatory ideologies.

References

Christenson, J.A., Garkovich, L.E. and Taylor, G.S. (1983). Proruralism values and migration behavior. *Population and Environment*, **6**, 166–78.

Cloke, P.J. (1983). *An introduction to rural settlement planning*. London: Methuen.

Clout, H. (1976). Rural–urban migration in western Europe. *In* J. Salt and H. Clout (Eds), *Migration in post-war Europe: Geographical Essays*. Oxford: Oxford University Press.

DiGiuseppe, R.A., Miller, N.J. and Trexler, L.D. (1979). A review of rational-emotive psychotherapy outcome studies. *In*: A. Ellis and J.M. Whiteley (Eds), *Theoretical empirical foundations of rational-emotive therapy*. Monterey, Calif.: Brooks/Cole.

Ellis, A. (1977). The basic clinical theory of rational-emotive therapy. *In* A. Ellis and R. Grieger (Eds), *Handbook of rational-emotive therapy*. New York: Springer.

Ellis, A. (1979). Rational-emotive therapy as a new theory of personality and therapy. *In* A. Ellis and J.M. Whiteley (Eds), *Theoretical and empirical foundations of rational-emotive therapy*. Monterey, Calif.: Brooks/Cole.

Ellis, A. and Harper, R.A. (1975). *A new guide to rational living*. North Hollywood, Calif.: Wilshire.

Frederick, C.J. (1982). Violent behavior in rural areas. *In* P.A. Keller and J.D. Murray (Eds), *Handbook of rural community mental health*. New York: Human Sciences Press.

Husaini, B.A. and Neff, J.A. (1982). The prevalence of psychopathology in rural Tennessee and Oklahoma. *In* P.A. Keller and J.D. Murray (Eds), *Handbook of rural community mental health*. New York: Human Sciences Press.

Keller, P.A. and Murray, J.D. (1982). Rural mental health: An overview of the issues. *In* P.A. Keller and J.D. Murray (Eds), *Handbook of rural community mental health*. New York: Human Sciences Press.

Maultsby, M.C. and Ellis, A. (1974). *Techniques for using rational-emotive imagery (REI)*. New York: Institute for Rational-Emotive Therapy.

Mazer, M. (1982). The influence of the rural community on the mental health of its inhabitants. *In* P.A. Keller and J.D. Murray (Eds), *Handbook of rural community mental health*. New York: Human Sciences Press.

Murray, J.D. and Kupinsky, S. (1982). The influence of powerlessness and natural support systems on mental health in the rural community. *In* P.A. Keller and J.D. Murray (Eds), *Handbook of rural community health*. New York: Human Sciences Press.

Segal, J. (Ed.) (1976). *The mental health of rural America: The rural programs of the National Institute of Mental Health*. (DHEW Publication No. ADM 76–349; Formerly DHEW Publication No. HSM 73-9035). Washington, D.C.: US Government Printing Office.

Wagenfeld, M.O. (1982). Psychopathology in rural areas: Issues and evidence. *In* P.A. Keller and J.D. Murray (Eds), *Handbook of rural community mental health*. New York: Human Sciences Press.

Walen, S.R., DiGiuseppe, R. and Wessler, R.L. (1980). *A practitioner's guide to rational-emotive therapy*. New York: Oxford University Press.

Wilkinson, K.P. (1982). *Changing rural community mental health*. New York: Human Sciences Press.

Young, H.S. (1984a). Counseling strategies with working class adolescents. *British Journal of Cognitive Psychotherapy*, **2**(2), 21–32.

Young, H.A. (1984b). Practising RET with Bible-Belt Christians. *British Journal of Cognitive Psychotherapy*, **2**(2), 60–76.

Young, H.S. (1984c). Practising RET with lower-class clients. *British Journal of Cognitive Psychotherapy*, **2**(2), 33–59.

Chapter 12

Enhancing the psychological adjustment of school-age children: a rational-emotive perspective*

Michael E. Bernard

This chapter which presents an overview of how rational-emotive therapy (RET) can be modified for use with children and adolescents is organized into four sections. The first section focuses on the currently available research concerning the effectiveness of RET and rational-emotive education (REE) with younger populations. In the second section, the limitations of a child's developing cognitive and linguistic capacities are discussed and guidelines are presented for how RET can be made more concrete and specific to the child's developmental capacities. Section three presents a four-stage assessment-treatment model for applying RET with younger populations which includes rapport building, assessment, skill acquisition, and practice/application. Emphasis is placed on the importance in assessment for distinguishing between a child's emotional and practical problems. Three basic treatment strategies are described which RET practitioners typically employ to modify both a young client's dysfunctional interpretations and appraisals of reality as well as irrational beliefs (rational self-statements, empirical analysis and philosophical disputation). The final section of the article describes how RET can be employed with parents.

It has only been within the past 10 years or so that behavioural scientists have begun studying the extent to which the psychological problems of school-age children can be modified by psychoeducational and therapeutic programmes designed to teach them new ways of thinking about themselves and their environment. In so doing, they have opened the minds of child-oriented mental health practitioners to the collective wisdom of many great philosophers and social commentators of their day; namely, that what separates human beings from all other animals is their capacity to exercise

---

* Portions of this Chapter were adapted from Bernard and Joyce (1984) and Ellis and Bernard (1983).

control of their minds and in so doing to take a large amount of responsibility for their feelings, behaviour and, ultimately, their destiny. More and more practitioners are applying cognitively oriented techniques to help children and adolescents use their minds to help themselves overcome problems of adjustment and to live happier and more fulfilled lives.

Today, there are several different cognitive approaches which are being applied to enhance childhood adjustment (interpersonal cognitive problem solving: Spivack and Shure, 1974; Spivack *et al.*, 1976; self-instructional training: Kendall and Finch, 1979; Meichenbaum and Asarnow, 1979; cognitive social skill training: Camp and Bash, 1981; Halford, 1983; stress inoculation: Cormier and Cormier, 1979; Novaco, 1979; attribution retraining: Meichenbaum, 1977; Rotter, 1966; and rational-emotive therapy: Knaus, 1974; Ellis and Bernard, 1983). These approaches have idiosyncratic historical origins (e.g. cognitive psychology, semantic therapy, Soviet psychology) and do not derive from a single all-embracing cognitive model of psychological adjustment. They all do, however, consider *verbal mediational factors* (cognitive skills, irrational beliefs, self-instructions, attributions, negative thinking) as central to understanding and modifying childhood maladjustment. In practice, these approaches are being increasingly employed together in the form of multitreatment cognitive programmes to deal with the full range of childhood emotions and behavioural problems.

This article will describe the use of rational-emotive therapy (RET) with children and adolescents. While RET has been employed for over 25 years with younger populations, it has only been since 1980 that it has begun to be widely accepted by mental health professionals and written about (e.g. DiGiuseppe, 1981; Ellis and Bernard, 1983; Waters, 1982). (For a description of the theoretical background, research findings, assessment and training procedures of the other cognitive approaches, see Bernard and Joyce, 1984.) Initially, a summary of the research status of the efficacy of RET will be presented. This will be followed by a discussion of developmental factors which influence the use of RET with younger populations. A four-stage treatment model which describes how RET is applied with younger populations will be presented. The article will conclude with a discussion of how RET is employed with parents of children with problems of adjustment.

Research findings

Most of the controlled experimentation which looks at the application of RET with younger populations has taken place since 1970 (for a more intensive presentation, see Bernard and Joyce, 1984). A limited number of case studies have been reported in the late 1960s and early 1970s which indicate that RET principles are effective with children. Beginning with a study by Albert (1972) and continuing for the next 10 years (e.g. Meyer, 1982), experiments which have explored the effectiveness of RET with children and youth have followed a similar format. The typical experimental question of concern is generally an open-ended one: 'What is the effect of RET on ('normal', younger–older, fourth grade–eighth grade, dull–normal–bright, anxious, low self-esteem, learning disabled, emotionally disturbed, hearing-impaired) children?' 'Normal' subjects have tended to be randomly selected on the basis of availability and on a volunteer basis (e.g. Robbins, 1976; Ritchie, 1978). By and large, subjects who participated in treatment groups varied greatly in a host of personality and cognitive characteristics that were unrelated to treatment.

It is very difficult to make generalizations concerning the findings of these studies. It is clear that studies suffer from a lack of assessment instruments to measure changes in emotions. Dependent behavioural measures have been too global, masking more specific changes in behaviours. The heterogeneous composition of experimental groups and the use of parametric statistics also serves to mask potential changes in individual subjects. Certain early studies suffered from a number of difficulties which limit their internal and external validity, including (1) no pre-test was administered to assess differences, (2) an attention-placebo group was lacking to control for the 'Hawthorne' effect, and (3) only self-report dependent measures were used. The lack of replication studies makes the confirmation of valid findings difficult to make. With these reservations in mind, a number of tentative generalizations can be offered.

There is little question that RET concepts and emotional problem-solving skills can be acquired by groups of children as young as 10 years of age and that RET can be taught as part of a normal curriculum. A very strong and consistent finding is that children of all ages can acquire basic RET concepts and modify their beliefs as measured by the two available tests of irrationality in children – the Ideas Inventory (Kassinove *et al.*, 1977) and the children's survey of Rational Beliefs (Knaus, 1974). Changes in irrational beliefs of children have not generally, however, resulted in concomitant *large scale* changes in behaviour, such as increasing assertiveness or reducing aggression. Future studies will need to examine changes in specific behaviours in relation to changes in specific irrational beliefs.

In terms of bringing about causal attributional change, there is a consistent finding which indicates that RET does *not* bring about changes in causal attributions from external to internal.

It appears from reviewing the literature that the changes that are brought about by RET have up to now been limited to changes in specific emotions

and behaviours. Large-scale changes, as measured by standardized personality measures, have generally not be found. This has been probably due to the
relative inexperience of practitioners who conducted the studies (few ex-
perimenters have received either formal training in RET at any of the
Institutes for Rational-Emotive Therapy and Rational Living across the
United States or intensive supervision in RET at their university or college)
and to the limited time spent with children.

Cognitive–developmental considerations

Armed with the knowledge that basic learning processes and abilities (e.g.
attention, memory, verbal mediation, cognitive strategies) appear to systematically develop in complexity over the childhood period (e.g. Flavell,
1982), rational-emotive practitioners are increasingly taking into account a
child's cognitive–developmental maturity in deciding upon and identifying
maximally appropriate therapeutic style and assessment–treatment methods.
For example, children in the pre-operational period of development, as
defined by Piaget (approximately 5–7 years of age), do not seem to profit
from discovery therapeutic methods to teach rational self-statements but
rather require direct expository methods. Pre-operational children seem
unable to apply in a general way, cognitive self-guiding strategies.

   Also from a review of Piaget, it is known that it is only when children are in
the formal operational period (12 years of age plus), that they are *generally*
capable of the type of hypothetico–deductive reasoning that would appear to
be a necessary prerequisite for disputational examination of fundamental
irrational beliefs. Many children do not have the cognitive capacity to
(1) recognize their *general* irrational beliefs (e.g. 'The world should be fair and
bad people should be punished') *when they are presented as hypothetical* proposi-
tions; (2) understand rationally re-stated beliefs (e.g. 'The world is not a fair
place to live and people who mistrust others can be helped to correct their
ways'); (3) employ their rationally re-stated beliefs in all situations where
they are treated unfairly; (4) spontaneously generate rational self-talk regarding others' behaviour (e.g. 'It's okay to make mistakes'); and (5) employ
rational self-talk to 'cool' down emotions and guide behaviour.

   We know from Piaget and others that children between the approximate
ages of 7 and 11 (concrete operations) structure the world in an empirical and
inductive manner. As a consequence, RET child practitioners employ very
concrete examples and many teaching illustrations. The underlying logic of
this approach is that the child in this period can be taught general attitudes and
beliefs through extensive and intensive rational analysis of specific situations.
For example, when working with aggressive and conduct disordered younger boys (7–11 years of age) we find that they frequently believe that people

whom they perceive 'doing them in' deserve to be 'done in' themselves. We have achieved good success in getting this population to change their beliefs by:

1. Discussing a specific situation (e.g. being unfairly treated in a maths class by a teacher).
2. Defining the concept of 'fairness' and having them empirically analyse whether the current situation is unfair or not; this step frequently involves puppets, so that the child can view the situation from another's perspective.
3. Discussing the concept of 'mistake making' and explaining the different reasons why a maths teacher may act unfairly and make mistakes.
4. Providing a set of rational self-statements (e.g. 'It's okay to make mistakes. No-one's perfect, I can handle this situation, I don't have to get upset') which are modelled and role-played.
5. Discussing the concepts of 'fairness' and 'mistake making' in the context of other problematic situations (e.g. other teachers, parents, siblings, in-class, at play, at home).
6. Giving practice in applying the rational self-statements to novel situations.
7. Reinforcing the child (and getting him to self-reinforce) for using rational self-talk with the practitioner and in 'real-life situations.'

In working with young pre-operational children, rational–emotive practitioners are especially conscious of their difficulty in *readily* taking into account the perspective of others (egocentrism) as well as considering more than one relevant dimension. As children during this period rely heavily on perceptual analysis rather than conceptual inference, extensive rational analysis of irrational concepts is de-emphasized and, instead, reliance is placed on the child's more advanced capacity for dealing with pictorial and imaginal representation. A great deal of concrete and simple materials are employed (pictures, diagrams, stories) which young children can more readily learn from. At the same time, developmental work in verbal mediation (e.g. Flavell *et al.*, 1966) indicates that children between the ages of 6 and 9 who fail to produce spontaneously relevant self-guiding verbal mediators may learn to do so from instruction.

Therefore, it is important to spend a great deal of time with younger children, teaching them through a variety of different methods or techniques, first instructing them in acquiring rational self-talk and, secondly, in spontaneously uttering the self-talk.

In working with children (and to a somewhat lesser extent with adolescents) it is relevant to recall that children, especially at younger developmental levels, are active learners, and that knowledge acquisition is facilitated by 'doing' as much as 'seeing'. Use of pictures and stories may serve as imaginal mnemonic devices and enhance the experiential aspect of the learning episode which may also facilitate memory.

While cognitive–developmental research consistently indicates that all children appear to demonstrate an invariant sequence in which they pass through different stages of development, the ages which encompass each stage have proven to be only approximations and that there are fairly wide individual differences with which children attain different stages. With this finding clearly in mind, it is possible to provide broad guidelines for RET practitioners in considering the relationship between the age of the young client and selection of a RET intervention procedure. Whereas instruction in rational self-statements can be employed with children of all ages, we generally do not cognitively dispute irrational concepts with children who are much less than 7 years of age and do not dispute irrational beliefs with children much below the age of 11 or 12.

Stages in therapy

There are four discernible stages in applying RET with children and ado-lescents: (1) rapport building, (2) assessment, (3) skill acquisition, and (4) practice and application. Although each stage usually requires attention, one need not hold to this particular order. For example, one could be developing a relationship while defining a problem.

Relationship building

While the practice of RET is traditionally characterized by an active-directive style of therapy and by a de-emphasis on the importance of the practitioner–client relationship, such is not the case when RET is employed with younger populations.

The relationship a RET practitioner builds with a young client is often a necessary precondition for change. However, it needs to be kept in mind that it has been reported in the literature that in upwards of 20–25 per cent of child and adolescent referrals, positive and lasting results were achieved using RET without the practitioner actively establishing a high level of rapport. For the majority of young clients, there is a need to employ as many techniques as possible to establish a positive relationship. For many children who are referred to a RET practitioner, they often have a history of being in trouble and are suspicious of and distrust adults. If a youngster arrives with this attitude, it will be almost impossible to enlist his or her support and cooperation. And for many children and adolescents, self-disclosure may be difficult. Therefore, with some young clients, encouragement, gentle confrontation, and a slower pace of therapy is recommended (Walen *et al.*, 1980). Child-oriented RET practitioners recognize the value of relationship factors such as *positive regard, congruence or genuineness*, and *empathic understanding*.

The attitude RET practitioners take to their role with a child is important in determining the effectiveness of intervention. RET practitioners, in trying to respond appropriately to the developmental level of the child, model their approach after someone who has proven successful with interacting and communicating with children, rather than after someone who has proved his or her effectiveness with adults (e.g. Rossi, 1977). Enthusiasm, liberal applications of praise, humour, treating the child as an equal, concrete and down-to-earth language, healthy amounts of physical contact, being friendly and not overbearing, being non-judgemental and open to suggestions, and pointing out to children that you as a practitioner are not out to force a child to become perfect as parents might desire but rather to help the child change some of the hassles, hurt feelings, or worries about the future he or she may be experiencing, have been suggested as facilitative of the practitioner–young client relationship.

To increase rapport and self-disclosure it is a good idea to dispel a child's misconceptions regarding the role of the RET practitioner. The following information can be provided: 'I'm a psychologist (counsellor). I help people solve different kinds of problems' (Walen *et al.*, 1980). Other suggestions for increasing self-disclosure include having the practitioner be a good model for self-disclosure, accepting whatever the child says without putting him or her down, reinforcing the child for self-disclosure, *not* being overly business-like, always being honest, going easily and carefully on questions, telling the child what information you have as a practitioner, *not* beginning the relationship by asking questions, *not* asking what you already know, and *not* asking the same question more than once (DiGiuseppe, 1981; Waters, 1982).

For working with very young clients, additional concrete suggestions for developing rapport include the following (Bernard and Joyce, 1984):

1. Tell them your name.
2. Find out what they like to be called ('Tom', 'Tommy' or 'Thomas').
3. Show interest in their real-life context – family, friends, hobbies, pet.
4. Find ways to set the relationship apart from other adult–child relationships. Sit beside the child or adolescent, never behind a desk, or, for early sessions with very young children, choose a relaxed setting such as bean bags, the floor or garden swings.
5. Guide the child as to what you expect. State the rules for the relationship: 'This is not like other places. You can say anything you like. You can say just what you think and what you feel.'
6. Early disclosure of feelings is helped by first suggesting to the child a

general statement about children: 'Children sometimes feel afraid about someone new' (or . . . 'cross at *having* to do something'). 'Do you think children feel this way?' 'Maybe you feel this way right now?'

7. For an inhibited youngster, the practitioner may 'read' the body language and tentatively put the feeling into words for the child. This can give the child confidence that the practitioner knows how he or she feels inside.

8. Show that you are a person who *listens* by not continuously interrupting, and by responding to what they have said.

In working with adolescents who tend to be more reluctant, vague, defensive and hostile in sharing details with a stranger, the following suggestions can encourage a positive practitioner–client relationship, which may lead to the adolescent accepting an open, problem-focused and problem-facing format (from Bernard and Joyce, 1984; Young, 1983):

1. Listen for the adolescent's preconceived ideas about the practitioner and therapy.
2. As soon as possible, give the adolescent an idea of the time span (e.g. 6–8 sessions or 3 months) you think will be needed to work on the problem.
3. Where the adolescent is not self-referred but sent by a parent or teacher, it is especially important to establish rapport on a basis apart from authority – adult to child. You may wish to allow the adolescent to call you by your first name.
4. Find opportunities to be with the client at other times than treatment sessions.
5. Help define the problem for the adolescent by providing a simple statement which reveals your knowledge of their difficulties.
6. Simplify the definition of a problem by describing the problem as involving hurt feelings, hassles with others, or doubts about the future.
7. Use a representative example from the life of another young person.
8. Offer a problem out of your own life.
9. Use visual aids.

Assessment

RET assessment can be seen as being composed of a *problem identification* and a *problem analysis* phase. Problem identification involves determining whether, in fact, a problem exists and, if it does, who owns it. Children and adolescents are frequently referred to a practitioner by their parents (or teachers). The initial task of the practitioner is to determine whether the youngster, the parents and/or the teachers are actually demonstrating an emotional or a behavioural problem. During problem identification, it is important for the practitioner to be aware of developmental, peer, and cultural–familial norms in the area of concern. It is quite common for the problem to be shared by both a child and his or her significant others.

Once it has been established that a problem does exist and the problem ownership has been determined, the problem analysis phase of RET assessment takes place. The practitioner may interview the child, the parents and the teachers to determine the extent of their respective cognitive, emotive and behavioural dysfunction.

A distinctive aspect of RET assessment is the separation of emotional (non-manipulative) from practical (manipulative behaviour) problems. Waters (1982, p. 233) differentiates among these types of problems as follows:

> Emotional problems are generated by self- and goal-defeating belief systems, and are characterized by extremely uncomfortable, stagnated feelings, while practical problems are realistic difficulties in the environment resulting in unsatisfactory situations, which one wishes to change. . . . When one is in the midst of an emotional problem, it is analogous to creating a dense fog which obscures one's view of the practical problem and also renders any logical or reasonable thinking about the problem virtually impossible. In order to clear up the emotional fog so that practical problem-solving can proceed, it is necessary to identify the beliefs generating the fog and replace them with more rational beliefs. Practical problem solving is best attempted when emotions are appropriate to the situation.

Hauck (1983, p. 337) further distinguishes between manipulative and non-manipulative behaviour:

> Non-manipulative behavior is shown by children who would show their symptoms if they were alone on a desert island. The behavior has no ulterior purpose, it comes solely from within the interaction of the child with him or herself over some event in the person's life. Such behavior is not meant to impress, to control, or to influence anyone at all. It is simply a reaction to the irrational thoughts the child has expressed and because they are irrational, they have unfortunate consequences. . . . When a child develops a symptom and uses it for secondary gain, we call such behavior manipulative. Depression may now exist in order in order to get sympathy. Anger may gain in intensity because a child hopes to scare his parents into acquiescing to his desires. If he becomes nervous, perhaps his mother will let him stay home from school. Or, if a girl will not do her chores on time, or

complete her homework, she may be doing this for revenge against a frustrating parent. I determine that behavior is manipulative if it seems goal directed.

The choice of intervention will differ depending on whether the behaviour appears to be manipulative or non-manipulative. Children manifesting non-manipulative behaviour would be good candidates for RET. Typical emotional problems include inappropriately high levels of anger, anxiety or depression (self-downing), which are generated by irrational beliefs and which lead to extreme reactions that prevent goal attainment. Their parents would be provided with rational arguments to help their child whenever he or she gets upset. Practical problems are revealed in either aggressive or avoidant behaviour and stem from the youngster's not knowing how to behave appropriately in a situation (i.e. being teased). Emotional problems often precede practical problems, although children may upset themselves emotionally about their practical problems. When behaviour appears to be primarily manipulative, much of the work of the practitioner is conducted with parents and teachers in teaching them how to manage misbehaviour more constructively.

The problem analysis phase of child assessment is instituted after it has been decided that the young client 'owns' at least part of the problem. At this time, more analytical methods are employed to characterize not only emotional and behavioural strengths and weaknesses, but also the role of the client's cognitions. This second phase of assessment results in the determination and prioritizing of emotional, behavioural and cognitive targets for change.

Most of the assessment information the practitioner collects from a young client is from a one-to-one interview. The practitioner at first seeks to ascertain the young client's perception of the problem and begins by helping the client define the nature of the problem and having the client describe when and where the problem occurs, its frequency, intensity and duration, persons who are generally present when the problem occurs, what they are saying, doing and feeling, and how they react after it occurs. The young client is asked to describe his or her behaviour carefully, so that the practitioner can get a measure of the degree of correspondence between his or her view and the view of others. The practitioner is concerned with behavioural over-reactions (aggression) and under-reactions (withdrawal).

The client is also asked to describe his feelings in the problematic situation, to indicate the variety of feelings experienced, and to rate the intensity of feelings from strong to weak. If the youngster has difficulty finding an appropriate label for the emotion, a list of possibilities and their definitions from which to choose is provided. In the main, the practitioner is on the lookout for the three primary emotions of anger, anxiety (worry) and depression (self-downing), and the related feelings of jealousy and guilt (see Bernard, 1984, for a RET analysis of different emotions in childhood). The practitioner who at this point has an initial idea of activating events (A) and emotional and behavioural consequences (C), is able to infer what a child is most probably feeling if he or she is behaving in a certain way, and what his or her behaviour might be which accompanies specific emotional reactions. These inferences are also useful when the child does not provide full details of feelings and behaviour.

When practitioners begin to analyse the different cognitions which might be influencing the emotions of a young client, they begin to listen for any indication of irrational self-talk, concepts and beliefs which the client may be thinking during problematic situations. Generally, RET practitioners attempt to isolate the following types of cognitive distortions (e.g., Grieger and Boyd, 1983): (1) errors of inference which refer to predictions or conclusions that falsely represent reality, and (2) errors of evaluation which involve affective judgements concerning the 'goodness' or 'badness' of the client's interpretations of reality from which are inferred the presence of irrational beliefs. Waters (1982) suggests the following problem areas to assess: (1) Is the child distorting reality? (i.e. 'Nobody likes me, they're all against me'); (2) Is the client evaluating situations in a self-defeating way? (i.e. 'This situation shouldn't exist. It's awful!'); and (3) Does the client lack appropriate cognitions? (lack of task-appropriate verbal self-instructions). Probing, questioning and listening occurs to determine if the client's self-talk aids or prevents the client from coping with stressful situations, whether the client thinks about different ways of handling situations in terms of possible positive and negative consequences, and whether the client attributes the cause of the problem to himself or to outside events which he has no control over.

Direct questioning and a variety of less direct elicitational techniques are combined to get the young client to verbalize and become aware of self-talk. General prompts include:

What were you thinking when ———— happened?

What sorts of things were you saying to yourself when ———— ?

What name did you call your brother when he ———— ?

Tell me the first things which come into your mind when you think about ————.

Picture yourself back in class; what did you think when ———— ?

It is extremely difficult for some youngsters to become aware of and discuss their innermost thoughts, feelings, wishes and fantasies. Some of the reasons include the fact that this information is 'hidden away' in their private thoughts (see Bernard, 1981), that they have had little practice in discussing these matters with anyone, that they are afraid, hostile and embarrassed, and that some youngsters (especially boys) are taught that it is not right ('masculine') to show and discuss feelings. Younger children find it much harder to introspect than older populations and the amount of cognitive material they provide is usually much smaller. With older children more didactic-expository teaching methods can be employed, whereas younger children need slower paced and experiential learning activities. The use of pedagogical games and materials serves to build rapport, relax and disinhibit the young child. Bernard and Joyce (1984) provide a description of RET assessment techniques and activities such as emotional scales, emotional flashcards, the emotional detective, feeling charts, thought bubbles, the sentence completion technique, thinking aloud, expansion–contraction, and peeling the onion.

Skill building

RET is primarily oriented to teaching skills for the solving of emotional problems. Its aim is to have clients of all ages acquire an attitude of emotional responsibility; that is, to take control of their feelings through the operation of rational thinking and problem-solving skills. The main goal of emotional problem solving is to teach children and adolescents how to change inappropriate to appropriate feelings. Waters (1982, p. 234) indicates:

> Appropriate feelings are generated by rational beliefs, are an appropriate response to the situation, facilitate goal achievement, and are usually moderate as opposed to extreme reactions; whereas inappropriate feelings are generated by irrational beliefs, are an inappropriate response to the situation, impede goal achievement, and are usually extreme reactions.

Examples of inappropriate and unhelpful emotions are when children feel very angry, enraged, hostile, depressed and anxious, while more appropriate feelings would be irritation, annoyance, disappointment, sadness, apprehensiveness and concern. Secondarily, RET practitioners help young clients acquire practical problem-solving skills in order that they may more readily handle problematic situations.

The focus of RET with school-age children is to both help them correct irrational ideas and irrational thinking and acquire rational thoughts and skills so that their emotions become more appropriate and their behaviour more goal-oriented. Independent application of emotional problem-solving skills to a variety of problems across time would represent an ideal solution. For younger children, the goals of RET can be expressed as follows (Waters, 1981):

1. Correctly identify emotions.
2. Develop an emotional vocabulary.
3. Distinguish between helpful and hurtful feelings.
4. Differentiate between feelings and thoughts.
5. Tune into self-talk.
6. Make the connection between self-talk and feelings.
7. Learn rational coping statements.

For older children and adolescents, a more complex set of goals may be pursued in addition to the ones already listed (from Young, 1983):

1. Teach the ABC's.
2. Dispute 'awfulizing'.
3. Dispute 'shoulds, oughts, and musts' (personal imperatives).
4. Challenge 'I-can't-stand-it-it is' (low frustration tolerance).
5. Teach self-acceptance.
6. Correct misperceptions of reality.

There are two aspects of cognitive activity which can lead to childhood emotional and behavioural disturbances and which are corrected through RET. *Distorted interpretations and perceptions of reality* are brought about by errors of logical inference and reasoning (arbitrary inference, selective abstraction, over-generalization, magnification and minimization, personalization, and absolutistic/dichotomous reasoning), and can lead to moderately maladaptive levels of emotional arousal and dysfunctional behaviour. A second, and from a RET point of view, major aspect of dysfunctional cognitive activity, is the evaluations and appraisals the individuals make of their misinterpretations. These *evaluations of interpretations* which can be rational or irrational are seen to be the main source of emotional disturbance, since rational appraisals of a distorted perception of reality will generally not lead to extreme and unproductive levels of emotional arousal.

An example provided by DiGiuseppe and Bernard (1983, pp. 48–9) will illustrate the differences between faulty inferences which lead to misinterpretations and self-defeating appraisals of distortions of reality:

George, a ten year old, moved to a new neighbourhood and has not met new friends. He is sitting quietly in the neighbourhood playground while the other children are running about. He feels frightened and his associated action potential [behaviour] is withdrawal. He sits alone leaning up against a wall reading a book. As he sees the other children coming, George thinks 'They'll never like me, they'll think I'm not very good at their games and they won't play with me, no matter what I do.' George has drawn these inferences about the other children's behavior. In fact they are predictions about what might happen, but which never actually have. Inferences alone are not sufficient to arouse fear. Some children, although not George, might be perfectly happy to sit by themselves and read books, but George appraises the situation quite negatively and catastrophizes 'It's awful that I don't have anyone to play with, I must be a jerk if they won't play with me.'

RET practitioners decide on the basis of the age of and goals for a young client whether they wish to target the client's interpretation of reality ('They'll never like me') for change, which Ellis would consider a limited solution, or whether the evaluative assumptions and beliefs ('It's awful . . . I must be a jerk . . . ') are challenged.

Before the practitioner begins the teaching of emotional and problem-solving skills, it is most important to make young clients aware that not only are changes in their emotions and behaviours possible, but also that change is desirable (DiGiuseppe, 1981). Many children can only conceive of one way of dealing with and feeling in a situation, and some find it illuminating to learn both of the possibility of alternative courses of action and emotional change. Many children have few words for emotions and a narrow vocabulary may limit their ability to conceptualize a situation. Two of the first stages in using RET with a young client are to (1) provide a schema which incorporates a continuum of responses and feelings and contains a vocabulary for these reactions; and (2) to discuss the negative consequences of present behaviour in relation to the positive consequences (or less negative consequences) of feeling less upset and behaving more appropriately. In conjunction with these steps it is frequently useful to explain to a young client that being very upset is like being in an 'emotional' fog and that until one calms down, one will not be able to see how best to solve a problem.

After a young client is made aware of the possibility and desirability of change, the next step is frequently teaching the basic RET insights concerning thoughts, feelings and behaviour. It is most important that the young client possess some understanding of emotions. Children of all ages vary a great deal in their ability to understand and express emotions. It is often the case that a young client is unable at first to express what he or she is feeling let alone identify what others are feeling. The practitioner had better make sure that the young client has a good grasp of emotional concepts and is able to express them before proceeding (see Bernard and Joyce, 1984, for a discussion of emotional awareness activities).

There are a variety of ways in which a young client can be taught that feelings come from thoughts and not situations. Demonstrating how our feelings change if our thoughts change is one way. Another is by illustrating with a concrete example how people react and feel differently to the same situation and discussing why this should be so.

As a prerequisite to teaching young clients how to challenge and dispute irrational beliefs, it is sometimes necessary that the concepts of 'rational' and 'irrational' are formally taught. In working with younger clients and, especially children, Waters (1982) substitutes the terms 'helpful' and 'hurtful' for 'productive' and 'unproductive' beliefs. Waters explained that rational beliefs follow from reality, are self-enhancing, are apt to lead to achievement of goals, and result in appropriate emotions, whereas irrational beliefs do not follow from reality, are self-defeating, usually block one from achieving goals, and result in inappropriate feelings.

In working with older children and adolescents, it is desirable to teach them a 'disputation' or 'challenging' strategy for deciding if their thoughts are rational or irrational. They can be shown that challenging means 'to question yourself to see if your thought is rational or irrational' and be taught that 'to find out if a thought is rational or irrational, ask yourself "is there enough evidence for me to say the thought is true?" ' If there is, the thought is rational, if not, the thought is irrational. This strategy is used in teaching the basics of empirical analysis and philosophical disputation. Waters (1982, p. 576) suggests that children can learn to challenge their irrational beliefs by asking themselves and answering the following series of questions:

1. Is this belief based on fact, opinion, inference or assumption? Where is the evidence that this is really so?
2. Is it really awful? Is it true I couldn't stand it? Is it the worst that it could be?
3. Is this belief getting me what I want?
4. Why shouldn't it be so? Do I always have to get what I want?
5. Where is the evidence that this makes me worthless? How can this make me worthless or less than human?

There are a few basic strategies which RET practitioners typically employ to modify dysfunctional interpretations and appraisals and to teach rational thinking skills. *Empirical analysis* involves the practitioner and young client working collaboratively to design a simple experiment to test the client's interpretation of reality. In arriving at an *empirical solution*, the 'truth' of the client's inference is tested by having the client collect data which the client and the practitioner agree would be sufficient to either confirm or reject the client's assumption. In George's case, George and the practitioner could define those reactions of other children which would indicate that George was liked and those which would suggest dislike. George could then test his prediction that 'no-one will like me and play with me' by initiating a limited number of contacts with the children in the neighbourhood he would like to know, to see if, in fact, there was any evidence to support his self-defeating interpretative conclusions that he would be rejected. If little or no evidence was collected which supported George's conclusion, then his anxiety would, hopefully, decrease to a point where he would feel free and more relaxed to pursue other contacts. The practitioner could point to the fact that George's thinking was untrue and could help him to re-state his ideas more objectively.

A second basic cognitive approach for changing cognitions is what Albert Ellis calls *philosophical disputation*, and is the core and distinctive RET intervention. Disputation can occur at a number of levels of abstraction. The client can be taught to question the specific appraisals of particular interpretations by examining the irrational content (and concepts) contained in the appraisal. This limited form of disputation is appropriate for children who are not able to discuss irrational concepts and beliefs in the abstract. George might be able to re-evaluate his appraisal of social rejection rationally by disputing concepts of 'awful' and 'jerk' in the context of the presenting problem, whereas discussion of concepts such as 'exaggeration' and 'self-acceptance' as they apply in the general case might be well beyond his grasp. If George was aged 12 or older, he might be a better candidate for a more general consideration and application of philosophical disputation to the irrational concepts and beliefs which underly his negative appraisals.

Both empirical analysis and philosophical disputation at whatever level they are applied constitute the basic components of emotional problem-solving and rational-thinking skills taught in RET. There are two other general interventions approaches which RET practitioners frequently employ. *Rational self-statements* are provided by the practitioner to the client for rehearsal and subsequent utilization in situations which tend to occasion in the client inappropriate levels of affectivity. The contents of the self-statement incorporate rational concepts and help the client overcome whatever emotions are interfering with behaviour. George might be instructed through modelling to verbalize covertly self-statements which would compete with his social anxiety: 'just relax, George, just go up and introduce yourself. Don't worry, you can cope with whatever happens; be brave.'

Another cognitive procedure which is being increasingly employed by RET practitioners with younger clients is Rational-Emotive Imagery (REI). REI involves asking the young client to recreate as vividly as possible in his mind a mental picture of a situation in which he experiences an extreme emotional reaction. When the feeling is as strong as possible, the client is asked to try to change the feeling from being extreme to a more moderate level; for example, from extreme anxiety to moderate worry and concern. When the client is able to do this, it is pointed out that the way the emotional change took place is through a change in thoughts.

As indicated, RET practitioners also help younger clients to solve practical problems which are not emotional. In teaching practical skills, RET tries where possible to provide instruction in both how to *think about* a practical problem as well as how to go about solving it. While RET practitioners sometimes have to simply tell the client how best to handle a situation without going into what he should be thinking and saying, most practical problems involve the use of rational self-statements or more general cognition strategies (e.g. consequential and means-end thinking), combined with rehearsal of behavioural skills. A number of RET practitioners (e.g. DiGiuseppe and Bernard, 1983; Waters, 1982) have arrived at a practical problem-solving format which can be readily employed even with very young children, and includes defining the problem in concrete behavioural terms, generating as many alternative solutions without evaluating them, evaluating each alternative solution in terms of positive and negative consequences, choosing the best alternative and planning step-by-step procedures, and putting the plan into action and evaluating its results.

Practice and application

The final stage of RET involves helping the young client apply rational thinking skills outside the practitioner's office in real-life situations. While the task of teaching the basics of RET can usually be accomplished, it is quite another thing to see young clients spontaneously applying RET. RET stresses the importance of practising the skills in a variety of settings and of specific homework assignments.

The main way RET accomplishes the goal of this final stage of therapy is through *homework*. As a general rule, RET practitioners request that the young client practices and applies rational ideas, beliefs and skills acquired during sessions. Typical homework assignments include:

1. Monitoring feelings.
2. Writing down upsetting thoughts a young client might have during the week.
3. Practice of behaviours role-played and rehearsed with the practitioner such as verbal assertion or extinction.
4. Making a list of personal demands.

5. Filling out a chart which lists thoughts, feelings and behaviour as a consequence of some event.
6. Practising changing feelings and thoughts in a real situation.
7. Reinforcing oneself with positive self-talk.
8. Asking other people to write down positive things about the young client.
9. Filling out a self-concept inventory which elicits both positive and negative qualities of the young client.

This final phase is really the most taxing on the personal resources of the practitioner. It is at this time when young clients begin to realize that the practitioner, whom they had up until then perceived as someone understanding and friendly, is going to ask them to do things that they do not want to do, often because it involves hard work. At this point, the young client may quickly reinterpret the value he or she places on, and the trust in, the practitioner.

Another point to keep in mind is that clients who tend to complete their school homework, will tend to do what you ask them to do, while those who have a history of not handing in homework at school, will tend not to follow through with you. The problems faced in getting a young client to cooperate are the same as those faced by the young client's parents and teachers. If you doubt that the young client is likely to do what you ask, either do not ask or make sure that the client is prepared to change past behaviour by working further on the relationship he or she has developed with you. Frequently, a token reinforcement system is set up for younger clients to ensure appropriate levels of motivation. Communication and cooperation with parents is obviously essential. RET practitioners also focus on those irrational beliefs which may cause a young client's 'resistance' to homework.

The final stage of therapy is completed when the practitioner assesses that the goals of therapy have been achieved. Evidence of success is manifested when a young client demonstrates skills in solving emotional and practical problems and when both parent and child or adolescent are satisfied with the changes.

Working with parents

While advocates of RET have consistently maintained that some children have an inborn propensity for irrational thinking, faulty reasoning and cognitive distortion, they have also argued that the manner in which parents react to and communicate with a child who manifests signs of maladjustment can either help or hurt the child. Moreover, RET practitioners seem to agree that 'disturbed' parenting styles can create problems in relatively 'normal' children. Overly permissive child-rearing practices which are based on a number of unfounded assumptions ('children should never be frustrated'; 'I must always be loved and approved of by my child') can lead to self-indulgent, egocentric, demanding, easily frustrated children, with low self-esteem. Parents who are overly strict, blaming and unaffectionate hold a variety of erroneous ideas ('Children should not disagree with their parents'; 'Praise spoils a child'; 'Children must do well and behave correctly all the time'), which can lead to their children becoming anxious, tense, guilty and depressed.

Irrational beliefs of parents can adversely influence their behaviour patterns in two ways. One is through their emotions. Parents frequently get very upset when their child breaks a rule because they believe that: (1) 'For me to be a worthwhile parent and person, my child *must* be good all the time'; (2) 'I find it awful when my child is not – I can't stand it'; and (3) 'My child deserves to be yelled at and punished because he has made me so angry and for being such a bad child.' These irrational beliefs lead to extreme anger which produces intense and non-constructive disciplinary action. Alternatively, parents may employ inappropriate and counterproductive methods of child management because of *ignorance*. That is, they believe what they are doing is the correct thing to do and, often, it is the only way they can conceptualize relating to their children. Their maladaptive behaviour is not associated with extreme emotional arousal but is directly motivated by their 'unjustified' and 'outdated' assumptions. For example, some fathers who are basically mis-informed administer physical consequences to their children whenever they are caught misbehaving. At these times, they are not particularly angry though they may feel mildly irritated. These fathers hold the anti-empirical assumption that 'severe punishment after my child breaks a rule is a good way to teach him a lesson' and employ this rule as a basis for knowing what to do in problematic situations.

The actual goals of RET parent counselling and education are guided by the results of the assessment of parental involvement in the problems of their children. Bernard and Joyce (1984) have summarized these goals as follows:

1. Teach parents ways of conceptualizing the goals of families and roles of family members as well as appropriate attitudes of child rearing.
2. Teach parents family relationship and child management skills which are necessary for them to accomplish the goals of families as well as to solve problems.
3. Teach parents the ABC's of emotions so that they can overcome their own problems and, as a consequence, are able to prevent them from being transmitted to their child.
4. Teach parents how to calm down so that they can deal with problems level-headedly.

5. Teach parents the ABC's of childhood emotions so that they know what to teach their child who is having a problem.

The same four-stage flow-chart used to characterize work with children can describe RET parent counselling. As is the case with younger clients, the building of rapport with parents occurs across assessment and intervention stages. Similarly, assessment and intervention are interdependent and often take place together during a single session with parents.

The cultivation of a good relationship with parents is frequently a necessary but not a sufficient condition to bring about change in their attitudes and child-rearing practices. This is because many parents do not recognize their own involvement with their child's problems, do not have the expectation that they will have to talk about their feelings to a total stranger, and that they may be required to change. Getting parents to self-describe emotional problems, to work collaboratively with the RET practitioners, and to take an active role in helping their child, frequently requires the practitioner to work hard on developing a good relationship before the establishment of a contract to proceed becomes viable. While active RET therapy can be initiated with some parents during the first visit, highly emotional and defensive parents may need to be 'won over'.

There are two aspects of parent assessment which RET practitioners need to be concerned about. *Problem identification* determines the types of problems that exist in the family (emotional, practical–manipulative), who owns them, and the type of service (direct advice, direct assistance or psychotherapy) which will be most appropriate and helpful to the parents. The second phase of RET assessment, *problem analysis*, involves a more detailed consideration of parental thinking patterns, child-rearing philosophies and irrational beliefs which lead to dysfunctional family relationships, emotional stress and inappropriate behaviour. The unravelling of the mental world of parents is a cornerstone of RET practice. The assessment of parents takes place in a parent interview. Important aspects of the parent interview include:

1. An explicit behavioural detailing of the parents' concerns about their child including their frequency, intensity and duration.
2. An explication of the specific situations in which problematic behaviour occurs and an inquiry into parental expectations or rules (i.e. 'shoulds') the parents have about their child's behaviour.
3. An identification of immediate consequences following the child's behaviour, including what parents think, feel and do when their child behaves as he or she does.
4. A definition of goals for their child explicitly and behaviourally stated.
5. An explanation of the more general, on-going patterns of positive and

negative interactions between parents and child (Grieger and Boyd, 1983, p. 230).

The focus of RET work with parents is to teach them, when necessary, new child-rearing attitudes and emotional and practical problem-solving skills which will enable them to overcome their own difficulties as well as those of their child. Important insights for parents are that:

1. It is their beliefs and thoughts about what to do in situations, rather than the problem itself, which influences their approach.
2. The way parents may over-react emotionally and behave towards their child can frequently be hurting rather than helping their child.
3. No matter how poorly children behave, parents and not their children are responsible for how they (the parents) feel.
4. Change in parents, while difficult, is eminently possible.

There are two foci of disputation. One is the correction of erroneous beliefs of parents through the practitioner presenting objective evidence, anecdotal stories, self-disclosure, and authoritative facts which refute the ideas of parents. The second is the use of cognitive, emotive and behavioural disputational methods to challenge and change the irrational beliefs of parents which create emotional difficulties (extreme anger, anxiety, depression, guilt):

> The goal is a profound understanding of the illogic, lack of empirical support, and self-defeating and child-defeating nature of their basic beliefs, as well as an awareness of more plausible and constructive alternatives (Grieger and Boyd, 1983, p. 235).

At the same time as parents are acquiring basic RET insights, attitudes and skills and more appropriate child-rearing practices, the practitioner encourages them to implement their new knowledge and skills at home with their child. *Homework* is the principal means by which parents are given the opportunity to apply and generalize RET skills and attitudes. Homework that is assigned during the week basically involves three things. First, parents learn to control their emotions in situations where they previously became overly upset and reacted poorly. Secondly, parents carry out self- or practitioner-generated behavioural strategies for improving relationships among family members and managing the difficulties family members may be experiencing. Thirdly, in learning to distinguish irrational from rational ideas which underlie emotions, parents communicate this knowledge to their children in helping them overcome major emotional problems such as fear, anxiety and low self-esteem, and anger. Additionally, there are now a variety of materials and child literature written specifically for use by parents with children. Depending on the age of the child, the books and pamphlets can either be read to children by their parents or by the children themselves (e.g. Bedford, 1974; Garcia and Pellegrini, 1974; Waters, 1979, 1980; Young, 1974).

The future

The future for RET as applied to childhood maladjustments is promising and a number of trends can be anticipated:

1. The use of cognitively oriented preventative mental health and affective education programmes will increase.
2. The extent to which the irrational beliefs of parents and teachers influence childhood maladjustment will be more fully analysed.
3. The popularity of RET parent and teacher education programmes will grow.
4. Behaviourally oriented practitioners will begin to recognize more fully that children and their significant others have emotions which influence behaviour as well as the effects of behavioural treatment programmes.
5. There will be an increasing cross-fertilization of cognitive approaches to the problems of childhood.

References

Albert, S. (1972). A study to determine the effectiveness of affective education with fifth grade students. Unpublished Master's thesis, Queen's College.

Bedford, S. (1974). *Instant replay.* New York: Institute for Rational Living.

Bernard, M.E. (1981). Private thoughts in rational–emotive psychotherapy. *Cognitive Therapy and Research,* **5**, 125–142.

Bernard, M.E. (1984). Childhood emotion and cognitive behavior therapy: A rational–emotive perspective. *In* P.C. Kendall (Ed.), *Advances in cognitive-behavioral research,* Vol. 3. London and San Diego: Academic Press.

Bernard, M.E. and Joyce, M.R. (1984). *Rational-emotive therapy with children and adolescents: Theory, treatment strategies, preventative methods.* New York: Wiley.

Camp, B.W. and Bash, M.A.S. (1981). *Think aloud. Increasing social and cognitive skills – problem-solving program for children.* Champaign, Ill.: Research Press.

Cormier, W.H. and Cormier, L.S. (1979). *Interviewing strategies for helpers. A guide to assessment, treatment and evaluation.* Monterey, Calif.: Brooks/Cole.

DiGiuseppe, R.A. (1981). Cognitive therapy with children. *In* G. Emery, S.D. Hollon and R.C. Bedrosian (Eds), *New directions in cognitive therapy.* New York: Guilford Press.

DiGiuseppe, R.A. and Bernard, M.E. (1983). Principles of assessment and methods of treatment with children. *In* A. Ellis and M.E. Bernard (Eds), *Rational-emotive approaches to the problems of childhood*. New York: Plenum Press.

Ellis, A. and Bernard, M.E. (Eds) (1983). *Rational-emotive approaches to the problems of childhood*. New York: Plenum Press.

Flavell, J.H. (1982). On cognitive development. *Child Development*, **53**, 1–10.

Flavell, J.H., Beach, D. and Chinsky, J. (1966). Spontaneous verbal rehearsal in a memory task as a function of age. *Child Development*, **37**, 283–299.

Garcia, E.J. and Pellegrini, N. (1974). *Homer the homely hound dog*. New York: Institute for Rational Living.

Grieger, R.M. and Boyd, J.D. (1983). Childhood anxieties, fears and phobias: A cognitive-behavioural psychosituational approach. *In* A. Ellis and M.E. Bernard (Eds), *Rational-emotive approaches to problems of childhood*. New York: Plenum Press.

Halford, K. (1983). Teaching rational self-talk to help socially isolated children and youth. *In* A. Ellis and M.E. Bernard (Eds), *Rational-emotive approaches to the problems of childhood*. New York: Plenum Press.

Hauck, P.A. (1983). Working with parents. *In* A. Ellis and M.E. Bernard (Eds), *Rational-emotive approaches to the problems of childhood*. New York: Plenum Press.

Kassinove, H., Crisci, R. and Tiegerman, S. (1977). Developmental trends in rational thinking: Implications for rational-emotive mental health programs. *Journal of Community Psychology*, **5**, 266–274.

Kendall, P.C. and Finch, A.J. Jr (1979). Developing nonimpulsive behaviour in children: Cognitive-behavioral strategies for self-control. *In* P.C. Kendall and S.D. Hollon (Eds), *Cognitive-behavioural interventions: Theory, research and procedures*. London and San Diego: Academic Press.

Knaus, W.J. (1974). *Rational-emotive education: A manual for elementary school teachers*. New York: Institute for Rational Living.

Meichenbaum, D. (1977). *Cognitive-behavior modification*. New York: Plenum Press

Meichenbaum, D. and Asarnow, J. (1979). Cognitive-behavioral modification and metacognitive development: Implications for the classroom. *In* P.C. Kendall and S.D. Hollon (Eds), *Cognitive-behavioral interventions: Theory, research and procedures*. London and San Diego: Academic Press.

Meyer, D.J. (1982). Effects of rational-emotive group therapy upon anxiety and self-esteem of learning-disabled children. Unpublished Doctoral dissertation, Andrews University.

Novaco, R.W. (1979). The cognitive regulation of anger and stress. *In* P.C. Kendall and S.D. Hollon (Eds), *Cognitive-behavior interventions: Theory, research and procedures*. London and San Diego: Academic Press.

Ritchie, B.C. (1978). The effect of rational-emotive education on irrational beliefs, assertiveness and/or loss locus of control in fifth grade students. *Dissertation Abstracts International*, **39**(4B), 2069–2070.

Robbins, S. (1976). REE and the human development program. A comparative outcome study. Unpublished Doctoral dissertation.

Rossi, A.S. (1977). RET with children: More than child's play. *Rational Living*, **12**, 21–24.

Rotter, J.B. (1966). Generalized expectations for internal versus external control of reinforcement. *Psychological Monographs*, **80**, 1–26.

Spivack, G. and Shure, M.G. (1974). *Social adjustment of young children: A cognitive approach to solving real-life problems*. San Francisco, Calif.: Jossey-Bass.

Spivack, G., Platt, J. and Shure, M. (1976). *The problem-solving approach to adjustment*. San Francisco, Calif.: Jossey-Bass.

Walen, S.R., DiGiuseppe, R. and Wessler, R.L. (1980). *A practitioner's guide to rational-emotive therapy*. New York: Oxford University Press.

Waters, V. (1979). *Color us rational*. New York: Institute for Rational Living.

Waters, V. (1980). Series of stories for children: *Cornelia Cardinal learns to cope; Fasha, Dasha and Sasha Squirrel; Flora Farber's fear of failure, Freddie Flounder; Maxwell's magnificent monster*. New York: Institute for Rational Living.

Waters, V. (1981). The living school. *RET work*, **1**, 1.

Waters, V. (1982). Therapies for children: Rational-emotive therapy. *In* C.R. Reynolds and T.B. Gutkin (Eds), *Handbook of school psychology*. New York: Wiley.

Young, H.S. (1974). *A rational counseling primer*. New York: Institute for Rational Living.

Young, H.S. (1983). Principles of assessment and methods of treatment with adolescents: Special considerations. *In* A. Ellis and M.E. Bernard (Eds), *Rational-emotive approaches to the problems of childhood*. New York: Plenum.

Chapter 13

Weight control:
a rational–emotive approach

Al Raitt

Introduction

The working assumption, that emotional and behavioural problems are determined mainly by faulty thinking and irrational beliefs (I/Bs), is central to most of the modern cognitively based approaches to psychotherapy and, in particular, to that of Albert Ellis (1962), the inventor of rational–emotive therapy (RET). In essence, RET philosophy argues that people respond to various events in their lives (point A) according to a set of beliefs which they currently hold (point B). To the extent that such beliefs are based upon reality, appropriate behavioural/emotional consequences (point C) are most likely to follow. If the beliefs are irrational, then inappropriate consequences are more likely. Ellis (1977) has called this way of formulating human problems the ABC theory of emotional disturbance, although RET theory recognizes that emotions and behaviours are often closely related. The closeness of this relationship between emotions and behaviour will, I hope, also become apparent in this Chapter, although I will be using the ABC model essentially as a model of behavioural disturbance, to attempt to explain the behaviour of clients who want to lose weight but who act in ways which would tend to hinder or prevent them doing so. I will argue that I/Bs, in one form or another, are the principal determinants of dieting difficulties and that, with the exception of clients who suffer from some form of pathology, such as an under-active thyroid gland, anyone who really wants to lose weight and is prepared to work in order to reach this goal, can do so. In other words, I am saying that failure to succeed with a given diet is almost always due to irrational thinking.

In a very general sense, rational thinking can be regarded as thinking which helps us to behave in ways which maximize the probability of our achieving what we set out to and which minimizes our emotional distress; irrational thinking tends to decrease the probability of our reaching our desired goals and to increase emotional distress. While such a definition is all very well in a general sense, it is not particularly useful operationally, being somewhat vague and imprecise. RET therapists, therefore, prefer to talk of irrational thinking, or rather of irrational beliefs, in more specific terms. This, however, is more easily said than done, since as Wessler and Wessler (1980) have pointed out, RET therapists are by no means always in agreement as to what constitutes an irrational belief. Some, such as the Wesslers, restrict the term to mean only the appraisal or evaluation which clients make about the events in their lives. Others, such as Diekstra and Dasson (quoted in Wessler and Wessler, 1980), argue that all symbolic behaviour (i.e. thoughts, images, inferences, attitudes, etc.) can, for practical purposes, be regarded as 'beliefs' and, therefore, any illogicalities or cognitive distortions in such symbolic behaviour would, by their definition, be regarded as irrational. As we can see then, the notion of an irrational belief is somewhat controversial and not easily defined. Personally, I would prefer to avoid the term and to talk instead about evaluations, inferences, etc., and the rationality or otherwise of these. However, the term 'irrational belief ' has now become firmly entrenched in RET literature and cannot easily be avoided. Moreover, it does have some use as a form of linguistic shorthand when dealing with clients. I therefore offer the following definition of what I regard as a irrational belief at least within the context of dieting and weight control. When referring to this definition I will use the symbol I/B.

First, any belief, thought, attitude, self-statement, etc., which is not based upon factual evidence, and/or sound logic, can be regarded as an I/B. Secondly, any of the above thought processes which are likely to be counter-productive, in that they would tend to produce emotions or behaviour which is likely to hinder or prevent the client reaching some stated goal, can also be regarded as an I/B, even if factually correct.

Alternatively, a belief can be regarded as rational if it is both true, as far as can be determined, and will be found helpful by the client.

Irrational beliefs and dieting behaviour

I/Bs can undermine a client's efforts at any time from the first tentative thought, that it might be a good idea to lose some weight, onwards. Thus they could prevent a potential dieter from even making an inquiry ('Dieting is too hard for me'), could hinder or halt progress once a start has been made, and could result in relapse and subsequent regaining of weight after satisfactory weight loss has been achieved. In this Chapter, however, I will be dealing only with the effect of I/Bs during active attempts to lose weight. The reason for this is simply that, in the normal course of events, I do not come into contact with diet clients until they have made at least a tentative decision to lose weight. Similarly, once they have reached their target weight, treatment is normally terminated unless the client wishes to work on some additional problem. I therefore have little direct experience of the effect of I/Bs before treatment has started or after it has finished. Occasionally, however, I get the opportunity to talk to clients who have relapsed, or who come to see me with some other problem after losing weight, or who are contemplating dieting. From these conversations I get the impression that these clients' I/Bs take the same general form as do clients' I/Bs which emerge during active attempts to lose weight.

In principle, diet-related problems are no different from any other type of problem in that they are brought about and maintained mainly by I/Bs. In practice, however, I have usually found it best to deal with the two aspects of possible irrationality (accuracy and helpfulness) as distinct, although related, issues. This is useful because, in a sense, successful dieting requires two types of knowledge. In the first place the client has to have accurate information regarding the purely dietary aspects of weight control; the possible effect of spaced small meals as opposed to one or two large meals, the calorific values of given foods, etc. Although diet books abound nowadays, many of them are somewhat misleading; some are simply inaccurate, so that many dietary misconceptions exist, e.g. the notion that one must eat sugar in order to maintain energy. This sort of information comes under the heading of telling the client *what* to do and is a necessary, but by no means sufficient, condition for successful dieting. The second sort of information comes under the heading of telling the client *how* to do it, and it is on this aspect of dieting that RET principles are mainly employed.

The way in which I/Bs can influence eating behaviour is essentially similar to the way in which they influence other forms of behaviour. Likewise, the nature of such I/Bs is broadly similar, although the precise form of self-statements may, in some respects, differ from the type of self-statement which would likely lead to emotional problems. To some extent, of course, the degree of similarity between 'diet-related' as opposed to 'emotion-related' I/Bs depends upon how one defines irrationality. I have argued that unless a belief is both true and helpful it qualifies as an I/B. Clearly, then, according to this definition clients who believe some of the dietary myths and misconceptions which currently exist are thinking irrationally. To that extent, they are less likely to reach their goal of weight reduction. It is important, therefore, that the therapist check out that clients are in possession of accurate information on the 'what to do' dimension. Providing accurate dietary information, however, seldom presents much of a problem, since clients will normally accept new dietary information quite readily. More-over, many clients are quite knowledgeable on such matters, having dieted quite successfully in the past. Therefore, although it is wise to check the accuracy and extent of dietary information of clients before starting a diet programme, it is when we come to deal with the '*how* to do it' side of dieting that RET skills are, as stated earlier, most required. If we therefore exclude I/Bs which are, in essence, based upon dietary misconceptions from the remainder of this discussion and focus instead on the motivational aspects of the '*how* to do it' dimension, I/Bs can be divided into two main categories.

First, by far the largest category, can be subsumed under the more general heading of I/Bs which lead to Low Frustration Tolerance (LFT). A second, very much smaller but more diversified category is found where clients have a weight problem which is related to an emotional problem. The most commonly found example of this is where the weight problem is part of an anxiety problem, although clearly other emotional problems such as jealousy, tension, or lack of more suitable sources of gratification, can be found which relate to weight problems in this way. I believe that it is important that the therapist, as far as possible, tries to keep in mind this distinction between LFT-based problems as opposed to problems which are part of a more general problem, since quite different approaches are indicated – a point which I will address later in this Chapter.

LFT-based problems

It is perhaps not very surprising that LFT heads the list of I/Bs which lead to dieting problems, given the requirements of dieting. Successful dieting requires not just a single decision to diet, but a daily choice between satisfying an immediate short-term desire by eating some favourite food, as opposed to satisfying the much more remote, long-term desire of reaching and staying at a desired weight. Most would-be dieters genuinely want to lose weight. They also, however, want to go on eating and drinking their favourite foods. Contrary to what is often claimed, such clients do not lack motivation, but suffer from having two opposing and mutually exclusive motives. One of the first tasks of the therapist, therefore, is to help clients to recognize and examine *both* of these motives openly before making a commitment to either. The client is then in a better position to decide which motive or goal is the one desired *most* and also what price will have to be paid in renouncing the other. If this step is omitted, clients sooner or later start to show resistance. Many LFT clients, for instance, have never seriously considered the idea that it would be possible to be happy *and* overweight. This is mainly because they have been evaluating themselves negatively for being overweight. One of my first tasks, therefore, is to try to convince such clients that, while being overweight does carry considerable health and other hazards, they need not also regard themselves as second-class citizens because of their weight. As Presby (1979) would say, I try to 'take the must out of the dieting'.

Once clients come to realize that they do not have to diet, but have a choice which carries some costs but also some benefits (as do all choices), they are usually much less likely to offer resistance later. When LFT clients do show resistance they seldom do so directly. The illogicality of trying to lose weight while also demanding to eat as they have always done is apparent to most LFT clients. LFT beliefs are therefore normally expressed in more subtle and indirect forms. Some clients, for example, will report that a given diet is 'too expensive', 'too hard to follow', 'too boring', and so on. Now while one cannot simply dismiss these claims out of hand, a little careful probing soon reveals their true nature.

One client for example, who found the diet too expensive, regularly spent in excess of £15 per week at the hairdressers. Another client who 'couldn't live without bread and biscuits' was actually waiting to undergo major surgery for a cardiac condition, but was currently considered too great a risk because of her weight (18 stone). Clearly, clients have a perfect right to spend their money or even risk their lives as they wish to, and I have no wish to deny them that privilege. However, I also retain the right not to believe clients when their 'reasons' do not match their behaviour, as in the above examples. What such clients are saying, when translated into RET language, is 'I don't choose to work so hard in order to lose weight. Dieting should not be so hard.' Now, again, clients have a perfect right to make such decisions.

However, all decisions or choices seem to entail what I earlier called 'costs' and 'benefits', and decisions about whether or not to follow a particular diet are no exception to this rule. I usually therefore find that a useful intervention with LFT clients is to examine these costs and benefits with them and also help them examine not only the costs of a given decision, but how they are going to meet these costs. Putting this into a dieting context, this means examining not only which foods they would be required to give up, or reduce greatly, for the duration of the diet, but also just how they intend integrating such new eating habits into their life-style. Someone, for example, who normally conducts a large part of their business at a particular pub or restaurant, because that is where their business associates normally lunch, had better consider not only which foods are to be resisted, but also whether alternative foods are available at that venue and, if not, what other arrangements can be made. If these matters are not considered carefully then the pressures to give up the whole business of dieting are going to be greatly, and needlessly, increased. Incidentally, this notion of costs and benefits being attached to all choices we make is, I have found, a particularly useful intervention when dealing with perfectionistic clients, i.e. clients who are apparently paralysed into inactivity because they are afraid of making a wrong (less than perfect) decision. It is particularly effective when I also point out that deciding not to decide yet is also a decision and also carries costs and benefits.

The above examples, where clients complain of the diet being 'too hard', etc., are fairly obvious examples of LFT-type thinking and are quite easily dealt with. Often, however, LFT can be expressed much less obviously. For example, clients can be progressing quite well when, perhaps unintention-ally, they eat something which is not allowed on their particular diet. Instead of merely recognizing and regretting their error, LFT clients say to them-selves, 'Oh well, I have made a mistake and ruined the diet. That proves that I can't stick to it so I might as well go back to my old way of eating.' Another indirect way in which LFT can be expressed is where clients claim that they 'can't bear to see good food wasted', and thereby give themselves an alibi for the times when they eat up food which has been left over by other members of the family. Yet another disguised expression of LFT is where clients claim that they need more food because of the cold weather, or that they cannot sleep without hot milk or a few pints of ale at bedtime. While some clients may genuinely believe their own reasons – they may, for instance, experience some initial difficulty when trying to sleep without their usual nightcap – the majority are merely inventing excuses so that they can justify reverting to their former way of eating without feeling bad about it. In any case, this is very easily checked out by giving clients correct information, i.e that we do not need to eat more when it is cold, and that we will be able to sleep without beer or hot milk if we will take the trouble to train ourselves to do so. The client who is merely misinformed will readily accept such information, whereas the client who is indirectly expressing LFT will reject it, or invent new reasons for not sticking to the diet.

Elegant versus inelegant solutions

Ellis (1977) has made a distinction between what he terms elegant *vs* inelegant solutions. An elegant solution is where the therapist helps the client to reduce emotional distress or change maladaptive behaviour by helping the client change I/Bs to more rational beliefs. An inelegant solution is where the therapist helps the client by changing the external circumstances, or rather, by showing the client how such changes could be made. Inelegant solutions may also entail persuading clients that their perceptions of events are incor-rect.

The main problem with inelegant solutions is that, in general, they may help the client to feel better while leaving the basic problem largely un-changed. An example of such a strategy would be where a client, who has developed a septic gum boil, takes painkilling drugs rather than visit the doctor or dentist and receive corrective treatment. When dealing with diet problems which are due largely to LFT, there can usually be very little doubt regarding which type of solution to attempt. In such cases the 'diet problem' is, in essence, LFT. Therefore, if the client is to make any real and lasting change in eating behaviour, then the various I/Bs which are producing the LFT had best be disputed and changed and an elegant solution attempted. There is, however, a smaller group of clients, it may be recalled, in which the diet problem is only one aspect of a more general emotional problem. Some clients, for example, seem to have what I call a 'need to be fat', in that their eating behaviour is best regarded as an attempt by the client to deal with some underlying emotional problem. I will provide a few examples of such problems later in the Chapter.

It is, of course, not always easy to distinguish LFT clients from those who are more properly regarded as clients with emotional problems. However, if we listen carefully to the underlying themes of clients' statements, it is often possible to spot essential differences. The general theme expressed by LFT clients is that 'dieting is too hard for me, and should not be so hard'. Similarly, where clients are suffering from an emotional problem and where their weight problem is essentially symptomatic of that problem, this also can often be deduced by careful and wide-ranging questions. In any event, it is important that therapists are at least aware of these possibilities and do not commit the error of assuming that every client who experiences difficulties with sticking to a diet is necessarily expressing LFT, and should therefore be persuaded to try to increase their frustration tolerance.

Anxiety as a source of dieting problems

Anxiety, in one form or another, is one of the main emotions underlying dieting failure and like LFT can appear in a number of guises. A typical example is the socially anxious client who eats whatever is offered rather than risk offending someone: 'Aunt Jean will not like it [me] if I don't have some of her cake.' A similar form of social anxiety is expressed by clients who dare not let friends know that they are following a diet, because 'they would laugh at me if they knew'. The implicit belief common to both these examples is that 'it would be *awful* to be disapproved of '.

Various approaches are possible when dealing with clients who become anxious in such situations. One could, for example, attempt the elegant solution and try to persuade clients not to be so concerned about the opinions of others. At first sight it might appear that this would be the best possible way to proceed. The client would learn to become more autonomous and hence would be less likely to break the diet just to please others. It has been my experience, however, that no matter how elegant this approach might be in theory, it is not usually the best approach in practice. Clients who consult me over their weight problem do not normally see themselves in need of therapy in the fuller meaning of that term. In other words, although they may well see the connection between their eating behaviour and their desire to please others, they do not regard themselves as having an emotional problem. They therefore are not prepared to take the risk, or 'pay the price' of offending someone, or being laughed at, in order to lose weight. In this context it is well to remember the words of Bard (1980), who points out that 'clients will tend to accept our services only to the extent that they see them as relevant to *their* goals'. The desired goal, from the client's point of view, is merely to lose weight.

From an ethical point of view also we would do well to remember that we have accepted a fee from the client on the understanding that we are to help them to reduce their weight and not for helping them to become more assertive, or to reach some other goal which we might think more desirable for them. Ethically, therefore, we can only offer the elegant solution as *one* of the options open to the client, while also pointing out that this solution is only strictly required to the extent that the client frequently eats unwisely in situations of social pressure. If this is not the case, the other, less drastic, and probably more acceptable solutions, from the client's point of view, are possible. For example, if the client wishes to minimize the risk of being laughed at, or of offending someone, a plausible excuse could be invented, such as 'My doctor has put me on this diet and I am not allowed to eat this.'

In a sense, such might seem to be a rather mild form of anxiety which, of course, it is. Nevertheless, even these mild anxieties may not seem quite so mild to our clients and do result in many clients giving up their attempts to lose weight if not handled appropriately by the therapist. With these social anxiety-based problems we are generally dealing with a fairly straightforward problem, in that the anxiety is a consequence (point C) of the belief that 'It would be awful to be laughed at (lose approval)' (point B) arising from some social situation (point A). In other words, the whole problem can generally be formulated within one ABC episode. However, this is by no means always so and anxiety, or for that matter other emotional problems, can, and do, relate to dieting problems in more complex ways, often involving two or more distinct ABCs.

June, an attractive 24-year-old, despite her weight problem, exemplifies such a case and also illustrates what I referred to earlier as a 'need to be fat'. June had been dieting for a few weeks and was progressing quite well when she suddenly announced that she wanted to stop dieting. On questioning her about her decision the following facts emerged. The reason why June had wanted to lose weight in the first place was that her husband had not approached her sexually for several months. June had decided that this was because she had put on weight and become unattractive in her husband's eyes. She had come along to see me in order to rectify this situation. However, as her weight started to come off she found, to her surprise and dismay, that her husband did not show any increase in interest and was still avoiding sexual relations with her. June now began to suspect that the husband may have formed a relationship with some other woman, but was afraid to confront him with her suspicions in case they were confirmed. She therefore decided to regain her weight so that she could pretend to herself that her husband's lack of interest was due to her being fat. If we put this into ABC form it would like this:

Initial ABC

A   = Husband's behaviour (no sexual interest shown).
B   = 'His lack of interest is due to my becoming fat. I will lose some weight and he will be interested once more.'
C   = Behaviour of consulting me, and starting to diet. Also a reduction in her anxiety over her husband's behaviour.

Secondary ABC

A   = Awareness that husband still showing no interest despite weight loss.
B   = 'Lack of interest means that husband has found another woman. I could not stand it if he has.'
C   = Increased anxiety.

Tertiary ABC

A   = Increased anxiety (i.e. point C of secondary ABC).
B   = 'I would rather not know about his affair and will pretend that it is not happening. I will therefore regain my weight so that this pretence can be sustained.'
C   = Reduction in anxiety as weight increases on stopping dietary effort.

June was not, of course, fully aware that she was engaging in such self-deception until questioned as to the reasons behind her decision to stop her diet.

Theoretically, the most elegant solution to June's problem might be seen as getting her to dispute the I/B that she 'could not stand it if her husband had found another woman'. This would help June to become less emotionally dependent on her husband and she could then feel strong enough to confront him about his lack of sexual interest instead of hiding behind her increased weight. However, although June could quite readily see, and admit, the relationship between her anxiety over her husband's behaviour and her weight problem, she was not prepared to work at becoming more emotionally independent of her husband in order to lose weight; not that this was in fact suggested to her. From my point of view also, I was mainly concerned with helping June to reach the goal *she* had stated, i.e. to lose weight, and would therefore only have suggested that she become less emotionally dependent on her husband if I believed that this was her best approach to the problem. As it transpired I was not at all happy about some of the inferences June was making about her husband's behaviour, i.e. that his apparent lack of interest implied that he had found another woman, or that his initial lack of interest was due to June being overweight, and thought that it would be a good idea to investigate this more fully.

With June's permission, therefore, I contacted her husband and asked him to come and see me. On discussing the situation with him he revealed that it was, in fact, June's appearance which was 'turning him off', but that he had not, as yet, looked for someone else. He had, however, contemplated doing so since June had started to gain weight. On being told of this June promptly resumed her diet and subsequently lost over two stones. If I had persuaded her to work on the elegant solution of becoming less dependent on her husband she would probably have lost her husband instead or, at best, the relationship might have been badly damaged. June's case, therefore, exemplifies this 'need to be fat' rather well and, in my opinion, this is by no means an uncommon problem when dealing with overweight clients, especially female clients. Many dietary problems which at first might appear to be due mainly to LFT are, in fact, due to this irrational 'need to be fat'. Another example of this 'need' in action may make this clearer.

Sue, an extremely attractive 34-year-old teacher, was only very slightly overweight when she contacted me, but was aware that her weight was steadily increasing. Like June, she had been progressing quite well with her diet when she suddenly announced that she wished to stop dieting. Her reasoning was as follows. Sue had always been aware that most men found her attractive but, being happily married, she was not in the least interested in encouraging this. Recently, her husband had been promoted and his new job meant that he was away from home for longish periods. It was shortly after her husband's promotion that Sue had started to gain weight. At first she believed that her weight increase was due to her eating chocolate in the evening when she was bored. She therefore enrolled in some evening classes but, although now no longer so bored in the evenings, she found that she was continuing to eat unwisely and to gain weight. It was this worry over her 'uncontrollable eating' which had prompted her to consult me.

My initial approach with Sue was to regard her 'uncontrollable eating' as an LFT problem and therefore to help her dispute the idea that her eating was, in reality, beyond her control. Initially, this approach had worked fairly well, so that Sue's decision came as quite a surprise; the suddenness of her decision suggesting, moreover, that I had been working on the wrong lines. At this time I had not yet clarified my thinking on what I now call the 'need to be fat' hypothesis. However, I was aware that LFT clients seldom respond in this way – i.e. initial good progress followed by a sudden decision to stop dieting – and that they more characteristically respond by coming up with a variety of excuses for breaking the diet, all of which can readily be seen as expressions of LFT. Further questioning indicated that Sue's problem was not in fact LFT but fear of promiscuity. In Sue's case:

A   = Increased interest from men due to weight loss.
B   = 'I can't handle this increased attention, especially since I am temp-
        ted to encourage it. It would be awful if I were to do so and become
        promiscuous.'
C   = Decision to terminate diet.

The problems of June and Sue were, in some respects, similar in that both were based on the notion that they needed to be fat in order to handle their problems. The way in which these problems were dealt with in therapy was, however, quite different. June's case, it may be recalled, was dealt with by working for an inelegant solution of helping June to correct her faulty inferences regarding what her husband's behaviour implied. (I helped June to change the A part of her problem). In Sue's case, I took quite a different approach and went for the elegant solution by helping her to dispute the two I/Bs which seemed to be undermining her dietary efforts, viz. 'I need to be fat in order to discourage attention from men' and 'It (I) would be awful if I were to become promiscuous.' So, apart from encouraging her to dispute this idea, she was given some basic assertion training so that she became more skilled at saying 'No thanks', as if she really meant it. Similarly, I worked to persuade Sue that extramarital sex might not be a very good move for her since she might put her marriage, which she valued very highly, at risk. However, if she did choose to engage in such behaviour, that would not mean that she was an awful person; merely someone who might be regarded as having acted unwisely. Working along these lines I was able to convince Sue that she did not in fact need to be fat in any logical sense, but had a right to be as fat or as thin as she wished to be. She resumed her diet and, as far as I am aware, has not found it too difficult to handle advances from men. She is now an even more attractive lady and a more confident one.

Summary

In this Chapter I have tried (1) to spell out the relationship between I/Bs and the problems clients who are trying to lose weight typically encounter, and (2) to show how emotional and behavioural problems often interrelate in complex ways. For mainly pragmatic reasons I have defined I/Bs as beliefs which are either untrue or unhelpful in terms of the client's long-term goal, although recognizing that this definition of I/Bs would not be accepted by all RET theorists. Successful dieting requires two related types of knowledge, namely knowing *what* to do but also knowing *how* to do it. In general, most dieting problems are due to a deficit in the latter.

By far the most common source of dieting difficulty arises in the form of LFT, since many clients subscribe to the I/B that 'Dieting should be easy for me.' Not all clients who experience difficulties in sticking to their diet, however, can be regarded as LFT clients, since emotional problems such as social anxiety can undermine dietary effort.

In particular, I have tried to encourage therapists to recognize, and be on the look out for, clients who suffer from an irrational 'need to be fat' and not to confuse such clients with LFT clients. When dealing with these clients considerable care is required when deciding whether to opt for an elegant or an inelegant solution, although this applies to some extent with any type of client. This uncertainty over whether an elegant or an inelegant solution would be better is to some extent more clearly obvious when dealing with behavioural problems such as diet behaviour, as opposed to the more emotive problems such as anxiety, jealousy, etc., commonly dealt with so effectively by RET therapists. This is so because we have accepted fees from our clients in payment for helping them to pursue *their* goal of losing weight, and not in payment for helping them to become more assertive or some other goal which *we* might think would be to their advantage to have. Moreover, most diet clients definitely do not see themselves as in need of therapy in the sense of someone who presents with what is clearly an emotional problem. They will therefore often quite strenuously resist attempts by us to engage in the normal therapy-type interventions we would employ when dealing with emotional problems, should we be rash enough to attempt this with them. Even in situations where we are dealing with what could quite unambiguously be described as an emotional problem, it is not always very apparent which way to proceed, as June's case demonstrated.

Finally, I would like to discuss briefly the issue of relapse rate and whether the use of RET principles improves the rather high relapse rate frequently found when dealing with any of the appetitive behavioural disorders. Let me state from the outset that I simply do not know the answer to this question, for reasons already given. Let me also state that I think that this question is, to a large extent, irrelevant despite the adverse comment weight reduction programmes, especially those based upon psychological principles, frequently receives on this issue. I would, of course, be very pleased to report that RET principles, when applied to weight problems, produce lower relapse rates than those found with other approaches. To a large extent though, this is out of the hands of the therapist once the client has stopped treatment. There is, as stated at the start of this Chapter, no such thing as a permanent weight loss. The best any therapist can do is to show clients an effective way in which to lose weight, plus showing them various ways in which irrational thinking could result in unwise eating behaviour which would likely result in their regaining weight. We cannot, however, ensure that they will employ such principles ever after, any more than a driving instructor could ensure that former pupils will always drive carefully. In other words, I do not think in terms of RET producing a 'cure' in the sense that a medical doctor might cure some acute infectious disorder. RET is best seen as more of a teaching process in which effective methods of behavioural and emotional control are taught. Therefore, I maintain that the question of relapse rate is largely irrelevant.

References

Bard, J.A. (1980). *Rational-emotive therapy in practice*. Champaign, Ill.: Research Press.

Ellis, A. (1962). *Reason and emotion in psychotherapy*. Secaucus, N.J.: Lyle Stuart.

Ellis, A. (1977). The basic clinical theory of rational-emotive therapy. *In* A. Ellis and R. Grieger (Eds), *Handbook of rational-emotive therapy*. New York: Springer.

Presby, S. (1979). Taking the must out of dieting. *Rational Living*, **14**(2), 29–32.

Wessler, R.A. and Wessler, R.L. (1980). *The principles and practice of rational-emotive therapy*. San Francisco: Jossey-Bass.

Chapter 14

Withdrawal from heroin and methadone with RET: theory and practice

Emmett Velten

Most treatment programmes for addicts emphasize social/vocational rehabilitation, elimination of illicit drug use and criminality, and growth of a productive and fulfilling life. Many treatment personnel are ex-addicts, who may have relapsed into addiction many times and who accept the Alcoholics Anonymous/Narcotics Anonymous creed, 'Recovery is a lifelong process.' Most programmes offer after-care services, and the possibility of relapse is not ignored. Graduating clients are nearly always urged to establish or join positive support systems such as Narcotics Anonymous, and common sense as well as street-wise ideas are offered, such as good health and nutrition habits, exercise, avoiding old drug associates, never using 'mind-altering' drugs even once, dealing with stresses without chemicals and the development of new pleasures and excitement. The cognitive psychological component to most programmes' efforts towards relapse prevention revolves around the concept of 'addictive personality' and usually does not go beyond the idea that recovery is a lifelong process, so 'ABC' (always be careful). This Chapter adds another ABC, that of rational-emotive therapy (RET), in which A is activating experience, B the belief system or cognitions, and C the consequent emotions and actions. The RET aim for recovering addicts would be resistance to relapse (C) with a new set of ideas (B) despite possible occurrence of stresses and temptations (A).

The aim of this Chapter is to (1) describe patterns of opiate addiction and relapse to opiate addiction, (2) develop theoretical perspectives for the clinician within a cognitive–behavioural context, specifically RET, and (3) offer a brief manual of therapeutic strategies and tactics for problems of relapse prevention/abstinence maintenance.

How to become an addict

Heroin addicts appear obsessed with experiencing euphoria and freedom from discomfort, but they tend in the long run to find disproportionate dysphoria and discomfort. The more they insist upon experiencing only pleasure and no displeasure, the more displeasure and less pleasure they seem to get. They refuse to endure frustrations and delays in gratification necessary for longer-range happiness. It seems likely that addicts' tendencies towards hypophoria, impulsivity, egocentricity, and exaggerated needs and wants preceded their use of addicting substances (Martin, 1977). American service-men in Vietnam had a very high availability of heroin, high acceptance of its use, and enormous stress. There has been a common belief that service in Vietnam 'caused' the continuing drug addiction of Vietnam veterans after their return to the USA. In fact, it appears that those who remained addicts upon return to the USA tended to have had adjustment problems, scrapes with the law, and problematic drug use before they ever went to Vietnam (Robins, 1979).

Whatever the biological predispositions making people's experimentation with and devotion to heroin more likely, the behavioural pattern achieved by addicts is this: they try heroin, usually in a social context, and like it. They use more and their tolerance of it rises, necessitating more frequent use and larger amounts for the same subjective experience. As physical dependence de-velops, they begin to experience various flu-like withdrawal symptoms between 'fixes'. Soon, their use of heroin does not give them the sought-after high, but merely allays withdrawal symptoms, and they struggle to 'get well' and 'feel normal'. Addicts train themselves to be hypervigilant and phobic for signs of withdrawal, and eventually their obsession with euphoria and relaxation gives way to obsession with avoiding withdrawal symptoms.

Especially in America, the desired drugs are illegal and available mainly on the black market at inflated prices, so addicts encounter many problems in feeding their habits. The inconveniences they face – arrest, high prices, drugs of poor quality, unreliable dealers, overdose, illness, treachery from their associates, unpaid bills, hassles by 'straight' family members and loved ones – in obtaining the increasing amounts of money and drugs needed to keep them 'well', contribute to their becoming more obsessive and compulsive and to their deeper immersion in the drug/crime underworld.

Eventually, the tolerance of addicts for heroin is so high that they are mainly struggling to avoid withdrawal symptoms, and their physical/emotional/financial resources become exhausted. They have to 'clean up', or break their habit, at least temporarily. This means enduring acute withdrawal symptoms without chemical assistance ('kicking cold turkey') or registration at a formal detoxification programme with a regimen of withdrawal from opiates ('getting on detox').

Cleaning up

Detoxification in America is usually a 21-day programme of methadone doses. Methadone is a long-acting synthetic narcotic with several outstanding features:

1. It works well orally administered, which interrupts the needle fixation.
2. It reduces heroin withdrawal symptoms and usually eliminates them within a few days,
3. It tends to block the euphoric effects of heroin, so that additional use of heroin is a waste of money.

Acute cold turkey withdrawal from heroin lasts only 7–10 days, and in detox programmes the extra 10–14 days of low, decreasing doses of methadone, is designed to give addicts moe time, in theory, to obtain counselling, look for work, clear up legal hassles, and to stop illegalities, since their expenses are reduced. The cost-effectiveness to society of methadone detoxification seems adequate to justify such programmes (Des Jarlais *et al.*, 1981). Regrettably, the short-term relapse rate after detoxification is quite high (Lipton and Maranda, 1983). Whatever the reason, 21 days is not enough for well-trained addicts to change their behaviour over the long-term.

Methadone itself creates physical dependence equivalent to morphine (Isbell *et al.*, 1947), a fact which is crucial in methadone maintenance. Very few hardcore heroin addicts would remain in methadone treatment long unless they were physically dependent upon the methadone. They cannot withdraw rapidly from methadone because of resultant unpleasant symptoms, and this fact is a buttress against their impulsivity. A non-addicting opiate antagonist, naltrexone, which causes no euphoria, has relatively few takers among post-addicts and a high, rapid rate of drop-out from treatment with it (Martin, 1977; O'Brien and Greenstein, 1981). In Britain, recognition of the need for an addicting treatment to entice and retain addicts in treatment led to heroin maintenance. Opium, morphine and, increasingly, methadone, are also available at clinics in Britain.

Ideally, definitive direct addiction studies are needed, comparing and contrasting the objective and subjective effects of various opiates in terms of tolerance, physical dependence, withdrawal and craving. Such studies do not exist and possibly never will, given the extreme complexity of the phenomena to be studied (Jasinski, 1977; Martin *et al.*, 1973; Skoutakis, 1982). It is known that withdrawal from even well-established methadone dependence is easier but lengthier than withdrawal from heroin (Kleber, 1981). Some authorities (Nyswander, 1972) question methadone's psychological addictiveness, despite the fact that its chronic use leads to at least as much tolerance and dependence as heroin and morphine (Martin, 1977). This is because addicts graduating from methadone maintenance and who later relapse usually report they craved heroin, not methadone. This is despite the fact they may have been physically dependent upon methadone for years and may not have used heroin at all during that time.

Indeed, the intensity of physical dependence using objective scoring criteria (Himmelsbach, 1942) may not be the prime indicator of a drug's correlation with compulsive drug-seeking behaviour, but rather the immediacy and quality of the euphoria (Jasinski, 1977). Nearly all the methadone in detox/maintenance programmes (and available on the street) is in a liquid form for oral consumption, which is unsuitable for injection, and oral methadone is infrequently sought as a drug abuse for euphoric effects (Cohen, 1981). Only about 5–10% of clients signing up for detox have methadone in their intake urines, usually in combination with heroin (Gregory, 1984). Such clients typically state they were trying to avoid heroin withdrawal symptoms by using illicitly obtained methadone, which is far longer-acting than heroin and which reduces withdrawal symptoms, but which has a relatively paltry euphoric effect. Thus, perhaps as much for psychological as physical reasons, 21 days of low, decreasing doses of methadone probably leaves relatively few addicts with any significant methadone addiction. It may leave them with a mild physical dependence on a drug to which they have little psychological addiction, and of course it may leave them with the protracted syndrome of abstinence from heroin which they would have had in any case (Martin and Jasinski, 1969). It also leaves them with their underlying personality disorders which made them apt candidates for heroin addiction in the first place.

Relapsing into heroin use

At their next admission to detox many addicts blame the previous methadone detox for their latest relapse into heroin use. They state they 'felt sick' or 'didn't feel right' at the end of the previous detox because of the addictive power of the methadone, and so began to use heroin then (or, often, well before the completion of the detox), to ameliorate the discomfort of withdrawal from methadone. Were it not for the methadone, they claim, they would not still be addicts. Such clients may obsess about subtleties in the particular schedule by which their future methadone doses will be reduced, and strive to have just the right tapering of milligrams so that they will experience zero discomfort after detox is completed.

The second most popular reported reason for immediate relapse into heroin use is that the programme 'took me down too fast', that is, reduced the methadone dose too much, too fast to counteract alleged continued heroin withdrawal symptoms. Clinically, these two groups of immediate relapsers – those who imply they got too much methadone and were addicted to it, and those who say they did not get enough methadone long enough to beat their heroin habits – are typically found to have retained high access to heroin.

Despite the fact that these two groups of relapsers attribute their relapse to a deficiency of methadone or to a methadone addiction, and despite the fact that illicit methadone is fairly available on the streets and especially available near clinics (due to the diversion of 'take-home' doses), few relapsers seek additional methadone; they seek heroin, since they rate its euphoric effect far superior to that of methadone.

Other clients who eventually relapse, but not so fast, may mention not having felt well at the end of detox, but do not attribute their relapse to this. They tend to attribute their relapse to some special or unexpected circumstance, e.g. being approached by a known drug user; unexpected cravings which occurred when they entered old drug procurement areas; negative emotions or special stressors, such as job loss, death in the family, or illness or injury, which requires an appetite-whetting prescription of painkillers; or to positive emotions or situations, such as having a birthday or getting a paycheck, which they then celebrate by treating themselves to drugs.

Methadone maintenance

In America, clients who have had numerous unsuccessful detoxes often choose to enrol in methadone maintenance. They take methadone daily on a regular basis, are physically dependent upon it (or else might not persist in treatment), receive counselling and medical care, and theoretically can terminate their criminal involvements and adopt a pro-social life-style. Long-term follow-ups show this happy expectation does come to pass in a sizeable percentage of cases (Martin, 1977), and methadone maintenance compares favourably with other major forms of treatment (Simpson and Sells, 1983). However, for those clients who are not methadone 'lifers' and who choose to reduce their methadone doses gradually to zero, or 'to taper off ', as it is called in methadone clinics, withdrawal from methadone poses a problem similar to that of withdrawal from heroin faced by detox clients: it is not entirely pleasant and it is characterized by some feelings of withdrawal and of craving, usually for heroin.

The methadone doses at which long-term methadone clients are maintained depend largely upon two factors. One factor in dose determination is illicit drug use, as shown by analysis of urine specimens taken randomly at clinics. If the client uses illicit opiates, generally the methadone dose is raised to the point that the urge to use other opiates is curbed. This tradition in methadone maintenance is questioned by intriguing studies which suggest the possibility that some clients will give clean urines, that is, stop using illicit drugs, in order to earn various rewards, including dose increases (Hall *et al.*, 1979; Stitzer *et al.*, 1979, 1980).

A second factor in dose determination is the client's reported feelings of well-being. If the client reports subjective discomfort or temptation to use illicit drugs, often the methadone dose is increased by the programme. Typically, clients resist assessment of what is going on in their lives, because to them the problem is not having enough methadone to achieve uninterrupted comfort. Staff members, even counsellors, may learn to focus their attention largely on the client's main worry, which is whether the amount of methadone he or she is getting is 'enough'. The client's underlying addictability is not confronted. Thus, when the client does elect to 'taper off' methadone some day, his or her addictive personality traits may not have been modified. In fact, they may even have been exacerbated by the constant focus on achieving such minute gradations in methadone dose reduction that no discomfort at all is experienced.

Abstinence maintenance

Methadone maintenance programmes usually emphasize jobs, vocational counselling, relationship issues, and the development of positive ways to deal with stress, but typically no formal attention is given during programme enrolment to methods of relapse prevention/abstinence maintenance. With clients tapering from methadone maintenance over a period of months, or detoxing from heroin with methadone over a 21-day period, a counselling or psychotherapy component in programmes would be better aimed at relapse prevention/abstinence maintenance. This Chapter explores rational–emotive therapy applications towards that goal.

An important first point neglected by many practitioners is to determine the client's goal. Does the client intend to remain abstinent from opiates after methadone doses have ended? Some do not, and they would not be suitable for concentrated programme efforts to teach relapse prevention methods. In these cases, it might still be appropriate to explore their reasoning. Starting with the client's likely goal of a greater balance over displeasure in life, the therapist can explore how resumption of heroin use, with its many predictable negative consequences, is congruent with that goal. A few clients who admit they plan to relapse may be found to have a fixed self-concept as an addict, and in those cases therapeutic work on reducing self-labelling and self-rating may help.

But what of clients who do not plan to relapse? Most of them will agree that some planning to prevent relapse could be helpful, but others will decline the opportunity since they believe relapse is unthinkable and rigidly refuse to prepare for the possibility. They say, 'Why look at the negative?' Others will not consider preparation because they know it will require hard work. In either case, the decision not to think about the possibility of relapse may be buttressed with a misused Alcoholics Anonymous/Narcotics Anonymous slogan – 'One day at a time' – which does not mean 'do not have a plan', but in fact is an anti-perfectionism injunction. Beyond making relapse prevention training available to such clients, should they decide to utilize it, the therapist can give them information about how to sign up for the programme again if they need to do so.

Getting at and changing the ABC's

For those clients who do participate in relapse prevention training, the first step is to help them identify their previous patterns of relapse. For instance, the therapist may ask 'How did you decide to resume using heroin?' This question immediately introduces ideas of personal choice and responsibility, and begins to lay the foundation for work on decision making. Next, clients can be helped to identify specific thoughts, feelings and situations which they see as having contributed to their past relapses. Many clients will be puzzled in searching for specific thoughts, because they are looking for something dramatic and 'deep' and consider it insufficient simply to have thought 'I wanted to [use] because it would feel good.' In fact, that thought is most commonly reported and reflects selective forgetting of negatives and selective focusing on positives connected to drug use.

Clients can make a double column, with the left column labelled 'fiction' and the right column labelled 'fact'. Under 'fiction' ask them to list thoughts which justify their resumption of heroin use. Common ones are 'I'll just use once', 'I won't spend all my money', 'I can control it this time', 'I'll just use on weekends', and 'What the hell?' Have them evaluate the rationality of each of these thoughts, using some of Maultsby's (1978, 1984) criteria: (1) Is it (the thought) based on objective reality? (2) Does it help me reach my goals and feel happier in the long run without causing trouble for me or others? Then suggest that clients construct, in the 'fact' column, a rational dispute of each 'fiction'. It can help if these disputes are catchy slogans the client may be familiar with, e.g. Narcotics Anonymous's warning, 'One time is too much, 1000 times is not enough', which refers to the addict's typical resumption of compulsive drug use after a modest start. Next, develop with clients a plan for learning and rehearsing the list and reviewing it and practising it on a regular basis. Clients will claim quite factually that they 'know' the truth of the disputes. Emphasize that insight alone into the foolishness of the self-defeating thoughts has not been enough in the past to prevent relapse. Their job is to teach themselves to think correctly at the right time, namely before they relapse, not after.

Addicts usually tend to forget the negative aspects of their past addictions faster than they forget the positive aspects, a tendency which helps them in talking themselves into relapse. A simple but powerful procedure to help counteract this tendency is the 'shitlist'. Have clients list all the negative aspects of using the drug, such as expense, health problems and prison. Then, as in the double-column technique, have them develop a plan for frequent review of the list whether they think they need to or not. Explain that they usually forget the suffering they caused themselves with past drug use, so they had better train themselves to think about those past sufferings *before* deciding to relapse. This technique and others which provide perspective about negative consequences of drug use, are variations of the general semantics technique of referenting (Danysh, 1974). The idea is to help clients teach themselves to think of drug use in perspective before choosing to use, rather than only or mainly thinking of it in terms of positives before relapse and in terms of negatives after relapse, when it is too late. A few clients will resist this since they are frightened to think about the negatives. Teach them that they had better be appropriately concerned about things that could hurt them and learn to avoid poor results rather than merely refusing to think about such prospects.

Low Frustration Tolerance

Practically all heroin addicts exhibit abysmally low frustration tolerance (LFT) (Martin, 1977). One of the few personality factors which seem to differentiate addicts from others is their intolerance of delay (Wallace, 1979). The least delay or inconvenience in getting anything they want, drugs or otherwise, any hassle or discomfort, may be viewed with utter horror and reacted to with tantrums, hostility, whining, depression, impulsive action, and so on. Practically any RET procedure for improving frustration tolerance can prove helpful with addicts in preventing relapse (Ellis and Knaus, 1977).

No matter how slow a detox from heroin or a taper from methadone may be, there is bound to be some discomfort. Addicts tend to be so phobic of discomfort that many will refuse to think about such a possibility and choose simply to hope there will not be any. Rather brisk confrontations of this attitude may be required. Teach clients the idea that some discomfort might even be desirable, since they will benefit from learning that they *can* stand discomfort. They might be asked to list and review the advantages of tolerating discomfort and the disadvantages of refusing to tolerate it, to remember instances where they did stand discomfort successfully, and to engage in difficult actions on a regular basis for practice.

Clients may be taught self-instructions regarding any feelings of withdrawal, such as 'This discomfort is time-limited, it won't last forever, so I had *better* stop snivelling and get on with life!' Teach them to dispute such addict rationalizations as 'I can afford it' (using drugs) with facts like 'You've said that before and always ended up stealing to support your habit.' Ask them to assume the worst, that there will be some discomfort, and ask them how they will enable themselves to cope with it. Work this plan out in detail. Help them develop high frustration tolerance beliefs, as well as practical plans to minimize discomfort and distract themselves from it. Have them repeatedly rehearse their plans, in images and written or spoken words. The same self-instructional procedures may be applied in helping addicts curb their impulsivity. 'Stop and think', 'waiting won't kill me', and 'take the time to do it right' are examples of self-instructions which can counteract impulsivity.

Another aspect of building higher frustration tolerance involves teaching clients to cope with occasional unexpected thoughts about drugs or unexpected access to drugs after they have successfully passed beyond withdrawal. Teach them to question the idea that they *have* to have, rather than *desire* to have, the good drug feelings, particularly since they have reported that the good feelings pale in comparison with the inevitable ensuing bad feelings. Teach them to wait some specific period of time, say 30 minutes, before taking drugs when they get the impulse to do so. Emphasize that they have a whole lifetime in which to use to their heart's content, so why not wait 30 minutes and think it over? Rational-emotive imagery (REI) and desensitization may be helpful in teaching tolerance to this seemingly small amount of delay. While learning to delay in imagery, addicts can be taught to review past undesirable consequences of drug use and to visualize rewards for having been able to resist and escape temptation. Have them play the role of a patient person (Kelly, 1955) or instruct the therapist in how to act patiently.

High-risk situations

Another set of procedures overlaps and extends the techniques already described. It involves carefully identifying the high-risk situations in which clients have a history of relapse, or in which temptation to use drugs could be expected in the future. It also involves exploring the chains of events, behaviours and cognitions which preceded the specific high-risk situation and which helped place the client in the situation. Marlatt (1979) calls these 'apparently irrelevant decisions'. An example would be a recovering alcoholic's deciding to have beer in the house so his non-alcoholic buddies can drink while they watch the big game on TV. He has no intention to drink and does not drink, but he now has the idea he can have beer around without drinking. In retrospect, such decisions can frequently be identified as having brought clients to the launching pad of relapse.

The most common high-risk situations in heroin use relapse are:

1. Invitations to use by (usually) economically interested former drug associates, otherwise known as 'peer pressure' (Wallace, 1979).
2. Exposure to cues indicating availability, e.g. returning to procurement areas, seeing drug associates and dealers, knowledge that someone else is using drugs nearby.
3. Experiencing some negative emotion or situation.
4. Experiencing some positive emotion or situation, such as a love infatuation, which is related to a desire to 'celebrate'.

In each case a possible treatment format is as follows. Have clients:

1. Link in imagery serious negative consequences to a 'yes' decision in the high-risk situation. If 'apparently irrelevant decisions' have been identified, the clinician might better help the client link them to the ultimate high-risk situations and the negative consequences after a 'yes' decision.
2. Practise verbalizing the linkages. For example, 'If I go to that party, I'll see people using and will take drugs myself, and I'll get strung out and end up with a parole violation.'
3. Practise repeatedly in imagery linking positive consequences to saying 'no', escaping the high-risk situation, or avoiding the high-risk situation.
4. Rehearse verbally the linkage between 'no' and positive consequences.
5. Rehearse the entire cognitive-behavioural coping response, identify the high-risk situation(s), verbalize the possible negative consequences from saying 'yes', verbalize the possible positive consequences from saying 'no', and describe and practise the behaviours needed to avoid/escape such situations.

The latter might involve extended work in assertion skills, including work on the I/B's (irrational beliefs) which often underlie lack of assertion skills, e.g. need for love, approval, acceptance and comfort (Lange and Jakubowski, 1976). Additional methods of changing responses to high-risk situations may involve flooding/response prevention in imagery, and desensitization.

Factors affecting severity of withdrawal

Clients withdrawing voluntarily from either heroin or methadone, even those who do so very slowly, are convinced they have some withdrawal symptoms. They do, of course. The question is how some of them achieve the horrors they describe. Several psychological factors seem to play a part in the horror quotient of withdrawal. One is LFT. The more devoutly clients believe they must never and can never have or endure discomfort, the bigger the fuss they will tend to make over any objective amount of discomfort.

Another factor in severity of withdrawal is the degree to which clients remain in their drug routine and drug habitat. Numerous clinical observations as well as research (Meyer and Mirin, 1981) suggests that withdrawal symptoms are classically conditionable. Years after having left locations where they trained themselves as addicts, clients who return to those areas frequently experience verifiable withdrawal symptoms, which appear to be classically conditioned responses to cues, including thoughts, occurring in the old drug settings. For instance, ex-addicts returning from prison to their home training grounds frequently report withdrawal symptoms. An abstinent addict whose drug connection was encountered accidentally may report that he then sweated for several days after the encounter.

In addition, addicts have a long history of anxiety at the prospect of 'no drugs', and acute discomfort when having no drugs. 'No drugs' becomes a conditioned stimulus (CS) both for anxiety and withdrawal symptoms as well as for initiation of compulsive drug-seeking. Desensitization, flooding/ response prevention, and stress inoculation methods may be helpful in disconnecting and defusing this CS.

A factor related both to low frustration tolerance and to conditioned emotional responses is the perception of availability/scarcity of the drug. In general, the easier it seems to terminate withdrawal symptoms with a return to heroin, the more withdrawal symptoms addicts will tend to feel. A wealth of clinical observations supports this theory. Clients repeatedly mention how they kicked cold turkey more easily in jail (where access to narcotics was limited or nil) once they knew they could not get bail, than at home. Again, those who retreat to a mountain cabin to kick will usually report it was easier than in town. Clients may report that they did not develop acute withdrawal symptoms until the moment the drug was physically in their presence or the moment they smelled the sulphur from the match they used to prepare the heroin for injection.

The anxiety component to withdrawal seems at its highest when addicts are unsure whether they can obtain drugs within a certain time period. Once they know the relief is certainly available or, on the other hand, certainly not available (as is usually the case in jail), anxiety may abate. For instance, a frequent observation at detox clinics is that once certain addicts know they will be able to register for the programme that day, they calm down and indeed sometimes drop off to sleep, despite the fact that they might have to wait for hours to register. Some addicts report purchasing drugs on the street, going home, and then feeling so much better that they do not consume the drugs right away. Anxiety abates after they know they can stop withdrawal with the drugs they have purchased.

The situation with systematic gradual withdrawal from methadone maintenance to a dose of zero, or tapering, as it is called in methadone clinics, is more complex. The most anxious tapering clients are those who are leaving the programme voluntarily and who intend to try to remain drug-free after cessation of methadone. They are anxious because the prospect of 'no drugs' has been repeatedly linked to enormous discomfort for them in the past. Involuntary tapering clients, on the other hand, are rarely anxious about returning to a condition of 'no drugs', since they are often being dismissed from the programme for continued illicit drug use. The degree to which tapering clients experience craving for drugs seems related to exposure to cues, including thoughts, connected to past drug use. Those who have moved away from addict areas and life-styles seem less subject to major cravings, presumably partly because they have fewer reminders. Those who relapse into drug use may exaggerate the horror of their past withdrawal symptoms as a justification for relapse.

How to feel normal

Even many of those post-methadone maintenance clients who do not relapse into illicit drug use mention they did not feel 'right' or 'normal', sometimes for months after cessation of methadone. Often they believe that permanent physiological havoc has been done to them by drug, usually methadone, use. Indeed, subtle physiological indices of abnormal function have been found to persist up to 6 months after cessation of methadone maintenance (Martin *et al.*, 1973) even though most clinically significant symptoms disappear within 3 weeks. The same is true after withdrawal from morphine (Martin and Jasinski, 1969). Psychological factors of low frustration tolerance, conditioning and perception of access, are likely to play a part in this phenomenon. Those post-addicts most closely connected to their former drug lives will probably tend to feel less 'normal' and 'right' and for longer periods of time than those who have made a clean break.

The clinician may help clients by attributing this 'not right' phenomenon partly to the fact that not being on any drugs is *not* normal for addicts. The clinician can also suggest that it will take a while for the feelings of normality to come and try to persuade clients that in the meantime they can tolerate 'abnormality'. Clients can list possible reasons other than withdrawal for bad feelings, and be asked to poll non-addicts about their experiences of bad feelings. Clients can be helped to dispute the ideas that they *must not* have had feelings and *cannot stand* them.

Some of those bad feelings are treatable. High scorers on the Beck Depression Inventory are found to report more withdrawal symptoms than low scorers with equal heroin habits (Batki, 1984). In addition, the high depressives drop out of treatment significantly earlier. Identifying certain bad feelings as depression for which there are rather effective treatments, may help reduce a compulsive return to heroin.

All the changes in attributions suggested above are designed to provide addicts with new concepts to explain their experiences and thus to combat old beliefs such as 'I'm dope sick and can't stand it', and 'once a junkie, always a junkie', 'I'm weak', 'I'm born to lose', or other crude and erroneous versions of the disease model of substance abuse, all of which tend to make relapse more likely and effort at change less likely.

Living with and without craving

One of the clinician's objectives with recovering addicts may be to help them change their attitudes about the experience of craving. The medical theory which was part of the initial development of methadone maintenance was that long-term use of heroin led to permanent changes in the brain structure or function, so that addicts were metabolically defective and 'needed' opiates/opioids, and this need was to be filled by methadone (Dole and Nyswander, 1965, 1968). All the modern focus on endorphins continues the quest for physical changes in the brain that 'make' the addict crave and go on to do bad things. However, if permanent physical changes existed which cause craving and relapse, then why do so many well-trained addicts who move away from their training grounds to new locales report they felt fine and did not think of heroin? They, of course, could not feel fine no matter what their locale, if previous drug addiction had caused any crucial physical changes. At best, endorphin depletion may prove to be a mediator of discomfort, not a primary cause. Addicts may take craving as an indication of their fate or their weakness. Instead, they had better be taught that craving is largely a result of thinking about drugs in particular ways. Appetites for, say, foods and sex, may arise after related thinking. Thought is father to desire as well as deed. Thought-stopping (Wolpe, 1982) and referenting (Danysh, 1974) procedures may help clients curb their dysfunctional thoughts.

Rational-emotive theory holds that there may be biological leanings towards many disturbances, and addiction is no exception. However, clients had better be taught that regardless of the possible fact that they were born carrying the ball, they themselves ran with the ball and have spent long hours and years and sometimes decades training themselves into their disturbances.

They *can* retrain themselves and had better start promptly, given their leanings and learnings. RET, as well as AA and NA, holds that recovery is a lifelong process. Incidentally, Gamblers Anonymous recognizes that the psychological components of addiction to gambling, drugs and alcohol are virtually identical. Yet no one has ever received disability benefits for addiction to gambling, whereas many people in the USA receive disability benefits for their drug/alcohol addictions, which are thought to be 'physical'.

The cognitive attributional changes discussed above can be buttressed with other suggestions, for instance, about changing routines and associates, engaging in various distractions and pleasures, and adopting proper nutrition and exercise practices. In particular, addicts can use alternatives in two contrasting areas. Rather obvious is their typical need to learn more adaptive ways to cope with stresses. Standard recommendations are psychotherapy/counselling/recovery meetings, relaxations, hobbies, distractions, and natural remedies, such as improved nutrition and exercise.

Rather less obvious is the need many recovering addicts have for the development of positives, pleasures and rewards other than drugs. Usually they are deficient in forms of relaxation, hobbies, entertainments, legal excitements, sports, involvement in causes, and enjoyment of non-drug friends. Often, after addicts become abstinent, they do not return spontaneously to or seek out 'normal' pleasures and activities. They may tend to sit in their rooms, feeling bored, put upon, and deserving of some kind of pleasure (we know what kind), and feel so deprived they think, 'Why not?' Often they have trouble imagining any reward beyond drugs, or what they do imagine or remember pales in comparison with the drugs. Push them into some positive activities. Tell them they may not feel like doing them, but they do not need to feel like it in order to do it. After they do the activities, they may enjoy them and likely will feel more like doing them.

Clients who attempt to withdraw from heroin/methadone had better be told about the factors associated with abstinence, such as working, breaking with drug associates, avoidance of drug procurement areas, change of routines, getting exercise, participation in some type of therapy/counselling/recovery meetings, and disputation of low frustration tolerance philosophies. Prepare them for the possibility of a slip. Teach them to think of a slip as a discrete instance of behaviour, a behaviour with causes which can be identified and studied and modified, so that different behaviour occurs next time. Help clients dispute and replace ideas that they are born addicts.

Conclusion

Phenomena associated with addiction, such as addictive personality traits, cravings for drugs, and severity of withdrawal symptoms, as well as relapse prevention/abstinence maintenance issues, were examined in this Chapter from the viewpoint of rational-emotive theory. Various therapeutic strategies and interventions have been suggested for practitioners working with addicts.

References

Batki, S. (1984). Personal communication. Substance Abuse Service, San Francisco General Hospital.

Cohen, S. (1981). *The substance abuse problems.* New York: Haworth Press.

Danysh, J. (1974). *Stop without quitting.* San Francisco: International Society for General Semantics.

Des Jarlais, D.C., Deren, S. and Lipton, D.S. (1981). Cost effectiveness studies in the evaluation of substance abuse treatment. *In* J.J. Lowinson and P. Ruiz (Eds), *Substance abuse: Clinical problems and perspectives.* Baltimore: Williams and Wilkins.

Dole, V.P. and Nyswander, M.A. (1965). Medical treatment for diacetyl morphine (heroin) addiction. *Journal of the American Medical Association*, **193**, 645–56.

Dole, V.P. and Nyswander, M.E. (1968). Methadone maintenance and its implications for theories of narcotic addiction. *In* A. Wiler (Ed), *The addictive states, Association for Research in Nervous and Mental Diseases*, **46**, 359–66. Baltimore: Williams & Wilkins.

Ellis, A. and Knaus, W.J. (1977). *Overcoming procrastination.* New York: Institute for Rational-Emotive Therapy.

Gregory, H. (1984). Personal communication. California Detoxification Programs, Inc., San Francisco.

Hall, S.M., Bass, A., Hargreaves, W.A. and Loeb, P. (1979). Contingency management and information feedback in outpatient heroin detoxification. *Behavior Therapy*, **10**, 443–51.

Himmelsbach, C.K. (1942). Clinical studies of drug addiction: Physical dependence, withdrawal and recovery. *Archives of Internal Medicine*, **69**, 766–72.

Isbell, H., Wikler, A., Eddy, N.B., Wilson, J. and Moran, C.F. (1947). Tolerance and addiction liability of 6-dimethylamino-4-4-diphenyl-heptanone-3 (methadone). *Journal of the American Medical Association*, **135**, 888–94.

Jasinski, D.R. (1977). Assessment of the abuse potentiality of morphinelike drugs (methods used in man). *In* W.R. Martin (Ed), *Drug addiction I: Morphine, sedative-hypnotic and alcohol dependence.* New York: Springer-Verlag.

Kelly, G. (1955). *The psychology of personal constructs.* New York: Norton.

Kleber, H.D. (1981). Detoxification from narcotics. *In* J.H. Lowinson and P. Ruiz (Eds), *Substance abuse: Clinical problems and perspectives.* Baltimore: Williams and Wilkins.

Lange, A.J. and Jakubowski, P. (1976). *Responsible assertive behavior: Cognitive/behavioral procedures for trainers.* Champaign, Ill.: Research Press.

Lipton, D.S. and Maranda, M.J. (1983). Detoxification from heroin dependency: An overview of method and effectiveness. *In* B. Stimmel (Ed), *Evaluation of drug treatment programs.* New York: Haworth Press.

Marlatt, G.A. (1979). Alcohol use and problem drinking: A cognitive–behavioral analysis. *In* P.C. Kendall and S.D. Hollon (Eds), *Cognitive–behavioral interventions: Theory, research, and procedures.* London and San Diego: Academic Press.

Martin, W.R. (1977). Chemotherapy of narcotic addiction. *In* W.R. Martin (Ed), *Drug addiction I: Morphine, sedative-hypnotic and alcohol dependence.* New York: Springer-Verlag.

Martin, W.R. and Jasinski, D.R. (1969). Physiological parameters of morphine dependence in man – tolerance, early abstinence, protracted abstinence. *Journal of Psychiatric Research*, **7**, 9–17.

Martin, W.R., Jasinski, D.R., Haertzen, C.A., Kay, D.C., Jones, B.E., Mansky, P.A. and Carpenter, R.W. (1973). Methadone – a reevaluation. *Archives of General Psychiatry*, **28**, 286–95.

Maultsby, M.C. Jr (1978). *A million dollars for your hangover.* Lexington KY: Rational Self-Help Aids.

Maultsby, M.C. Jr (1984). *Rational behavior therapy.* Eaglewood Cliffs, N.J.: Prentice-Hall.

Meyer, R.E. and Mirin, S.M. (1981). A psychology of craving: Implications of behavioral research. *In* J.H. Lowinson and P. Ruiz (Eds), *Substance abuse: Clinical problems and perspectives.* Baltimore: Williams and Wilkins.

Nyswander, M.E. (1972). Personal communication. *In* E.M. Brecher and Editors of Consumer Reports, *Licit and illicit drugs.* Boston: Little, Brown.

O'Brien, C.P. and Greenstein, R.A. (1981). Treatment approaches: Opiate antagonists. *In* J.H. Lowinson and P. Ruiz (Eds), *Substance abuse: Clinical problems and perspectives.* Baltimore: Williams and Wilkins.

Robins, L.N. (1979). Addict careers. *In* R.L. Dupont, A. Goldstein and J.A. O'Donnell (Eds), *Handbook on drug abuse.* Rockville, MD: National Institute on Drug Abuse.

Simpson, D.D. and Sells, S.B. (1983). Effectiveness of treatment for drug abuse: An overview of the DARP research program. *In* B. Stimmel (Ed), *Evaluation of drug treatment programs.* New York: Haworth Press.

Skoutakis, V.A. (1982). *Clinical toxicology of drugs: Principles and practice.* Philadelphia: Lea and Febiger.

Stitzer, M.L., Bigelow, G.E. and Liebson, I. (1979). Reducing benzodiazepine self-administration with contingent reinforcement. *Addictive Behavior*, **4**, 245–52.

Stitzer, M.L., Bigelow, G.E. and Liebson, I. (1980). Reducing drug use among methadone maintenance clients: Contingent reinforcement for morphine-free urines. *Addictive Behavior*, **5**, 330–40.

Wallace, C. (1979). The effects of delayed rewards, social pressure, and frustration on the responses of opiate addicts. *In* N. Krasnegor (Ed), *Behavioral analysis and treatment of substance abuse* (NIDA Research Monograph No. 25, pp. 6–25). Washington, D.C.: US Government Printing Office.

Wolpe, J. (1982). *The practice of behavior therapy*, 3rd edition. New York: Pergamon.

Index